THE
# LION
THE
# CHURCH
AND THE
# WARFARE

Ephesians 3:14-19

*[signature]*

THE
# LION
THE
# CHURCH
AND THE
# WARFARE

David E. Schroeder, Ed. D.

# OTHERS COMMENT ON
## *The Lion, the Church and the Warfare*

David Schroeder's The Lion, the Church and the Warfare *will help you understand the invisible war around us, whether we like it or not! You'll be both enlightened and inspired by this masterful book.*

— *Jim Cymbala*
*The Brooklyn Tabernacle*

*With a surgical finger on the pulse of our age, David Schroeder offers a physician's vital biblical reality check and a warrior's stirring rallying cry. Our Enlightenment-conditioned minds — even for those of us who have bowed in repentance and faith before the Lord Christ of Scripture — are inclined to diminish an aspect of reality that is essential to a biblical worldview: that we are at war. Like our spiritual forebears Bunyan and Luther, Schroeder urges upon us an embrace of the combat duty into which we have been enlisted and yet too often remain unengaged. Schroeder's focus, however, is not on the combat but upon the Captain — the victorious Lion — who, as Paul teaches, "always leads us in triumphal procession" (2 Cor. 2:14).*

— *Ralph Enlow*
*President, Association for Biblical Higher Education, Orlando, FL*

*It's been some time since our attention has been pointed to the Lord's Church as a weapon of warfare. We often read and hear about the individual believer in spiritual warfare, but rarely do we hear about the Church in warfare. And we are in warfare. This book is a must-read, particularly in our contemporary Western context where the Church of the Lord Jesus seems to be losing ground. To be sure, we have the optics right; but, I am not sure if we have the objective right. And that is our calling: to worship and war in the name of Jesus. Dr. Schroeder unmasks the prince of the air, Satan, and ends with the ultimate triumph that the kingdom of this world is to become the kingdom of our Lord, and of His Christ!*

*— **Bishop Donald Hilliard, Jr., D. Min.***

*Senior Pastor and CEO, Cathedral International Church, Perth Amboy, NJ*

*Fulfilling the Great Commission requires a paradigm shift in every member of the Lord's Church. Christianity is not a cruise ship. It's a battleship! Cruise ships dock during wartime. Battleships sail during wartime. On a cruise ship, God is seen as a jovial entertainment director. On a battleship, God is seen as the fearless general. My friend David Schroeder eloquently and compellingly reminds us that we're soldiers not civilians. Let the Lion awaken the spiritual warrior within you, so you may passionately accomplish all the will of God for your life.*

*— **David D. Ireland, Ph.D.***

*Lead Pastor and Author, One in Christ; Raising a Child Who Prays*

*www.DavidIreland.org*

*Most Christians in the West have become too complacent to take seriously the spiritual battle presently being waged in the heavenly realms. This book is a sobering wake-up call for the Church to embrace her calling as Christ's warrior and engage in the battle of the highest stakes for the human soul. Combining solid biblical scholarship with lived experience in the trenches of ministry, Dr. Schroeder offers a jewel of spiritual discernment for our precarious time.*

*—**James Kang***

*Pastor, First Baptist Peddie Memorial Church, Newark, NJ*

Addressing both the theological and practical matters of spiritual warfare, Dr. Schroeder provides every believer a fresh look at and an emboldening call to our victory in Christ. Far from being helpless victims or passive observers, true believers are commissioned as transformed, empowered, and fully-equipped warriors for the advancement of His Kingdom. Encouraging deep fellowship, obedience, and agreement with our Commanding Officer, this exceptional book will strengthen every reader in the ultimate victory at hand.

— **Dr. Thomas W. Keinath**
*Former Senior Pastor of Calvary Temple and Author of Conquest & Glory:*
*A Pastor's Journey Through the Book of Revelation*

The Christian life is not a playground; it's a battleground! Sadly, the modern church is often apathetic and unaware of the intense spiritual battle raging all around it. Dr. Schroeder's power-packed book is a clarion call that unmasks the enemy's schemes and wakes up believers to the true reality of spiritual warfare. It's time for Christ's bride to put on her battle armor and engage our enemy as David vividly describes. Discover God's battle plan for your life — how to walk in authority, pull down strongholds, and claim victory in the name of Jesus!

— **Pastor Tim Lucas**
*Author of Liquid Church: 6 Powerful Currents to Saturate Your City for Christ*

David Schroeder has brought in a most timely message in The Lion, the Church and the Warfare. *Nowadays, Christians are either unaware or fearful of satanic attacks. Dr. Schroeder reminds us we are in fact the battleground of spiritual warfare. As we are fully conscious of the divine power and the protection given us and fearlessly live as transformed beings in Christ, we can fight with God to negate the influences of Satan! This is a book that would prepare and strengthen our hearts to become mighty warriors of God on earth.*

— **Gordon Sau-wah Siu**
*Senior Pastor, North Point Alliance Church, Hong Kong*

*As followers of Christ, we have an enemy and we are in a battle. Satan hates us and wars against us. The Lion, the Church and the Warfare will remind you that Jesus Christ is our Commanding Officer — the One who already won the battle through His death and resurrection. Dr. Schroeder highlights the important truths that our battle plan must focus on Jesus Christ through prayer and worship and that we have authority in Christ that enables us to overcome Satan's opposition and march to victory. Your faith and endurance will be bolstered as you read these pages.*

*— **Terry D. Smith***

*Vice President for Church Ministries, The Christian and Missionary Alliance*

*When you know who you are, then you know your authority and can stand firm against the strategies of the enemy. That is the key takeaway I received from Chapter 14. The Lion, the Church and the Warfare is a significant work on understanding the schemes of the enemy, understanding our identity in Christ, understanding our mission as people of God when it comes to warfare and understanding the purpose of worship and prayer — in our lives and as weapons of warfare. Dr. Schroeder has given a wonderful gift to the Church. I pray that as you read it, the eyes of your understanding would be open.*

*— **Rev. Kelvin Walker***

*Superintendent of Metro District of The Christian and Missionary Alliance*
*Corporate Vice President of The Christian and Missionary Alliance*

# DEDICATION

Armies of spiritual warriors have served alongside me during the past few decades.

To the trustees, faculty, and staff of Nyack College, 1993-2005, thank you for keeping pace during twelve years of furious growth on campuses in Nyack, New York City, Washington, D.C., Dayton, and Puerto Rico. Thousands of young warriors were sent into many fields armed with spiritual fervor, intellectual depth, and professional expertise because of your influence.

To the trustees, faculty, and staff of Pillar College, 2007-2019+, thank you for weathering floods and famines to plant Christ-centered campuses in the Garden State. Alumni of diverse cultures, ethnicities, economies, societies, and generations are testimonies to your competence and compassion. The best is yet to come!

To alumni of these fine institutions, carry the banner of Christ high as you bring light into the dark sectors of society. You have overcome many adversities in one of the most difficult mission fields on earth, metropolitan New York, and New Jersey. You have my deep respect and confidence that you will finish well and bring many sons and daughters to glory.

# CONTENTS

# ACKNOWLEDGMENTS

If there is any subject one would not want to write on without an army of support, it would be spiritual warfare. This long-contemplated project took seed in my soul two decades ago from experiences I had as president of Nyack College and Alliance Theological Seminary. Occasional ministry trips in Africa, Asia, and South America cultivated my soil; meeting with a band of spiritual warriors in prayer each week for several years (thank you, Chuck, Ron, Lonnie, Frank, Shino, Mike, Peter, and Kurt) planted the seeds; hearing stories of victory over dark powers from some students planted the seeds; and reading the books found in the bibliography at the end of this text gave growth to the plant. Now, it is my hope that the fruit from these influences will bring health and nourishment to many.

A great gift to this venture has been Dr. Diane Zimmerman, who has saved me much embarrassment and enriched your reading pleasure by doing macro- and micro-editing. Thank you, Diane, for the scores of hours you poured over several drafts of the manuscript, for forcing me to clarify my audience, for suggesting greater structural logic, for professionalizing the textual presentation and for keeping me on task by eliminating much extraneous material.

Betzi Schroeder has also helped polish the text by scrutinizing its punctuation and spelling, and by researching and formatting the footnotes and bibliography. My ever-ready wife and companion has also been an emotional and prayer support through the arduous months of writing.

Two men of God, seasoned in spiritual warfare, have been foundational to my views and many comments in this book. They have been like field generals in the Lord's army. Seated with Christ in the heavenly realms is

Dr. John A. MacMillan, author of *The Authority of the Believer*. In the Preface and in footnote 2, I credit him for awakening me to the present realities of spiritual warfare and for helping make sense of encounters I have had with those living under the control of spiritual wickedness. Likewise, in the Preface, I give great appreciation for the incomparable work of Dr. Neil T. Anderson, whose writings and personal practice have been used by God to release untold scores of people from spiritual bondage. I am very grateful to Harvest House Publishers for giving me permission to quote extensively from *The Bondage Breaker*.

Those spiritual heroes who have endorsed this book have had profound influences in my life in ways they probably do not know. I am grateful for their encouragement and modeling of lives of victory over the enemy.

It has been a delight to work with the friendly professionals of Equip Press. Special thanks to Michele, Kara and Stephanie.

Colleagues at Pillar College, especially Dr. Peter Amerman, chair of Biblical Studies, have also encouraged me to finish the work, as this book will likely be used in courses for undergraduate and graduate students.

Mostly, of course, I am eternally indebted to the Lord Sabbaoth, the Commander of heaven's armies, as He is my greatest delight, my deliverer from eternal darkness and my King.

# FOREWORD

The devil is real. We've crossed paths. More than once.

My very first encounter came one night in my freshman year of college, shortly after I found salvation in Christ. In my newly ignited faith, I was eager to start exploring hymns I had never sung before. So, under cover of darkness I slipped into a local church sanctuary near campus, sat down at the piano and in the dim light of one lamp began working my way through a hymnal.

Suddenly, I was aware of a "darkness" surrounding me that was not physical. A chill ran through my body, goose bumps formed on my arms, my pulse raced. *Something* was "there" that felt malignant, evil, oppressive, ominous. It seemed to be hovering, drawing nearer, ready to attack. Ready to devour.

If only at that moment the teachings in David Schroeder's new book on "engaging the battle of the ages" had been around to inform my new walk with Christ. I would have dealt with that night quite differently. Instead, I exited the building in a panic, unable to sleep the rest of the night.

Fortunately for you, however, you *do* get to dig into David's vital "battlefield manual," designed to equip you to understand and deal with any moment like what I experienced.

But a whole lot more!

For, you see, this book is about a conflict of breathtaking *cosmic* proportions — unfolding at a magnitude no one can fully grasp.

This book is about the sinister drama that embroils the entire human race — with huge implications for those of us in saving union with the Son of God, the Lion reigning on the Throne of heaven. Because, it is around *Him* the battle rages.

That is to say, at the end of the day this warfare — both its visible and invisible dimensions — is not about us. It is all about *Christ*.

Since I had my first-time exposure to the enemy of our souls, across decades of worldwide travel into every stream of the Church, I have witnessed many forms of this all-encompassing, life-and-death struggle.

At one end, I've seen its very *personal* manifestations (such as subtle demonic influences), but at another end, I've suffered its *institutional* expressions (such as at the hands of earthly regimes). In some cases, these "principalities, powers, and rulers" in domains of darkness appear to hold sway *territorially* (like over a certain city or country). In other cases, they gain obvious footholds in the minds and morals of whole *societies* (inciting addiction to pornography, for example).

Most surprising to many Christians, however, are passages like 2 Corinthians 10 and 11 where the Bible indicates that, more often than not, these deadly onslaughts take their toll *inside* our churches. This is where Satan erects his most strategic "strongholds." They are found among God's people, designed to diminish for us the glory of God's Son, to rob us of the "purity of devotion" he deserves.

*But, here's the good news.* David Schroeder makes an invaluable contribution to believers by bringing together under one cover a distillation of solid biblical teaching and time-proven practical insights to empower Jesus followers to triumph in the fight. What he's written is the best, most-balanced volume on this critical subject I've ever read.

To whet your appetite, here are just four of the key characteristics of *The Lion, the Church and the Warfare* I'm grateful for. The book is:

**Hopeful.** Its chapters will convince you there's every reason to be filled with eager anticipation about the glorious outcomes in this fight, both now and later. Right off the bat, in the Preface, the author leaves no doubt about the victory awaiting us:

*The Commanding Officer, Jesus Christ, has enlisted His people, the Church, to be His infantry, the boots on the ground, provided them with His authority, and has already won the war through His crucifixion, resurrection and ascension. ... As I write, I am trusting that the truths of Christ's victorious power and appropriation of our true identity in Him will have a liberating and empowering impact on individual readers.*

**Strategic.** You'll discover the battle, and our crucial place in it, is part of a much grander Eternal Plan moving toward triumphant consummation. We read:

*The intention of God's eternal purpose is, namely, to bring everything together under the authority of Christ — everything in heaven and earth (Ephesians 1:10) ...Christ's authority is over all principality, and power, and might and dominion (Ephesians 1:21).*

To fulfill this strategy you'll learn, for example, how our "Supreme Commander" organizes his battle tactics by: preparing a refuge from the forces of evil for all who are redeemed; building his Church in the face of and as a rebuke to our enemy; equipping his people to directly and effectively engage in the battle as he exercises divine authority *through* us; constantly interceding and advocating in the midst of the conflict for his troops to be fully supplied by Heaven. Just to name a few.

The "Last Days" of this Plan (as David Schroeder titles Chapter 28) come when Satan and all his minions are thoroughly destroyed so that the glory of Christ covers the earth as the waters cover the sea, never to be defied or diminished again.

**Practical.** For every reader, this book provides a treasury of helpful and proven suggestions, not only to enlighten us more fully to the scope of the cosmic conflict, but also to enable us to fully, and intelligently, engage the enemy right where we live — and in doing so, contribute meaningfully to his ultimate downfall.

Explore established biblical requisites for victory, including: claiming all the privileges of your position in Christ; learning how to put on the "armor" of Ephesians 6 (which is really all about putting on Christ); the powerful impact of worship and prayer — individual and corporate — to push back the darkness and make room for an increase of the light of Christ throughout the world.

In fact, there's a whole chapter describing the "Boot Camp" where, you may be surprised to learn, virtually *every* facet of Christian discipleship, seen from one perspective, forms a solid, proactive assault on the devil "who's like a roaring lion, seeking someone to devour" (I Peter 5).

**Christological.** Finally, David Schroeder — out of his decades of ministry throughout the world, in the Church and in academic arenas — is determined to make sure the reader understands how and why the combat, both in the heavenly realms and on the earth, is really all about *Christ*. It is because of Him, it is against Him, it is only won through Him and only won for Him.

An entire chapter is devoted to "The Commanding Officer," a comprehensive title applied to Jesus alone and to His reigning leadership today. He who right now leads believers across the globe in his on-going victory parade (2 Corinthians 2:14), has *already* been assigned the *supremacy* in everything, including over all the hosts of evil (Colossians 1:18). He reigns today as our everlasting champion! Devils tremble and flee.

Which is why it's so critical that the book keeps bringing us back to one great biblical doctrine — the *ascension* of Christ. The author writes:

> ... *central to God's plan of redemption as was the resurrection of Christ, His ascension and enthronement in heaven are seen ... to be the capstone of the victory as our Captain is placed well beyond the adversary's access, from which He will orchestrate the final campaign.*

A number of Christian leaders believe our generation of Christians is being prepared to share in a massive acceleration of the Gospel, both in America and among the nations, as a result of a broad-based "Christ Awakening" movement within the churches.

If there's any substance to this expectation — if the Holy Spirit truly is about to cause the whole Church to become *wholly alive* to the whole vision of the whole Christ — then we can be certain of one thing: Spiritual warfare, both local and cosmic, will unfold in full-throttled counter-attacks against all intensifications of Jesus' Kingdom — assaults more ferocious than anything the Church may have yet known.

Before this battle accelerates any further, therefore, *now* is the hour for Christians to dig into the valuable insights found in *The Lion, the Church and the Warfare*. Thank God — literally — that He directed David Schroeder to write this guidebook for such a time as this.

Read it, absorb it, pray it. Then, get ready to engage!

— ***David Bryant***
President, *Proclaim Hope!*
Founder, ChristNow.com
Author, *Christ Is NOW!*

*Now we see through a glass darkly*

*Take up the full armor of God, so that you will be able to resist in the evil day, and having done everything, to stand firm. Stand firm therefore …*

# A WORD FROM THE AUTHOR

## The Devil Made Me Do It

You have heard and maybe said, "The devil made me do it!" It's a joke, right? The idea that the devil made me do it? It is usually used as a somewhat humorous excuse nobody really believes, but it's a good way to trivialize our miscues. Even people who don't believe in a real devil may use that phrase. But hardly anyone believes it, and neither do I.

I don't believe the devil can **make** anyone do anything. But I do believe Satan has far more influence on individuals and society than we imagine. Am I unduly superstitious or naively paranoid? I don't think so (but as a friend says, just because you're paranoid doesn't mean they're not out to get you).

For the past three years I have been writing this book on spiritual warfare — not a topic I chose; it chose me. Let me explain. For the past few decades I have had the privilege and assignment of serving on international mission boards in Asia and Europe, requiring annual trips. I've also traveled in ministry in countries in Africa, the Middle East, and Latin America. Unless one goes strictly as a tourist to the countries I have been in and remains antiseptically remote from those cultures, or if one has no spiritual eyesight whatsoever, the presence of very dark forces is obvious. Our western, spiritually dumbed-down worldview cannot explain much of what I have seen.

To gain a better biblical handle on the spiritual worldview presented in the Bible and believed in by many supposedly less-advanced cultures, I began studying an old book I was exposed to as a teenager — *The Authority of the Believer* by John A. MacMillan. Then I supplemented that with heavy doses of Neil Anderson and Michael Heiser. Several more trips into animist, Buddhist, and Communist countries opened my eyes even more. Consequently, I felt compelled to write *The Lion, the Church and the Warfare*.

So, back to the question of whether the devil makes us do it, meaning commit sins. The answer, I believe, is a definite yes and no. All sin and evil are ultimately traceable back to the success of the tempter, the adversary, which is the meaning of *satan*. So, yes, he's to blame. But, no, he isn't. He can only tempt. Satan cannot force anyone to sin. True, the devil is deceptively seductive, and he knows how to play on our weaknesses, but we are ultimately responsible for our own sins. It just won't fly when you stand before God the Judge and say, "The devil made me do it."

So, how can we successfully "Just say no"? Two ideas come to mind: 1) Choose to fear the right lion; not the roaring lion who seeks to devour you (1 Peter 5:8), but the Lion of the tribe of Judah who has prevailed and has authority (Revelation 5:5). 2) Die. Die to yourself, a concept found in the Gospels and epistles. Die to your rights, your reputation, your plans, your amusements, your possessions — die to everything that Satan can get his claws on to take you down. And don't forget to die to your unbiblical worldview that tries to make a joke of God's enemy. Hopefully, as you read and apply the truths in this book, God will arouse you to be a spiritual warrior.

# PREFACE

Obviously, apologies or at least credit go to an intellectual mentor, C. S. Lewis, for the title of this book.[1] I'd like to think he would approve, both for its creativity and the worldview it portrays. The struggles of Peter, Susan, Edmund and Lucy may or may not suggest the spiritual warfare made more obvious in another of Lewis' famous works, *The Screwtape Letters*, but the imagery is apt.

Whether one takes the lion to be Jesus Christ, the *Lion of the tribe of Judah* (Revelation 5:5) or the devil who is depicted as a *roaring lion seeking someone to devour* (1 Peter 5:8), matters not, as both are the principal adversaries in the warfare.

Unlike *Chronicles* and Lewis' other marvelous fictions, the subject of this book is not fiction. It is the battle of the ages with the highest of stakes, the souls of all who are created in the image of God, that is, all human beings. The warfare is invisible to most, but all too real as many of its victims and prisoners can attest. The Commanding Officer, Jesus Christ, has enlisted His people, the Church, to be His infantry, the boots on the ground, provided them with His authority, and has already won the war through His crucifixion, resurrection, and ascension. We are in the mopping up phase, commissioned to rescue those Satan is still seeking to devour.

---

1    For those unfortunate ones who are unfamiliar with Lewis' *The Chronicles of Narnia,* the title of this book is a take-off on one of the seven novels of the series. Over 100 million copies have been sold and several popular movies have been produced based on the books.

A superstitious person would never think to write a book like this. Neither would a theological liberal. Nor, even a generic, lukewarm believer. And maybe a Spirit-filled pastor / college president would be wise not to venture into a treatise that, hopefully, will enrage the enemy of God.

I say "hopefully," not because I am trying to pick a fight with Satan, but because, on God's behalf, I want the devil to feel threatened by being exposed and rendered less potent in the life of the Church. We are living in the last days, the *eschaton*, and Satan's day of dominance on earth is nearly over. So, he is marshalling all his power and forces in rebellion to attack God's kingdom and take as many as possible down with him.

We see this in the clashing of nations and ideologies. King David was truly a warrior, but even he asked, *Why are the nations in an uproar?* (Psalm 2:1).Today, there are many answers to that question: religious radicalism (fundamentalist Islam), economic supremacy (oil), territorial greed (Russia), cultural hatred (North Korea), ethnic purging (antisemitism), technological espionage (many nations and individuals) and privileged protection (USA and the first-world nations of the West). Nations, cultures, and ethnic groups are clashing all over the globe.

One of President Franklin Delano Roosevelt's famous sayings was, "I hate war, Eleanor hates war, Fala hates war." Fala was their dog. Now, I suppose it's possible for dogs to hate war — but usually just the smaller dog hates war. Humorous as "Fala hates war" may be, it opens the question, "From where does the universal penchant for fighting and war come?" The Apostle James asks that question: *Where do wars and fights come from among you?* He answers his own question by saying that they come from our evil desires and our efforts to get what others have (James 4:1-2). Such selfish greed causes individuals, nations, and fanatics of an ideology to engage in war.

The great cosmic war taking place primarily in the heavenly realms is no different. Satan's evil desires, his greed, and, above all, his choosing to be his own god, make this a war we cannot avoid — not if we are God's people in His kingdom. His Church is both a fortress, in which through fellowship and learning we are protected and prepared for battle, and also a battle ground. Satan hates the Church almost as much as Jesus loves the

Church. He hates it because when God's people gather freely to worship, to lift up praises that glorify Him, and to encourage each other with the reminder of Satan's downfall as we share communion, for example, that is the most humiliating and hurtful thing Satan must endure. The worshipping Church is a reminder

> Satan is a fraud and a failure, and we are a rebuke to his rebellion.

to Satan that he is a fraud and a failure, and we are a rebuke to his rebellion. We reinforce his guilt by our submission to Christ and our love for Him. That's why I love attending and being part of a local church — as we gather with God's adoring children to praise Him and to do further damage to Satan's mutinous psyche. I love the Church at war because *the weapons of our warfare are not of the flesh, but divinely powerful for the destruction of fortresses* (2 Corinthians 10:4).

While this book is not a research text, I would be remiss not to draw on the wisdom of spiritual authorities from the past. Chief among them has been a literary mentor, John A. MacMillan, whose brief essays were compiled in a short book, *The Authority of the Believer.*[2] I credit him with opening my eyes to new dimensions of spiritual reality. His essays were mostly circulated among the people of the denomination he served in, The Christian and Missionary Alliance. He served as a missionary in China and the Philippines, and then became editor of *Alliance* magazine and a professor at Nyack Missionary College in New York. If I know of any work whose importance far exceeds its acclaim and circulation, it is *The Authority of the Believer.* Copies may be obtained, but it has gone in and out of print. For that reason, I have gained permission from the latest publisher to quote extensively from it. MacMillan's language may be a bit quaint (and advanced) for modern readers, but the content is so enlightening.

---

2    The contents of MacMillan's book first appeared as a series of articles in *The Alliance Weekly* (now *Alliance Life*). The first series appeared under the title *The Authority of the Believer.* A second series carried the title *The Authority of the Intercessor.* Both series were subsequently published as pamphlets. This volume combines both booklets, since they both deal essentially with the same truth, the authority of the believer.

A more contemporary author on the topic of spiritual warfare is Neil T. Anderson, and I have drawn from his excellent books *Victory Over the Darkness* (1990), *Walking Through the Darkness* (1991) and especially, *The Bondage Breaker* (2000).[3] In fact, while re-reading *The Bondage Breaker*, I nearly aborted this project, even while halfway through the writing. So much of what I was saying was said by Anderson and illustrated with real-life stories from his own vast experience. What persuaded me to continue was realizing I was writing for a slightly different audience and purpose. Neil Anderson's writing is directly personal and pastoral to help individuals find release or freedom from spiritual forces which torment or cripple them spiritually, psychologically, and socially. I have written *The Lion, the Church and the Warfare* to enlist more Christ-followers (the Church) for spiritual warfare, to expand their understanding of the unseen realm and to encourage them to use the authority Christ has conferred on His people for success against God's enemy. Beyond these purposes is my desire to help the people of God understand that spiritual warfare is not just about expelling demons, which very few Christians are engaged in (or even believe).

As I write, I am trusting that the truths of Christ's victorious power and appropriating our true identity in Him will have a liberating and empowering impact on individual readers. My hope is to help leaders enable their churches to become military academies for Christ's kingdom, not just hospitals for people who are hoping to recover or country clubs for spiritual socializing. So, I write to and for the Church, much as Paul was writing to the Ephesians, but certainly without his level of inspiration. As a Christian college president, I would be very pleased if the book would be used in the academy to further prepare students who intend to engage in many types of ministry.

Another source I have referenced freely is *Ephesians — God's Grace and Guidance in the Church*, which I wrote, and which was published in 1998 as

---

3    As cited on the copyright page, I am grateful to Harvest House for permission to quote extensively from *The Bondage Breaker*. Other useful sources for going deeply into the field of spiritual warfare are found in the bibliography at the end of this book.

part of the Deeper Life Pulpit commentary series (Christian Publications, Inc.). Reviewing that work nearly two decades later has been an exercise in humility. While the letter Paul wrote to the Ephesians[4] truly describes God's grace and guidance for the Church, when I wrote the commentary I was unaware of the importance of the spiritual worldview that Paul emphasized in each chapter. Unfortunately, I did not find that in other commentaries either. Most of us take the spiritual armor section in 6:10-17 to be sort of like Paul saying, "Oh, by the way, I almost forgot — you need to be careful and prayerful because the devil will try to destroy you." My more careful study revealed that spiritual conflict was the main point of all the other teachings in Ephesians, as I hope to show in this book.

Satan has deceived the Church in many ways, but his greatest deception is our unawareness that many of the dysfunctions and failures in Christian families, churches and organizations are due to Satan's influences in day-to-day activities and conversations. When the Apostle Paul wrote, referring to Satan, *for we are not ignorant of his schemes* (2 Corinthians 2:11), he certainly must not have meant twenty-first-century Christians because we truly are unaware of Satan's schemes. Look in the cracks in a relationship between a Christian husband and wife, and you will find Satan smiling at you. Check closely the "exaggeration" on the resume of a Christian pastor, salesman or executive, and the devil's fingerprints will be evident. Look at the empty chair in the living room as a depressed widow seeks to drown her sorrow in alcohol and afternoon soap operas, and you will find Satan to be her invisible companion. Glance quickly at the porn site that the teenage youth group leader is addicted to, and be aware that lurking behind the sensual scenes of the digital hookers are satanic pimps. Visit the hospital room of the teenage girl whose cutting and anorexia have put her there, and you may

---

4    I am aware, of course, of the uncertainty of Paul's intended recipients and the reasons for that uncertainty. Earliest manuscripts do not indicate the addressee. Quite likely, the letter was intended to be a circular letter for churches in the province of Asia, much as Colossians seems to have been. Nevertheless, I will be referring to the letter as traditionally understood — to the "saints in Ephesus." See also footnote 28.

see Satan enjoying her misery. And examine the digital device addiction that enslaves millions of modern "screen-agers," and you will see God's enemy enjoying his captive.

> Spiritual warfare includes living the Christian life the way God designed it to be lived.

Thousands of other illustrations of dysfunctions, even among Christians, could be cited — things that we tend to believe are just part of the weaknesses of humanity, or of sin in general — that are truly "schemes" of the devil, which we do not seek to acknowledge or confront, much to the enemy's pleasure. While we do not need to become paranoid or blame every human ill on Satan, we give him unnecessary victories when we do not see that our major weapon against his schemes is living in daily obedience to Christ. In other words, spiritual warfare includes living the Christian life the way God designed it to be lived. The many hortatory sections (strong exhortations for practical Christian living) of the Gospels and epistles must be taken seriously — such passages in Ephesians 4 and 5 which exhort us in the areas of wholesome speech, sexual purity, anger, theft, greed, coveting, drunkenness, and insubordination.

**Navigating *The Lion, the Church and the Warfare***

Chapters 1-4 of this book set the stage or, more properly, the field of the warfare, noting that it is not the world at large that is in active battle, but the Church of Jesus Christ which is fighting for the honor of His kingdom. Chapters 5-8 describe the enemy of God, known by various names, and his strategies which he exercises through his own armies of wicked beings. The battleground is really the souls of men and women, many of them being held captive and scheduled for eternal separation from God, as we see in Chapters 9-13. In Chapters 14-17 we meet the Commanding Officer, who is also the King. We see why He has already been victorious through God's eternal plan. Almost ready to engage the battle in earnest, Chapters 19 through 23 reveal the warriors who have been selected, trained, and prepped for battle. In Chapters 24 through 27, the warriors take authority over the enemy, confidently standing in their armor and waging warfare under the Commander's orders. Finally, in Chapters 28-30, we see what we have known all along: The ultimate triumph belongs to the God whose kingdom shall reign forever and ever.

But we are getting ahead of ourselves here. Before marching ahead, let us be aware that for neither the author nor the reader is this subject or activity merely intellectual or theological. God's enemy is very real and wicked. He delights in destroying individuals, families, churches, and nations. And he is apt to attack anyone who renounces and exposes the kingdom of darkness. As one incorporated in Christ, I do not fear him because *greater is he who is in (me) than he who is in the world* (1 John 4:4), but neither am I careless.

Just as I have prayed for spiritual protection throughout this writing, I implore the reader to do so as you read. I am convinced that if a reader's interest is merely academic, with no intended call-to-arms, he or she may not need to worry about being spiritually harassed. But if one is intent on joining the warfare, of seeking first God's kingdom, then the enemy will attack, but you, being grounded in God's Word and covered with His banner of blood and spiritual armor, will not succumb to his annoyances.

Over the past few decades, an entertainment fad has come and gone and come back again — wearing 3-D glasses in movie theaters. So, get ready for 5-D, not the fourth dimension of physics, which is time, but the fifth dimension of eternity. The fifth dimension is the *epouranios*, the heavenly realm, which means a lot more than heaven, the abode of God. Put on your 5-D glasses, the *eyes of your heart* (Ephesians 1:18), and get ready for a reality worldview you probably have not seen before.

# SECTION ONE
# THE WAR OF THE AGES

# 1

## CHURCH AT WAR

The name of this chapter suggests several possibilities:

- A local church with warring factions within, such as the church at Corinth, or a church split today over disagreement about worship styles.
- War, such as doctrinal disputes, between local churches or denominations. For example, disputes between Calvinists and Arminians, or Pentecostals and Presbyterians.
- Warfare between the church and the community or culture in which it lives, such as a publicly displayed cross or nativity scene, or the definition of marriage. This warfare seems to be growing as terrorism, secularism, humanism, and atheism are intent on eradicating Christianity from our culture.
- But scripture also indicates that there is a deeper war — the true cause of all war, and here's a hint — it isn't on earth. War was started and continues in the *epouranios*, the heavenly realms, a word we explore later in this book.

### The World of the War

When my wife Betzi and I moved to Colorado Springs in 1991, we were excited to be able to buy a beautiful house in the Pine Cliff section along the front range of the Rocky Mountains. From our back deck we had a magnificent view of Pike's Peak and Garden of the Gods. We were told by the realtor that our particular hill in Pine Cliff was known as Rattlesnake Hill, but no one had seen a rattler for quite some time — until Betzi came face to face with a three-foot-long rattlesnake as she was cleaning the rock garden in the back!

Now, anyone who has met Betzi knows her to be about the calmest person on the planet. And, fortunately, that quality probably spared her from being bitten. Gingerly, she backed away and came and informed me of the intruder, although by that time some fear had begun to overwhelm her tranquility.

Macho as I needed to be at that moment, I grabbed a shovel and went to the back yard. By this time, the snake had moved off the rock ledge onto the finely crushed rock part of our yard — perfect for my murderous intentions. Coming behind it, shovel poised to strike, I breathed a quick prayer, and, WHAM, with one stroke, I severed its head completely from the rest of its body. Mission accomplished, sort of. What I then saw really freaked me out. The body began coiling and uncoiling, at least six inches from the severed head. But even more freaky, the jaws kept snapping open and closed. I knew that although the snake was dead, if it bit me I would still be poisoned and in need of medical help.

Eventually, its primitive nervous system got the message that it was dead, and all the scary theatrics stopped. The next day, my freshman son Brian took the severed serpent to high school. I didn't know they still did show-and-tell in high school, but he enjoyed showing off the dead snake to his biology class.

## Killing Satan

Often since that serpentine assassination in my garden have I thought about another snake in the first earthly garden. Unfortunately, that snake seemed to have won the battle, as our human parents succumbed to its lying seduction, causing us to be banished from God's immediate presence and to die spiritually. The after-effects of that encounter are responsible for all the evil, sickness, sin, disease, and death in the world since that awful day.

But, back to my snake story. The lesson from the Pine Cliff snake that grips me most is the imagery of the dead snake still behaving as though it were alive. That's the story of Satan

> What Satan didn't know was that he was the one being killed on the cross.

today. The seed of the woman, Jesus Christ, struck the head of the serpent, as prophesied by God in Genesis 3:15. The atoning death of our Lord was the great victory of God that undoes the curse of the Garden of Eden and dooms God's adversary eternally. Satan's head has been crushed. God's enemy thought he had the victory as Jesus hung on the cross. What Satan didn't know was that he was the one being killed on the cross. Nevertheless, like our Pine Cliff rattler, Satan continues to writhe and seeks to strike every human he can. The day is coming soon when he will realize he is dead.

Martin Luther envisioned that in his hymn *A Mighty Fortress Is Our God.* [5]

The first stanza tells about God and the enemy:

1. *A mighty fortress is our God, a bulwark never failing;*
   *Our helper He, amid the flood of mortal ills prevailing:*
   *For still our ancient foe doth seek to work us woe;*
   *His craft and pow'r are great, and, armed with cruel hate,*
   *On earth is not his equal.*

The second stanza refers to our inability to have victory without Christ Jesus, Lord Sabbaoth, the God of heaven's armies:

2. *Did we in our own strength confide, our striving would be losing,*
   *Were not the right Man on our side, the Man of God's own choosing.*
   *Dost ask who that may be? Christ Jesus, it is He;*
   *Lord Sabbaoth, His Name, from age to age the same,*
   *And He must win the battle.*

---

5    *A Mighty Fortress Is Our God* was written by Martin Luther in 1529 and translated into English by Frederick H. Hedge in 1853.

The third stanza assures us that despite the real threat of the Prince of Darkness, God will triumph through one little word:

3. *And though this world, with devils filled, should threaten to undo us,*
   *We will not fear, for God hath willed His truth to triumph through us;*
   *The Prince of Darkness grim, we tremble not for him;*
   *His rage we can endure, for lo, his doom is sure,*
   *One little word shall fell him.*

The last stanza says that it is God's unfailing truth that wins the battle and establishes His eternal kingdom:

4. *That word above all earthly pow'rs, no thanks to them, abideth;*
   *The Spirit and the gifts are ours through Him Who with us sideth;*
   *Let goods and kindred go, this mortal life also;*
   *The body they may kill: God's truth abideth still,*
   *His kingdom is forever.*

But killing Satan? Unfortunately, I don't think that can or will be done, and certainly not by mere humans. Christ has already done that, and we know the end of the story (Revelation 20:10), but more on that later.

## Biblical Cosmology

For many modern people, my snake story and Luther's hymn would be seen as vestiges of past and primitive ideas. Satan — really? The cartoonish red guy with horns, hoofs, tail, and pitchfork? You mean, people really still believe in that stuff?

Well, yeah, they do. Even in the sophisticated, enlightened West, polls show that the majority of people believe in the realty of the devil. Hopefully, not the pitch-forked one, but an evil adversary who seeks to lead humans astray. Such people, and untold millions in other cultures and throughout history, have held to an open worldview that allows for the possibility of realities that are beyond our sensory experience.

Everyone has a worldview, and the worldview embraced by Christians may be called a biblical worldview or cosmology. A cosmology (*kosmos* — the world + *logoi* — words) is a view of the structure of the world or the universe. Depending on one's worldview, it may entail simply the material world of planet earth or layers of metaphysical reality that include the heavenly realms *(epouranios)*. A biblical cosmology encompasses realities and existences beyond what our five senses detect.[6]

Although other terms in Scripture, such as *third heaven* (2 Corinthians 12:2), may refer to the heavenly realms, we focus mostly on the adjective *epouranios,* which is a derivative of the Greek word for heaven. It occurs twenty-three times in seventeen verses according to the Greek concordance of the NASB: once in John 3:12; six times in Hebrews; the rest in four of Paul's letters, mostly Ephesians. The lexicon shows these uses:

1.  existing in heaven

    (a) things that take place in heaven

    (b) the heavenly regions

    >   (i)   heaven itself, the abode of God and angels

    >   (ii)  the lower heavens, of the stars

    >   (iii) the heavens, of the clouds

    (c) the heavenly temple or sanctuary

2.  of heavenly origin or nature[7]

An article by Matt Slick, a Christian apologist, shows how these understandings related to Jewish and Christian cosmology in biblical times:[8]

---

6   See Addendum 1, *Biblical Worldview Ideas and Scriptures.*

7   Thayer's Greek Lexicon, https://www.biblestudytools.com/lexicons/greek/kjv/epouranios.html.

8   Matt Slick, CARM, Christian Apologetics and Research Ministry, Dictionary of Theology, "Heaven." Scriptures are taken from the New International Version. Used by permission.

*At the time of ancient Israel, they did not have as complete an understanding of the universe as we do today. So, they wrote in terms with which they were familiar. The Jews spoke of three heavens. The first heaven consisted of the earth atmosphere where the clouds and birds were. The second heaven was where the sun, stars, and moon was* [sic]. *The third heaven was the dwelling place of* God. *When Paul said that he was caught up to the third heaven (2 Cor. 12:2), he was referring to the very dwelling place of God.*

### The First Heaven: Earth Atmosphere
- Deut. 11:17, *"Then the LORD's anger will burn against you, and he will shut the heavens so that it will not rain and the ground will yield no produce ..."*
- Deut. 28:12, *"The LORD will open the heavens, the storehouse of his bounty, to send rain on your land in season and to bless all the work of your hands."*
- Judges 5:4, *"O LORD, when you went out from Seir, when you marched from the land of Edom, the earth shook, the heavens poured, the clouds poured down water."*
- Acts 14:17, *"Yet he has not left himself without testimony: He has shown kindness by giving you rain from heaven and crops in their seasons ..."*

### The Second Heaven: Outer Space
- Psalm 19:4, 6, *"In the heavens he has pitched a tent for the sun ... It rises at one end of the heavens and makes its circuit to the other ..."*
- Jeremiah 8:2, *"They will be exposed to the sun and the moon and all the stars of the heavens which they have loved and served ..."*
- Isaiah 13:10, *"The stars of heaven and their constellations will not show their light."*

### The Third Heaven: God's Dwelling Place
- 1 Kings 8:30, *"(phrase repeated numerous times in following verses), then hear from heaven, your dwelling place ..."*

- Psalm 2:4, *"The One enthroned in heaven laughs; The LORD scoffs at them."*
- Matthew 5:16, *"In the same way, let your light shine before men, that they may see your good deeds and praise your Father in heaven."*

*The highest heaven, the third heaven, is indicated by the reference to the Throne of God being the highest heaven:*
- 1 Kings 8:27, *"But will God really dwell on earth? The heavens, even the highest heaven, cannot contain you."*
- Deut. 10:14, *"To the LORD your God belong the heavens, even the highest heavens, the earth and everything in it."*

### Which Heaven?

So, which is it? Where is the *epouranios?* The sky above our planet? Outer space? A spiritual dimension where God exists? To get at that answer, look at a few of the occurrences in Ephesians, which refer not only to the heavenly realms, but also to the warfare therein. Notice that I cite **in bold** a passage from each of the six chapters, supporting my contention that the spiritual cosmology underlies the teaching of the entire letter.

Ephesians 1:19-21
*I also pray that you will understand the incredible greatness of God's power for us who believe him. This is the same mighty power that raised Christ from the dead and seated him in the place of honor at God's right hand in the* **heavenly realms.** *Now he is far above any ruler or authority or power or leader or anything else — not only in this world but also in the world to come.*

Ephesians 2:2
*You used to live in sin, just like the rest of the world, obeying the devil — the commander of the powers in* **the unseen world** *(the prince of the power of the air — NASB). He is the spirit at work in the hearts of those who refuse to obey God.*

Ephesians 3:10, 11

*God's purpose in all this was to use the church to display his wisdom in its rich variety to all the unseen rulers and authorities in the **heavenly places**. This was his eternal plan, which he carried out through Christ Jesus our Lord.*

Ephesians 4:10, 26, 27

*And the same one who descended is the one who ascended higher than **all the heavens**, so that he might fill the entire universe with himself.*
*And "don't sin by letting anger control you." Don't let the sun go down while you are still angry, for anger gives a foothold to the devil.*

Ephesians 5:11, 12

*Take no part in the worthless deeds of **evil and darkness**; instead, expose them. It is shameful even to talk about the things that ungodly people do in secret.*

Ephesians 6:11, 12

*Put on all of God's armor so that you will be able to stand firm against all strategies of the devil. For we are not fighting against flesh-and-blood enemies, but against evil rulers and authorities of **the unseen world**, against mighty powers in this dark world, and against evil spirits in the **heavenly places**.*

(Verses cited from NLT, emphasis mine)

There may not be a definitive answer to the question of the location of the heavenly realms. It seems from the above verses that Jesus is seated next to the throne of God in the heavenly realms, and it also seems that Satan and his minions are somehow present in the heavenly realms, as well as being the princely leader of the powers of the air.

It's interesting that although Scripture makes it very clear that the earth is the Lord's and everything in it, presumably including the atmosphere above (Psalm 24:1), when Satan tempted Jesus, he *led him up and showed Him all the kingdoms of the world in a moment of time. And the devil said to Him, "I will give you all this dominion and its glory; for it has been handed over to me, and I give it to whomever I wish"* (Luke 4:5, 6). Jesus did not dispute this idea, which does not make it true, as Satan is *the father of lies* (John 8:44).

MacMillan writes:

> *It is necessary to state here what is commonly understood by those who carefully study the Word, that the kingdoms of this world are under the control and leadership of satanic principalities. The great head of these is, in the Gospel of John, three times acknowledged as 'prince of this world' by our Lord Himself. His asserted claim to the suzerainty of the world kingdoms, made to the Lord Jesus (Luke 4:6), was not denied by Christ. Although a rebel against the Most High and now under judgment of dispossession (John 12:31), he is still at large, and as the masses of mankind are also rebels, he maintains over them an unquestioned, because unsuspected, rule, their eyes being blinded to his dominance (2 Corinthians 4:4).*
>
> *The whole rebellious system is divided into heavenly and earthly sections (Isaiah 24:21). These are 'the host of the high ones that are ones that are on high' (the unseen powers of the air) and 'the kings of the earth upon the earth' (the rulers of mankind and their subjects).*[9]

My view is that *epouranios* refers to a spiritual dimension, which includes all three atmospheres. It should not surprise us that God does not intend or need us to have a full understanding of that dimension. But I believe He wants us to know that a cosmic warfare exists, and we are part of it.

---

9    John A. MacMillan, *The Authority of the Believer* (Harrisburg, PA, Christian Publications, Inc., 1997) p. 14.

## Summary Thoughts from Chapter 1, Church at War

- What Satan didn't know was that he was the one being killed on the cross.
- A biblical cosmology includes realities and existence beyond what our five senses detect.
- *Epouranios,* which is a derivative of the Greek word for heaven, occurs twenty-three times in seventeen verses and expresses the idea of heavenly realms.
- God's purpose in all this was to use the church to display his wisdom in its rich variety to all the unseen rulers and authorities in the **heavenly places** (Ephesians 3:10).
- The whole rebellious system is divided into heavenly and earthly sections (Isaiah 24:21).

# 2

## WORLDVIEW SHIFT

Many in our modern, scientifically driven society reject the idea of a heavenly realm, or any reality that is metaphysical,[10] or outside of nature. What naturalists do not accept or agree with is that every worldview is a faith-worldview, but truly, the naturalist has more faith than the believer because the naturalist has to believe that everything got here by way of nothing, rather than being created by an unseen Somebody. Both worldviews require faith; the believer is honest about his or her faith.[11]

> The naturalist has to believe that everything got here by way of nothing.

Commenting on worldviews, Neil Anderson provides these insights:

> *In stark contrast to Western rationalism and naturalism, other inhabitants of the world have a different view of reality. The reality of the spiritual world is part of their culture and worldview. Animistic and spiritistic cultures appease their gods with peace offerings and perform religious rituals to ward off evil spirits. In many Third World nations, religious practice or superstition has more practical relevance in daily life than science does.*

---

10    Metaphysical is a compound word; meta, meaning "with," "change," or "alongside."

11    See my article, *Being and Nothingness*, Addendum 2.

*It is easy for those who are educated in the West to dismiss Eastern worldviews as inferior on the basis of our advanced technology and economic success. But why then do we have the highest crime rate of any industrial nation and the greatest distribution of pornographic filth?*

*Between the two tiers is what Dr. Paul Hiebert calls the "excluded middle," the real world of spiritual forces active on earth. We must include the kingdom of darkness in our worldview because in reality there is no excluded middle! When Paul talks about the spiritual battle in the heavenlies, he is not referring to some distant place like Mars or Pluto. He is referring to the spiritual realm, the kingdom of darkness that is all around us and governed by the ruler of this world.*[12]

Not only is the Western, modern world dismissive of the supernatural worldview of the Eastern world, it also rejects the worldview of the ancients, which Michael Heiser persuasively demonstrates in his books *Supernatural* and *The Unseen Realm*.[13]

Neil Anderson confirms the demonic worldview held by church fathers and goes on to document their thought of the demons being apostatized angels.

*Nor did the early church fathers have a problem with the reality and personality of demons. Origen wrote:*

---

12    Neil T. Anderson, *The Bondage Breaker*, (Eugene, OR: Harvest House Publishers, 1990), pp. 30, 31.

13    Michael S. Heiser, *Supernatural* and *The Unseen Realm*, both published by Lexham Press, Bellingham, WA, 2015. As a Hebrew language scholar, Heiser examines the worldview of ancient Semitic cultures, demonstrating a very different picture of the heavenly beings (*elohim*) than is commonly presented in western theological texts and systematic theologies. Reading his books opens one to a much larger picture of the great drama that is the primary theme of the Bible. His material and the worldview he presents convincingly from Old and New Testaments also answer many of the thorny questions usually passed over by preachers and Bible teachers. Throughout this book, we try to be consistent with the perspective he shares, but it is often so unlike the theology we have been steeped in that this has been a learning exercise for this author.

> *In regard to the devil and his angels and opposing powers, the ecclesiastical teaching maintains that the beings do indeed exist; but what they are or how they exist is not explained with sufficient clarity. This opinion, however, is held by most: that the devil was an angel; and having apostatized, he persuaded as many angels to fall away with himself; and these, even to the present time, are called his angels.*[14]

Even two generations earlier, John MacMillan saw the worldview shift that is still taking place.

> *The rapidly approaching end of the age is witnessing a tremendous increase in the activity of the powers of darkness. Unrest among the nations, more intense than at any previous time in earth's history, is due largely to the stirring up of the ambitions and passions of men, while the spread of an almost wholly secularized education is quietly doing away with the scriptural standards which formerly exerted a restraining influence among the so-called Christian peoples. Our wealth and social culture have not made us thankful to the Giver of all good, but have centered us upon the material things of the world, and have produced a self-sufficiency that quite ignores our dependence upon the Creator of all.*[15]

The worldview of much of modern society does not recognize the battles we face daily as coming from spiritual forces that seek to corrupt and destroy the work of God, but we are in the eternal war of the ages, which can be seen in earthly wars.

## Spiritual Warfare

So, what, exactly, is spiritual warfare? We do not know a lot about the warfare that is waged in the heavenlies between spiritual beings, but spiritual

---

14   Anderson, *Bondage Breaker,* p. 116, as cited by Michael Scanlan, T. O. R., and Randall J. Cirner, *Deliverance from Evil Spirits* (Ann Arbor, MI: Servant Books, 1980), p. 16.

15   MacMillan, p. 3.

warfare also exists on earth and it involves humans, especially Christians, in ways we might not recognize. Here's an attempt at an explanation about spiritual warfare that involves humans. Satan battles against Christians and non-Christians through temptations that lead to sin, which increases his power over an individual. The non-Christian has very little defensive strength — mainly his or her best intentions and weak willpower — and no offensive strength. Satan's kingdom suffers no damage at the hands of nonbelievers. Christians have spiritual armor and prayer as defensive tactics (see Ephesians 6:10-18 and Chapter 24 of this book) and Spirit-filled righteous living as an offensive weapon.

How so? When Christ-loving, God-honoring, Holy Spirit-filled people live the way God intended, that is a huge victory over God's enemy. Our righteous living and deeds demonstrate and dramatize Satan's failure. So, you are doing spiritual warfare ...

- when you speak truth lovingly
- when you do not covet more riches
- when you do not lust after other people
- when you engage in social justice
- when you are honorable with your finances
- when you humbly help the less fortunate
- when you tell others the Good News about Jesus
- and when you read God's Word, pray, worship, and fellowship with God's people.

In other words, just by living the Christian life you are engaged in spiritual warfare.

## Cosmic Warfare

The world is at war today. It always has been from the beginning of time (and even before time). According to a 2003 *New York Times* article,[16] if war is defined as a conflict that has killed at least 1,000 people, the world

---

16    Chris Hedges, *New York Times*, July 6, 2003.

has been at peace for only 268 out of the last 3,400 years of human history, less than 8 percent of the time. But that is just earthly war, which is just a reflection of the super-cosmic battle that has been raging on earth since God allowed Satan into the Garden of Eden. Most people, even Christians, know nothing about this war, even though our souls are the battlegrounds. Earthly battles of all kinds are inspired and motivated by the enemies of God whose sole aim is to destroy God's creation, beginning with the beings created in God's image, human beings. Our self-centered agendas take us into all kinds of rebellion and perversion, which are intensifying as the Day of the Lord draws near.

The apostles Paul and Peter, and Jesus, of course, anticipated this *eschaton,* this last day:

> *But realize this, that in the last days difficult times will come. For men will be lovers of self, lovers of money, boastful, arrogant, revilers, disobedient to parents, ungrateful, unholy, unloving, irreconcilable, malicious gossips, without self-control, brutal, haters of good, treacherous, reckless, conceited, lovers of pleasure rather than lovers of God.*
>
> 2 Timothy 3:1-4

> *Let no one in any way deceive you, for it (the last day) will not come unless the apostasy comes first, and the man of lawlessness is revealed, the son of destruction, who opposes and exalts himself above every so-called god or object of worship, so that he takes his seat in the temple of God, displaying himself as being God. Then that lawless one will be revealed whom the Lord will slay with the breath of His mouth and end by the appearance of His coming.*
>
> 2 Thessalonians 2:3, 4, 8

> *Know this first of all, that in the last days mockers will come with their mocking, following after their own lusts.*
>
> 2 Peter 3:3

> *In First Timothy 4, the Apostle Paul makes a clear and emphatic prophetic statement. He says: 'Now the Spirit speaketh expressly, that in the latter*

*times' — during the closing part of the church age — 'some shall depart from the faith, giving heed to seducing spirits, and doctrines of devils' (I Timothy 4:1). We have entered into these latter times and are seeing about us what the writer mentions. Numerous cults have arisen or have split off from the churches which hold to the fundamental truths of the Word of God.*[17]

Now, truthfully, we have been in the *eschaton* since Jesus came, and none of us knows for sure when that last calendar day will be, presumably the same as the *parousia*, the coming of the Lord.[18] While we are never encouraged by Jesus to become preoccupied with trying to figure out the exact time of His coming (see Acts 1:7-8), He did admonish His followers to be watchful and be aware of the signs of His coming:

> *But of that day or hour no one knows, not even the angels in heaven, not the Son of Man, but the Father alone. Take heed, keep on the alert; for you do not know when the appointed time will come.*
>
> Mark 13:32-33

Nevertheless, Francis Schaeffer's question is even more relevant than in 1976 when he wrote the ten-part epic book and film series: *How Should We Then Live?*[19] The short answer is found in the Lord's Prayer and teaching: *Your kingdom come. Your will be done, on earth as it is in heaven* (Matthew 6:10); *Seek first the kingdom of God* (Matthew 6:33). So, the answer of how we should live in this turbulent, devilish time is to belong to another kingdom, one which will destroy and supersede the evil empire over which Satan holds sway.

---

> The answer of how we should live in this turbulent, devilish time is to belong to another kingdom.

---

17    MacMillan, p. 163.

18    "Coming," see Matthew 24:3, 27, 37, 39.

19    Francis A. Schaeffer, *How Should We Then Live?* (Old Tappan, NJ: Fleming H. Revell, 1979).

In this chapter we have seen that the realities of the worldview of people from biblical days are still very much in place in our day and in all cultures. Some of the non-humans that God created dwell in the heavenly realms, while others infect the earth and human beings. The popular shift in worldview ideas has not changed the fact that Satan still seeks to disrupt the purposes of God. Spiritual warfare is both a seen and an unseen reality due to satanic rebels against the kingdom of God, as we demonstrate in the following chapter.

## Summary Thoughts from Chapter 2, Worldview Shift

- In addition to rejecting biblical theism, the modern, Western worldview is dismissive of the transcendent worldview of ancient people and the majority of people in the world today.
- Spiritual warfare occurs as Satan battles against Christians and non-Christians through temptations that lead to sin, which increases his power over an individual.
- Spiritual warfare is not just the dramatic activities of confronting demons; daily living for Christ as God prescribes also defeats Satan's attempts to corrupt us.
- Spiritual warfare will continue and intensify as we approach the *eschaton*, the last days.

# 3

---○◦○---

# CLASHING KINGDOMS

---○◦○---

Whether you want to be or not, whether you are aware of it or not, whether you are actively engaged in it or not, you are at war. Planet earth and especially the humans who live here are a battleground of epic proportions and eternal consequences. In case your view of life on earth is that this is merely a staging ground or a waiting room for the next life, beware — you are on a battleground filled with dangerous landmines that the enemy has planted to destroy you. So, as the Apostle Paul told the Roman Christians, *Wake up ... Don't participate in the darkness* (Romans 13:11, 13; NLT). If you are a follower of Jesus Christ, Satan wants to destroy you, your family, and your church because you have abandoned his side and changed your allegiance.

As a follower of Jesus Christ, you are an expatriate. You are living in a country that is not your own. You have renounced your native citizenship and taken an oath of loyalty to a new nation. Your adopted "country" is not a democracy; it's a monarchy, a kingdom, and Jesus is King. He is not just the coming King, He is your King right now.

Philippians 3:20 tells us that our citizenship is in heaven; not "will be," but now. I don't know how you feel about your earthly, native country, but I have bad news for you — it is a fallen culture. In fact, all earthly cultures and nations are fallen. Only the kingdom that Jesus reigns over is

*... that culture — the kingdom of God — should be our first allegiance.*

not fallen, and that culture — the kingdom of God — should be our first allegiance. So, we need to know a lot more about that culture.

As His disciples, we need to learn about the kingdom of God because it is our new nationality, our Fatherland, the kingdom of which we are a part. Any other kingdom or nation we might belong to is not only fallen, it is under the authority of the powers of darkness. Proper decorum for living in God's kingdom must be learned, so we had better understand this kingdom. We wouldn't go to Buckingham Palace without first learning how to dress and behave appropriately. Nor is an alien granted citizenship without first learning the basic facts about his or her new country and government. So, we must learn more about this kingdom which demands our loyalty and spiritual patriotism, and for which we wage spiritual warfare. What, then, is the kingdom of God?

**The Kingdom of God**

The dominant theme of the teachings of Jesus was about His kingdom, which He also called the Kingdom of God.[20] His unique kingdom was recognized in His infancy when the magi from the East came to Jerusalem asking, *Where is He who has been born King of the Jews?* (Matthew 2:2). His kingdom teaching and signs continued until His trial before Pontius Pilate who asked Him, *Are you the King of the Jews?* Jesus responded, *It is as you say* (Matthew 27:11). John's Gospel reports that He went on to say to Pilate, *My kingdom is not of this world* (John 18:36).

If Pilate was confused, he wasn't the only one. A question begged to be asked, but no one dared or thought to ask — what, exactly, do you mean

---

20    The NASB shows "kingdom of God" used fourteen times in Mark's sixteen chapters, thirty-two times in Luke's twenty-four chapters, and four times in Matthew; however, "kingdom of heaven" is used thirty-three times in Matthew's twenty-eight chapters, parallel to the sayings in Mark and Luke, demonstrating Matthew's sensitivity to his Jewish audience in refraining from using the sacred name of God.

by "kingdom"? The King used the phrase frequently, usually in the midst of a parable or story. Like when He said, "The kingdom of God is like a mustard seed." But no one asked the obvious — "What do you mean by kingdom of God?"

And yet by His stories, and more by His life, an understanding of the kingdom of God gradually dawned on the disciples. They began to understand kingdom life because they were experiencing it!

The kingdom of God for King Jesus meant the rule of God in the hearts and lives of people who know, love, and obey God. It is not a geographical place where Jesus owns political control. It is a reign, not a realm. It is an active power in people due to the authority of God in their lives.

One time the Pharisees were asking Jesus about when the kingdom of God would come. He answered them,

> The kingdom of God is not coming with signs to be observed, nor will they say, "Look, here it is!" or "There it is!" For, behold, the kingdom of God is in your midst.

Luke 17:20-21

Jesus was affirming the presence of the kingdom in the lives of His followers, and yet it is obvious from many of the other teachings of King Jesus that there is a dimension of the kingdom that we know nothing about in this life.[21]

So where is the kingdom? What is the kingdom? **When God chooses to confront a situation — that is the kingdom of God.** His kingdom is His presence and power in authority. The kingdom of God was most clearly seen when Jesus used His power to defeat the effects of sin in the lives of people.

---

21   Writing about the resurrection of believers, Paul told the Corinthians:
    But each in his own order: Christ the first fruits, after that those who are Christ's at His coming, then comes the end, when He delivers up the kingdom to the God and Father, when He has abolished all rule and all authority and power (1 Corinthians 15:23, 24).

His authority astonished everyone who witnessed His mighty acts and teachings. Luke reports an interesting statement by King Jesus about His authority over demons and the nature of the kingdom. He had recently expelled a demon, and for doing that He was challenged by the Pharisees regarding the source of His authority. They were suggesting that His strength came from demons. King Jesus made a quick rebuttal to that foolish notion. Then He added, *But if I cast out demons by the finger of God, then the kingdom of God has come upon you* (Luke 11:20).

So, King Jesus saw and taught that the kingdom of God has power over the forces of evil and the damning effects of sin on God's creation. God's kingdom overrules every power that would attempt to undermine and diminish the creative work of God and His eternal plan.

**A National Kingdom?**

The concept of the kingdom of God was revealed first to the Jewish people. In fact, God told Moses that His people were to be a *kingdom of priests* (Exodus 19:6). Priests are those who represent others to God. Question: If all of Israel were to be priests, whom were they to represent to God? Obviously, other human beings, the Gentiles. The story of Jonah, the reluctant missionary-prophet to the Assyrians in Nineveh, illustrates this idea.

After the period of the judges, Israel, wanting to be like the other nations, wanted an earthly king, but God did not want Israel to have an earthly king. Israel was to be a theocracy, a monarchy in which Yahweh Himself would be their King. Yet Israel insisted on having a king, and God allowed their desire (see 1 Samuel 8).

After Israel's 1,000 years of failure at trying to be like the other nations with a king, a baby was born, the promised *seed of the woman* (Genesis 3:15), the subject of dozens of prophecies. As we have seen, He was immediately considered to be a king even as an infant, but He shunned that label (John 6:15), knowing it was a political king the people wanted. Nevertheless, the dominant theme of His life and teaching was about the kingdom of God.[22]

---

22   For those interested in seeing the extent of this theme, please see Addendum 3, *Outline of Matthew's Gospel of the Kingdom.*

As is readily seen in the first narrative section of Matthew's Gospel, both John the Baptist and Jesus came proclaiming the kingdom (Matthew 3:2 and 4:17). The message was a call to *repentance* (see Mark 1:4, 15), a clear indication that entrance into God's kingdom comes through repentance.

The good news (gospel) of the kingdom is the possibility of entering God's kingdom, and Jesus was clear about how that can happen. When the Jewish Sanhedrist Nicodemus visited Him, Jesus rather abruptly cut off Nicodemus' line of inquiry and said, ... *unless one is born again, he cannot see the kingdom of God.* Nicodemus couldn't quite fathom that, so Jesus repeated, ... *unless one is born of water and the Spirit, he cannot enter into the kingdom of God* (John 3:3, 5). The new birth is the entrance into God's kingdom.

Entering the kingdom through repentance and the new birth delivers us from slavery (see Romans 6:6-20). Through Jesus' death and resurrection, we are emancipated, freed from the kingdom of darkness and death, which is the *wages of sin* (Romans 6:23). Every person who experiences the new birth and deliverance from Satan's realm of darkness is saved from eternal damnation in hell.

But that is not all that the gospel provides. Those who now reside in God's kingdom are transformed. Key evidence of God's kingdom is the transformation of self-centered sinners (the way we all start out) into God-centered

> Evidence of God's kingdom is the transformation of self-centered sinners (the way we all start out) into God-centered disciples.

disciples. That is what King Jesus prayed for when He said, *Your kingdom come, your will be done on earth as it is in heaven.* God's will is done by kingdom citizens known as disciples. They are the ones He entrusts with spiritual authority over the demonic powers, as He told His disciples in Matthew 10:8; Mark 6:7, 12, 13; and Luke 9:1; 10:17.

How is all this Good News of the kingdom made possible? By the grace of God!

## Crazy Redeeming Grace

I was taught that when reading a book, especially from a secular author, it might be wise to read the last chapter first. Now, that may spoil a good novel or mystery, but it is often helpful to anticipate where the author wants to take you. In the case of the Bible and understanding the war of the ages, it is good advice. Early believers did not have the advantage of all written revealed truth, but they knew that Christ plans to return to earth so that they (we) will always be with Him in His kingdom (John 14:3). What a wonderful truth! But how is that possible, considering our fallen estate and Satan's powerful grip on creation and humanity?

The answer is summed up in one word: *redemption*. Jesus taught us our part[23] to enter the kingdom, and He also provided the means. God has chosen to pay the price justice demands to purchase our forgiveness and freedom from sin by the sacrifice of His Son, Jesus. What an amazing thought! We must be pretty special creatures for God to be willing to do that. Well, yes and no. We are not so amazing, but God's love and grace are amazing, and so is His *Crazy Love*.[24]

Interestingly, God's grace is at one and the same time unnecessary and essential. It is unnecessary from God's perspective in that nothing forced God to offer such a gift. In fact, nothing compelled God to create His earthly or heavenly families. No constraint or compulsion was on God to provide for man's forgiveness other than His eternal plan and loving kindness. On the other hand, His grace is entirely essential if God is to redeem His fallen creation. The effects of sin are so great that no part of the creation, including mankind, retained enough value to merit God's good pleasure or earn favor with God. Something from outside of creation needed to be offered to atone for the sins of mankind. Therefore, God, by His own free choice and loving kindness offered up His own Son to shed His blood as the payment for our redemption.

---

23     Our part is not what other religions, and even much of Christianity, teach, which can be called "religion" — man's effort to please God by human efforts, like good works, which fail to give the new birth that is necessary for entrance into God's kingdom. That new birth, which the Apostle Paul calls "justification by faith," is a gift which cannot be earned (Romans 6:23).

24     The title of Francis Chan's excellent book (Colorado Springs, CO, David C. Cook, 2008).

The Greek word for *redemption* means to set something free, to release it from bondage. In secular society *redemption* is used infrequently and, usually, incorrectly. People associate the term with trading in coupons for a gift. I recall as a boy going with my parents to a Green Stamp Redemption Center to exchange stamp books for gifts. Today, we can redeem points for flights, or upgrades, or hotel rooms, or car rentals. The idea is surrendering something for something of greater value to you.

Spiritual redemption, however, does not involve an exchange of value. Rather, the one being redeemed is entirely the object of God's grace. In the shameful past, when slaves were owned as property in this country and in others, occasionally, a kind-hearted person would pay for the freedom of a slave and then release him or her completely. The person was said to be redeemed. To be redeemed spiritually is to be set free from the bondage and penalty of sin. God has paid the price so that we may legitimately be released from the bondage of sin and brought into His family.

Ephesians 1:7 states that the primary benefit of redemption is the *forgiveness of our trespasses*. The New Testament uses at least five words that are sometimes translated by the English word *sin*.

- *Hamartia* is the basic word for sin, meaning to miss the mark.
- *Parabaino* is often translated transgression; going beyond an allowable limit.
- *Anomia* may be translated iniquity; lawlessness; rebellion against authority.
- *Adikia* is the opposite of righteousness, being unjust.
- *Paraptoma* is often translated trespass; a false step or a serious blunder.

The word "trespasses" in Ephesians 1:7 is *paraptoma*. So, the redemption received in Christ is the forgiveness of the false steps and blunders which took us into servitude to sin in the first place. Imagine walking through a wooded area, not knowing that hunters had put out traps to ensnare animals to sell or trade the pelts for money. Not seeing the hidden traps, you step into one. That is a false step or a serious blunder, a *paraptoma*. We have all made such false steps, and we need to be released, redeemed, from those sins.

What can set us free from Satan's snares? The source of the forgiveness and the payment of our redemption is the blood of Jesus, according to Ephesians 1:7. Blood, being the most valuable substance in the world, is the ultimate payment for sin. No other substance, regardless of its value, is acceptable to God as a payment for sin. The Cain and Abel story illustrates this vividly, as Cain was rejected by God for bringing a bloodless sacrifice. Through that example, the people of God learned that sin is of such serious consequence that only the shedding of blood would be acceptable to God for the remission of sins (see Hebrews 9:22). Even the pagan religions knew that, but they sacrificed their children. Some of the evil kings of Israel also did that.

So, yes, from God's point of view, we are so special that He has chosen to redeem us. But, there's more!

Are we truly the only reason God has entered our world through Jesus Christ and made Him go through a grisly, painful death — just to redeem us rebellious creatures? I think something bigger is in play here.

**Heavenly Conflicts**

We have already seen in Chapter 1 that the "heavenly realms" idea, using the Greek word *epouranios*, affirms clearly that spiritual warfare is waged beyond planet earth. Some members of the "heavenly council," alluded to in many biblical passages such as Psalm 82, do their nefarious, devilish work on earth, while others battle in the heavenlies. The passage in Daniel 10 demonstrates this, as the archangel (actually *chief prince*) Michael had to fight his way through to bring God's message to Daniel. Michael Heiser notes that the *prince of Persia* who resisted Michael is one of the rebellious heavenly court members sent with the scattered people (nations) at Babel.[25]

---

25    Michael Heiser, *The Unseen Realm*, pp. 119-120.

Sad to say for our human egos, but earth isn't the center stage of God's reality, and we aren't the main actors. This is not to diminish our standing with or importance to God. We who are believers are the prize of the battle God has won in the heavenly places. We are the bride of Christ. But we need to understand that God is still dealing with the great rebellion of Satan,

> Earth isn't the center stage of God's reality, and we aren't the main actors.

and in doing so, He is using His plan of redemption to fulfill His eternal purpose — to humiliate and further condemn His enemy, and to create and gather His forever-family, the Church.

This is explained brilliantly by MacMillan in what I call true replacement theology[26]:

*The 'God of the whole earth' does not purpose to tolerate forever this rebellion against His righteousness. "I have sworn by myself, the word is gone out from my mouth in righteousness, and shall not return, That unto me every knee shall bow, every tongue shall swear" (Isaiah 45:23). Ere this can be accomplished, the instigators to human rebellion must be cast down. In this regard the divine method is clear. 'The powers of the air' are allowed to retain their seats only while their successors are being prepared. God, having redeemed a people and purified them, has introduced them potentially into the heavenlies. When they have approved themselves, they will in actuality take the seats of the 'powers of the air,' thereby superseding those who have manifested their unfitness and unworthiness.[27]*

*This purpose, present and future, is very definitely stated in Ephesians chapter 3:9-11. Here it is revealed as the divine will that 'now (nun, the present time) unto the principalities and powers in the heavenly places might be made known through the church*

> The Church is God's instrument in declaring to these rebellious and now usurping powers the divine purpose.

---

26    "Replacement theology" customarily refers to a view that the Church has replaced Israel in God's plan.

27    MacMillan, p. 19.

*the manifold wisdom of God' (3:10).* **The Church is to be God's instrument in declaring to these rebellious and now usurping powers the divine purpose,** *and in administering their principalities after they have been unseated and cast down.*

*This is further declared to be 'according to the eternal purpose of the ages which he purposed in Christ Jesus our Lord' (3:11). That is to say, God, through all the past ages, has had in view this wonderful plan of preparing in Christ Jesus a people, chosen and called and faithful, whom He might place in these heavenly seats to rule through the ages yet to come. It is spoken of, in the verses just preceding, as 'the mystery, which for ages hath been hid in God,' one phase of this mystery being the wonderful veiling of the deity of the Son of God in our human nature, that we through Him might 'become partakers of the divine nature' (2 Peter 1:4)*[28] (emphasis added).

Could it be that the ultimate number of those "cells" of the body of Christ, the total number of saved people, will equal the number of fallen angels that are being dislodged from the *epouranios?* Speculation, for sure, but maybe the one-for-one idea was hinted at when Jesus heard the report of the seventy-two who returned from their mission exulting that the demons were cast out by the authority of Christ.

*Lord, even the demons submit to us in your name. He replied, "I saw Satan fall like lightning from heaven"* (Luke 10:17, 18).

Might it have been that every dispossessed demon was replaced by a new citizen of the kingdom of God? If that speculation is right, isn't it a lovely and motivating thought that every person who becomes a new follower of Christ, who crosses over from the kingdom of darkness to the kingdom of God, dislodges one of the enemies of God and brings His kingdom one member closer to completion?

---

28 MacMillan, pp. 19-20.

*The 70 disciples came back from their mission with a new perspective, a true perspective. Spiritual authority is not a tug-of-war on a horizontal plane; it is a vertical chain of command. Jesus Christ has all authority in heaven and on earth (Matthew 28:18); He's at the top of the chain of command. He has given His authority and power to His servants to be exercised in His name (Luke 10:17); we're under His authority, but we share it for the purpose of doing His will. And Satan and his demons? They're at the bottom, subject to the authority Christ has invested in us. They have no more right to rule your life than a buck private has to order a general to clean the latrine.*[29]

Christ's victory through His death and resurrection is really two-fold: it redeems repentant, fallen humans from the condemnation we deserve, and it triumphs finally and conclusively over God's enemy who began the warfare long before Eden in his rebellion against God. The redemption of humans from Satan's grip restores God's original purpose to have a family of free, moral agents who respond humbly and submissively to His fatherly love, living forever in His kingdom.

## Summary Thoughts from Chapter 3, Clashing Kingdoms

- Only the kingdom that Jesus reigns over is not fallen, and that culture — the kingdom of God — should be our first allegiance.
- When God chooses to confront a situation — that is the kingdom of God. His kingdom is His presence and power in authority.
- Disciples are the ones He entrusts with spiritual authority over the demonic powers.
- Earth isn't the center stage of God's reality, and we aren't the main actors.

---

29   Anderson, *Bondage Breaker*, pp. 79, 80.

# 4

## INTERNATIONAL CONFLICTS[30]

While the focus of this study is to strengthen God's people for their role in the warfare between God and the spiritual beings which revolted against Him, a greater understanding of the dimensions of the warfare will help us be more alert. The birth of God's kingdom through the people of Israel would not happen without conflict and warfare.

As I write, we are experiencing a time of much international conflict and terror. The foreign policy of the leaders of the United States is being challenged from within and from other nations.

Satan has always been working through the ages and the nations of the world. In the biblical book of Exodus, we see the colossal battles between Moses and Pharaoh, or really, between Yahweh and the gods of Egypt. Only after ten very destructive plagues which Yahweh used *so that the Egyptians will know that I am the LORD* (Exodus 7:5; NIV) did Pharaoh release God's people from slavery.

Upon entering the Promised Land, Canaan, forty years later, the younger generation — those who as children witnessed God's mighty arm of

---

30   See an expansion of this section in Addendum 5, *Satanic Workings through the Ages and the Nations.*

deliverance in Egypt and through the Red Sea and experienced His provisions in the desert — now faced a whole new world of gods. Unfortunately, despite repeated warnings by the prophets, the Israelites were seduced by those gods and drifted away from Yahweh. Satan had them worshipping Baal, Asherah, and even Molech, who enticed the people of God into ritual prostitution and child sacrifice.

Were the Jews aware of Satan's existence and activities? MacMillan describes how the dark kingdom was evident in the earliest times:

*We are sometimes prone to think that the saints of Old Testament times possessed little clear conception of the powers of the unseen world. But this is a misapprehension on our part. It is true that in the Book of Psalms the emphasis first appears to be laid upon visible and physical foes. Those the writer hates "with perfect hatred" (Psalm 139:22) because they were also the enemies of God. But we would be wrong in limiting the thought of the psalmist to what alone could be seen. It will be remembered that Satan is introduced in the very beginning of the Old Testament, and that he appears as the constant adversary of the people of the Lord. The facts also of possession by demons and contact with familiar spirits were well-known and often referred to with reprobation by the prophets and in the Law.*

*Furthermore, the book of Job was written long before the time of David and was unquestionably in his hands and those of the spiritual leaders of Israel. It was doubtless included among the Scriptures in which he meditated with great delight. In this remarkable narrative the veil of the invisible world has been drawn partly aside, and there is given a very startling view of the secret working of the great adversary who had been permitted to bring trouble upon God's champion. We see Satan so concealing his own working that the pious patriarch was actually deceived into believing that he had been set up as a mark for 'the arrows of the Almighty' (Job 6:4). Knowing these facts as they did, it is not too much to claim that David and his fellow saints realized that at least many of the bitter persecutions which they suffered originated from the same dread source that was responsible for the afflictions of Job.*[31]

---

31    MacMillan, pp. 69, 70.

Even though we too experience the reality of evil in our world and in our day, we need to keep in mind that Satan has always corrupted societies, cultures, and nations throughout history. Looking at the bigger picture historically and geographically helps us see that the *fiery arrows of the devil* (Ephesians 6:16; NLT) that we face as individuals are mere salvos in the battle of the ages. God's enemy hates God and all that He has created and called "good," including the nations of the world.

> The fiery arrows of the devil we face are mere salvos in the battle of the ages.

## Dark Days for Israel

Soon after David defeated Goliath, Israel would enter the international scene. It was necessary for the nation to realize that Yahweh was King even over the many other mighty nations. This kingship of the LORD of Hosts is vividly expressed in Psalm 24:10: *Who is this King of glory? The LORD of hosts, he is the King of glory!* (ESV). He is the glorious King of Israel, and Zechariah 14:6 tells us that He will be King of the world, over all the kingdoms of the earth (see also Isaiah 37:16).

But, sadly, that is not how Israel would experience God in the following generations. As both punishment and discipline for their waywardness, God first banished the ten northern tribes through the Assyrian conquest. One would think the remaining tribe, Judah, would have learned, but about 150 years later, the Babylonians, having defeated the Assyrians, captured and destroyed Jerusalem and the temple. Most of the Jews who were not killed by sword or famine were deported to Babylon. Satan was having his way with the people of God.

God had sent many warnings through the prophets. A few hundred years after David's kingship, Isaiah, God's Secretary of State, outlined how God related to foreign powers of his day, especially in Isaiah 10-23. The historical setting of Isaiah 10-23 was 8th century B.C., the Assyrian threat against all the nations and cities of the Fertile Crescent. Isaiah, whose name means "Yahweh has given salvation," was the advisor to Judah's kings Uzziah, Jotham, Ahaz, and Hezekiah. Isaiah's primary prophecies concern the nations of Israel and Judah, the twelve tribes that came from the lineage of Abraham, Isaac, and Jacob, but had split into two kingdoms after Solomon's reign. God would judge both nations, starting with Israel which fell to the Assyrians who destroyed Samaria in 722 B.C.

The prophecy against Jerusalem is in Isaiah 22:1-14. Isaiah rebuked the Israelites' frivolous attitude in the midst of national crisis and their cosmetic attempts to prepare for a siege. Human political efforts rather than repentance and trust were the strategies of Jerusalem according to verses 12 and 13. Though Jerusalem would be spared from Assyrian conquest, seen in Isaiah 37:36, the Babylonians would totally destroy the sacred city and carry off most citizens into exile in 586 B.C. The Jews no longer lived in the Promised Land. In exile, they would endure their own dark days.

**Dark Days for the Nations**

The days were dark also for the nations opposing or surrounding Israel. The main message of Isaiah 10-23 is God's policy toward the nations that oppose Him, not just those who oppose Israel.

To the "enemies" of God, Isaiah was to deliver separate messages, beginning with the most powerful empire of the day, **Assyria** (conquering west Iran, Iraq, Jordan, Syria, Lebanon, Israel, Sinai, and Egypt). Assyria's capital was Nineveh, the wicked city that had repented earlier under Jonah's reluctant ministry. Jonah had resisted going there because he hated the powerful, evil empire. Unfortunately, Nineveh's repentance did not last long. Assyria did not know or understand its role in God's sovereign ruling of the nations.

*What sorrow awaits Assyria, the rod of my anger, I use it as a club to express my anger.*

*I am sending Assyria against a godless nation, against a people with whom I am angry. Assyria will plunder them, trampling them like dirt beneath its feet. But the king of Assyria will not understand that he is my tool; his mind does not work that way. His plan is simply to destroy, to cut down nation after nation ....*

*After the Lord has used the king of Assyria to accomplish his purposes on Mount Zion and in Jerusalem, he will turn against the king of Assyria and punish him — for he is proud and arrogant.*

Isaiah 10:5-7, 12

Before God's judgment came on Assyria, however, He used that vile nation to judge other nations. **Damascus** (Isaiah 17) was and still is the capital city of Syria (Aram), just north of Israel. It also would be destroyed by an invasion of Assyria. But, there are hints of a remnant (verse 6) and repentance (verses 7-8). Though Israel, under King Ahaz, at first aligned with Assyria, Isaiah rightly predicted that God would use Assyria to punish both Syria and Israel, which He did by destroying their capital cities, Damascus in 734 B.C. and Samaria in 722 B.C.

The **Philistines**, who occupied the Gaza strip (now occupied by Palestinians), were the perpetual pesky neighbor to the west of Israel/Judah, along the eastern shores of the Mediterranean. Isaiah 14:28-32 predicts that famine and a northern power will destroy Philistia, and that happened in 721 B.C. when the Assyrians conquered them. Isaiah 2:6-8 describes Philistines as "fortune-tellers and idolaters." 1 Samuel 5 tells about their god and idol Dagon, whom Yahweh humiliated.

The people of **Moab** (east side of Dead Sea, central Jordan) were the descendants of Lot, Abraham's nephew. Ruth, King David's great-grandmother, was a Moabitess. Seeing the Assyrian threat and the coming devastation of Moab, Isaiah urged them in Isaiah 15 and 16 to take shelter in Judah, but the outcome, seen in 16:11-14, would be almost total destruction even though (or, perhaps, because), *The people of Moab will worship at their pagan shrines, but it will do them no good. They will cry to the gods in their temples* (NLT).

**Arabia** (Jordan, Saudi Arabia, Kuwait, and Yemen) consisted of nomadic Arabs. Arabia would also be overrun by the Assyrians (21:13-17).

**Egypt,** Chapter 19, as the competing power to Assyria for empire dominance and pagan practices including occultism, receives the harshest prophecies because with Israel worshipping Yahweh in their midst for 400 years, they had the greatest opportunity to know the true God. First, civil war (19:1-4), then economic disaster (19:5-10), then political folly (19:11-15), then spiritual panic and eventual revival (19:16-25) are parts of the prophecies to Egypt. **Cush (Ethiopia)** would fare no better through her alliance with Egypt (Isaiah 18 and 20).

God's message to **Babylon** was given in Isaiah 13:1-14:23 (modern Iraq, Jordan, Syria, and Lebanon). More than any other world power, Babylon is depicted as the most hostile to God, from the tower of Babel in Genesis 11 to the great mother of prostitutes in Revelation. Babylon stands for all that arrogantly opposes God. Two hundred years after Isaiah's prophecy, Babylon, which conquered Assyria in 612 B.C. and then destroyed Jerusalem in 586, was conquered by the Persians in 539.

In the 2,500 years since the fulfillment of Isaiah's prophecies, empires and nations have passed from the scene of history. Instigating international conflicts, inspiring genocidal warfare, oppressing the weaker nations, and undermining the faith of the people of God have been Satan's efforts to disrupt God's kingdom plans and assert his own evil nature.

**Honored by Every Nation**

What's the main message behind all this? God is very much involved in political, military, and international affairs. He uses nations to judge nations, and then judges them. He is sovereign. That is why David could say in Psalm 46:8-11 (NLT):

*Come, see the glorious works of the LORD: See how he brings destruction upon the world.*

*He causes wars to end throughout the earth. He breaks the bow and snaps the spear; he burns the shields with fire.*

*"Be still, and know that I am God! I will be honored by every nation. I will be honored throughout the world."*

*The LORD of Heaven's Armies is here among us; the God of Israel is our fortress.*

God is not a respecter of persons or of nations. His first disposition is to love and forgive Jews and Gentiles, but He will not tolerate sin. God will always judge sin, which is exactly what He did at Calvary. Eventually, Yahweh of armies will put down all rebellion (Isaiah 24:21-23) and establish His Kingdom from Mount Zion (Isaiah 31:4-5; 34:12). As the LORD of hosts, God is the all-powerful Ruler over the entire universe. All power and authority are His. He alone intervenes to provide victory for His people as they are faithful to Him. He alone brings world peace. At the same time, He is available to hear the prayers of His people (Psalm 80:19). There is no other God like this.

The sovereign LORD of hosts has the grace to always be there for the one who comes to Him through faith in the Lord, Jesus Christ. The King of glory, who commands the armies of heaven and who will eventually defeat all the rebellion of all His enemies in this world, including Satan, is none other than Jesus Christ. He is the LORD of hosts (Revelation 19:11-20). Cultures clash, but God's kingdom conquers them all.

We live in a kingdom of darkness (see Colossians 1:13), presided over by an imposter prince (see Mark 3:22) who temporarily holds power over this world and those who are not in the kingdom of God. Every generation, every culture, and every earthly kingdom has been dominated by the sin principle that is inspired by the enemy of God. Knowing about this satanic usurper, the enemy of God, is important for those of us who are in the resistance.

## Summary Thoughts from Chapter 4, International Conflicts

- For the time being, God allows Satan to influence the nations and promote war.
- The *fiery arrows of the devil* that we face as individuals are mere salvos in the battle of the ages.
- Satan plays into God's hands by instigating international conflicts, inspiring genocidal warfare, and oppressing the weaker nations.

- God is not a respecter of persons or of nations. His first disposition is to love and forgive Jews and Gentiles, but He will not tolerate sin.

# 5

## THE ADVERSARY[32]

### Satan's Biography, Before the Beginning

Headlines, newscasts, police reports, political fights, terrorism, recessions, human trafficking, and a myriad of other moral blights reveal we live in a messed-up world. How did the world get into such a mess today? We get a few hints of activity that occurred before the "beginning" of Genesis 1:1. While the primary purpose of the Bible is to tell the story of what God has done in human history to redeem mankind from the curse of the fall, which is recorded in Genesis 3, God gives us glimpses in several places of the Bible into pre-history.

The first hints are in the first book, Genesis. It's quite clear that other spiritual beings[33] were created before humans, existing in the heavenlies

---

32  See in Addendum 1: "Notes about Satan and Fallen Angels" for fuller information about the adversaries' attributes.

33  A major thesis of the enlarged biblical worldview that Michael Heiser exposes is that a "divine council" of beings (*elohim*), including *sons of God* created by God, existed with God before the creation activity of Genesis. See Addendum 1 for some of the scriptures that support this idea. Michael Heiser quotes Samuel Davidsohn, *An Introduction to the New Testament*, Vol. III, 1848, p. 282: "Hengstenberg stated that the Hebrew Bible text never uses *elohim* to refer to 'angels', but that the Septuagint translators refused the references to 'gods' in the verses they amended to 'angels.'

with God. It also seems that, originally, they were given some freedom of choice, and that one of them began a rebellion against God, whom God cast out of His immediate presence along with others who had joined the insurrection. That rebellion may have been over God's decision to create another order of beings in His own image, demonstrated in Satan's ongoing efforts to subvert God's plan, seen in every book of the Bible.

We may infer from Isaiah 14:12 that Satan's fall occurred in pre-history when angels or members of the divine council (see Psalm 82) had some freedom. The Isaiah passage seems to have multiple applications referring both to the king of Babylon and to Lucifer.[34]

*How you have fallen from heaven, O star of the morning, son of the dawn!*
*You have been cut down to the earth ...*

We will look at this passage more in depth, but for now our interest is to show what seemed to have occurred before creation. Subsequently, it seems that God may have removed free will from the remaining divine council, and possibly from angels who always do His will.[35]

There are many theories of the age of the earth and when God's acts of creation on earth began,[36] which are beyond the scope of this book, but it appears from Genesis 1:1-2 that the "pre-creation" earth was a dark, formless void (or, empty, a waste), covered with water. The word *earth* implies that

---

34 Commenting on multiple meanings in Scripture, Kenny Burchard in <u>ThinkTheology. org</u>, June 6, 2016, writes: "It's a popular notion to insist that a Scripture can only have one meaning or primary theological idea...While it is true that we need a way to guard against making a text of Scripture mean or say whatever we want it to, the solution to this mistake is not to make the mistake of claiming that a text can have only one meaning or theological idea. Good biblical interpretation insists that we work through a multi-layered interpretive process and then deal with either the one or the many things we discover as the process unfolds."

35 The most complete description of angels is in Hebrews 1:7, 14, where they are described as *ministering servants* and *spirits sent to care for God's people who will inherit salvation.*

36 See the article, Warren H. Johns, "Strategies for Origins," *Ministry*, May 1981.

matter existed from some previous act of God, but at the time when God decided to begin the present creation, the earth was a watery, dark wasteland. How much time lapsed and what else may have occurred on the earth before this present creation, if anything, is the speculation of many scholars.

The creation account of Genesis 1 ends by saying that everything God created in the six days *was good.* Move to Genesis 3, and, lo and behold, in the Garden of Eden appears a talking serpent who successfully tempts Eve to sin. Where did that serpent come from? What did it look like, and why could it speak? Obviously, it was not yet a snake, and obviously, not part of the creation of days 1-6, for it certainly was not "good." Might the serpent have been a pre-creation fallen "angel" (or member of the divine council) who was determined to disrupt God's purposes and defile God's creation? Obviously, or so it seems, Satan succeeded.

God had cast Satan to this planet after his rebellion and with him other rebellious members of the divine council. Perhaps this is referred to in Revelation 12:7-9.[37]

> *And there was war in heaven, Michael and his angels waging war with the dragon. The dragon and his angels[38] waged war, and they were not strong enough, and there was no longer a place found for them in heaven. And the great dragon was thrown down, the serpent of old who is called the devil and Satan, who deceives the whole world; he was thrown down to the earth, and his angels were thrown down with him.*

No wonder earth was a dark, watery wasteland.

A reasonable question is — why would God choose to create humans on the very planet where He had sent Satan? Why put humanity right on

---

37  There are four major schools of interpretation of *Revelation (Apocalypse,* in Greek), which we will not discuss here. Suffice it to say, my perspective is that God's revelation to John was not the revelation of just the future, but of Jesus Christ throughout history.

38  "Angel" literally means "messenger" or "emissary" and at times refers to an evil being. See, for instance, 2 Corinthians 12:7 — an *aggelos* of Satan.

the turf of the enemy in the path of temptation? No one can know for sure, but I believe God still wanted a family of free moral agents as His family; that may have been His purpose with the divine council originally. Satan's sin was not going to put an end to God's plan. By creating human beings, He chose to show Satan and all his rebellious comrades — the demonic beings that fell with him — that God could create free-willed individuals who would choose to respond to His love and grace and worship Him faithfully. So, He created Adam (mankind) right on Satan's turf. And while people continue to suffer from sin brought on by Satan's, Eve's, and Adam's fall from righteousness, God's redemptive plan for humans is still proceeding.

Another glimpse of Satan's history is seen in the oldest book of the Bible, Job.

> *Now there was a day when the sons of God* (ben elohim) *came to present themselves before the Lord, and Satan also came among them. The Lord said to Satan, "From where do you come?" Then Satan answered the Lord and said, "From roaming about on the earth and walking around on it."*

Job 1:6, 7

Apparently, Satan took a form other than a serpent, because God cursed the serpent to crawl in the dust (Genesis 3:14), but notice the text says he was on the earth. Then God began the drama that is the book of Job, a contest between God and evil (Job 1:8-11). Satan was given enormous freedom, which he still has, to destroy, defile, and seek to condemn sons and daughters of Adam and Eve. Although Job may never have found out why God allowed him to suffer so badly, we get an inside view in Chapters 1 and 2. The battle is between God and Satan, and Job is the battleground. Will God's goodness, seen in His love for Job, be strong enough to sustain him as a worshipper even in the midst of great loss, pain, and uncertainty? Satan, who had already failed in the faithfulness category, was betting "No." Just as he does in the cosmic battle that now rages. Thankfully, Satan lost the contest then as he did in the greater drama of God's redemptive plan in Christ. Job declared and stuck to his commitment: *Though He slay me, I will hope in Him* (Job 13:15).

The story of Job is a microcosm of the drama of the universe and the ages. The book does not give a closing conversation between God and Satan, but the point had been made. Not all free moral agents will remain in the rebellion that took Satan down, and subsequent history is showing that God's purpose in saving sinners is succeeding despite Satan's nefarious efforts. Paul would explain this in greater clarity in Ephesians 3, telling that God had commissioned him to declare the

> ...*mystery, which for ages past was kept hidden in God, who created all things. His intent was that now, through the church, the manifold wisdom of God should be made known to the rulers and authorities in the heavenly realms according to his eternal purpose which he accomplished in Christ Jesus our Lord.*

Ephesians 3:9-11, NIV

## Satan's Fall

We get an earlier impression of Satan's biography from some Old Testament passages. Keep in mind the principle of multiple interpretation, discussed in footnote 34.

The immediate subject of Ezekiel 28:11-19 was the king of Tyre, but it seems obvious that the prophet of God had in mind the inspirational force behind the king's ungodly activities, as he relates God's words:

> *You had the seal of perfection,*
> *Full of wisdom and perfect in beauty.*
>
> *You were in Eden, the garden of God;*
> *Every precious stone was your covering...*
> *On the day that you were created*
> *They were prepared.*
>
> *You were the anointed cherub who covers,*
> *And I placed you there.*
> *You were on the holy mountain of God;*
> *You walked in the midst of the stones of fire.*

*You were blameless in your ways*
*From the day you were created*
*Until unrighteousness was found in you.*

*By the abundance of your trade*
*You were internally filled with violence,*
*And you sinned;*
*Therefore I have cast you as profane From the mountain of God.*
*And I have destroyed you, O covering cherub, From the midst of the stones*
*of fire.*

*Your heart was lifted up because of your beauty;*
*You corrupted your wisdom by reason of your splendor.*
*I cast you to the ground; I put you before kings,*
*That they may see you.*

Notice these statements that could refer only to Satan, and how they give further insight to the enemy of God.

- *You were in Eden, the garden of God*
- *You were the anointed cherub who covers*
- *You were blameless in your ways*
  *From the day you were created*
  *Until unrighteousness was found in you*
- *I cast you to the ground*

God's plan for Satan is certain, and as Martin Luther penned, *For, lo, his doom is sure.*

Another Old Testament passage that seems to refer to the pre-creation history and fall of Satan is given in Isaiah 14:12-15. Here the immediate application is to the king of Babylon, but the phrases God inspired the prophet to write make it clear that this was not just about Nebuchadnezzar.

*How you have fallen from heaven,*
*O star of the morning, son of the dawn! You have been cut down to the earth,*
*You who have weakened the nations!*

*But you said in your heart,*
*'I will ascend to heaven;*
*I will raise my throne above the stars of God,*
*And I will sit on the mount of assembly*
*In the recesses of the north.*

*I will ascend above the heights of the clouds;*
*I will make myself like the Most High.'*

*Nevertheless you will be thrust down to Sheol,*
*To the recesses of the pit....*

David Guzik's Study Guide for Isaiah 14 adds to our insight about the fall of Lucifer.

A. ***How you are fallen from heaven, O Lucifer, son of the morning!*** *Here, the prophet identifies the king of Babylon as **Lucifer, son of the morning**. Some debate if **Lucifer** is a name or a title; the word means morning star or day star, referring to a brightly shining object in the heavens. Whether it is a title or a name makes little difference; this once brightly shining king of Babylon is now **fallen from heaven**.*

B. ***Fallen from heaven***: *In fact, there are four falls of Satan, and this refers to his final, fourth fall.*

C. ***Son of the morning***: *This is a title of glory, beauty, and honor, which fit Lucifer well before his fall. The morning is glorious, and in Hebrew thinking, the **son of** "x" is characterized by "x." So, before his fall, Lucifer was characterized by the glory **of the morning**.*

D. ***How you are cut down to the ground***: *What a contrast! This being, once so high, once so shining, once so bright, is now **cut down to the ground**.*

E. ***For you have said in your heart***: *Here, God tells us the reason behind the fall of the king of Babylon, both literal and spiritual. The fall was prompted by something he **said**, even though he may have never said it with his lips — it was enough that he **said** it in his **heart**.*

F.  *I will:* The pride, the grasping selfish ambition, the self-will of the king of Babylon is powerfully expressed in five *I will* statements. This is the essence of the self-focused and self-obsessed life.

    *i.*   **I will ascend into heaven.**

    *ii.*   **I will exalt my throne above the stars of God.**

    *iii.*   **I will also sit on the mount of the congregation.**

    *iv.*   **I will ascend above the heights.**

    *v.*   **I will be like the Most High.**

G.  *What prompted Satan's desire to exalt himself above all other creatures? What prompted the five I will statements?*

    *i.*   *Why did Lucifer rebel? Perhaps because he rejected God's plan to create an order of being made in His image (Genesis 1:26), who would be beneath the angels in dignity (Hebrews 2:6-7a; 2 Peter 2:11), yet would be served by angels in the present (Hebrews 1:14; 2:7-8; Psalm 91:11-12) and would one day be lifted in honor and status above the angels (1 Corinthians 6:3; 1 John 3:2). Satan wanted to be the highest among all creatures, equal to God in glory and honor, and the plan to create man would eventually put men above angels. He was apparently able to persuade one-third of the angelic beings to join him in his rebellion (Revelation 12:3-4, 7, and 9).*

    *ii.*   *If this is the case, it explains well Satan's present strategy against man: to obscure the image of God in man through encouraging sin and rebellion, to cause man to serve him, and to prevent the ultimate glorification of man.*[39]

---

39    David Guzik, *Online Study Guides* (2017). "Study Guide for Isaiah 14." Used by permission.

## Summary Thoughts from Chapter 5, The Adversary

- God chose to create humans on the very planet where He sent Satan.
- Passages in Ezekiel 28 and Isaiah 14 have multiple fulfillments, referring to Satan's fall.
- Satan's present strategy against man: to obscure the image of God in man through encouraging sin and rebellion.

# 6

## SATAN EXPOSED

While the archenemy of God delights in subterfuge and deception, his identity is not a mystery to Bible students. We may not always perceive his activities, but his identity is evident in Scripture. MacMillan brings together the various titles and descriptions given in the Bible.

> *The Dragon. This appellation seems to be applied with reference to his relationship to the world kingdoms. Unseen, he works among and controls them by an unnumbered host of agents of varied ranks. He is not in any sense gifted with omnipresence but is enabled to travel with the speed of light from place to place. His authority over his subjects seems unquestioned, and his will is absolute where he exerts it.*

> *The Old Serpent. This term alludes to his ministry of deception of mankind in general and of individuals in particular...The leaders of the world boast of the increasing light which is flooding over the world, and this is true of the advances made by science and by knowledge in general. But there is a widespread forgetfulness of God, so great that the nations of the earth are sitting in the darkness and in the shadow of death ...*

There is a widespread forgetfulness of God. The nations of the earth are sitting in the darkness and in the shadow of death.

*The Devil. This title means the slanderer or the malignant accuser, an attitude he bears toward the children of God. The Scriptures present him as 'the accuser of the brethren…which accused them before our God day and night' (Revelation 12:10).*[40]

Continuing with MacMillan's list and descriptions of the names and characterizations given in the Bible to describe our enemy, we come on a few more.

*Satan. The adversary of the believer, working through the multitude of principalities and powers, the world rulers of this darkness (Ephesians 6:12), whom the child of God is exhorted to wrestle against and overcome as he wears the whole armor of God.*

*Another set of titles is not grouped together but are used in varied places of the Word. One of these is 'prince of this world.' Three times our Lord Himself used it of Satan, the Prince of this World (John 12:31, 14:30, 16:11). A dignity conferred probably before his fall (Ezekiel 28:11-19). In the account of the temptation of our Lord (Luke 4:6), he claims suzerainty of the kingdoms of the world in the presence of Christ, who does not deny his claim. Since Satan is the lord of earth's kingdoms, there can be no such thing as a Christian nation.*

*The God of this Age (2 Corinthians 4:4). Satan seeks to supplant the true God in the hearts and the worship of mankind. Satan-worship is actually carried on in many places…even in so-called Christian lands there are large numbers who definitely acknowledge Satan as God.*[41]

## Satan's Colleagues

As we have seen, Satan was not the only rebel God cast out of His presence. A hierarchy of rebels is identified in Scripture by various names.

---

40    MacMillan, pp. 99, 100.

41    MacMillan, pp. 100-102.

Ephesians 6:12 refers to rulers and authorities, also called mighty powers in this dark world and ... evil spirits in the heavenly places.

MacMillan gives us insight in this passage:

*Who are these demons, which are everywhere distributed among mankind? Our knowledge of the unseen world does not permit us to state with assurance their origin. The Scriptures, while they speak frequently of them, give no definite information regarding whence they come. It details various orders of the angelic beings but tells little of their functions.*

*There seem, however, to be others than angels who were involved in the mighty conspiracy of the devil and who have shared in his ruin: these are the demons. In the enumeration given by the apostle of the malign forces with whom the Christian has to wrestle, four classes are mentioned (Ephesians 6:12). The first of these are called 'principalities,' mighty satanic princes, who have been appointed by their dread master to rule over the nations. Two of such princes are indicated, the 'prince of the kingdom of Persia' (Daniel 10:13) and the 'prince of Grecia' (Daniel 10:20). It would seem from this that earth's kingdoms are each presided over by one of these evil beings and that their councils of the nations are really dominated by unseen beings.*

*The second class is named 'powers' (exousias, authorities). We find them joined with principalities frequently (Romans 8:38; Ephesians 3:10; 6:12; Colossians 1:16; 2:15) but always in a secondary place, from which we judge that they are inferior in positions, probably as cabinet ministers associated in government.*

*The third class is called 'the world rulers of this darkness' (RV). The name suggests a ministry of deception, the keeping in darkness of the minds of men, especially of thought. To them is probably due the introduction into our educational systems of such heresies as evolution, to which men hold with strange tenacity, seeing there is no shred of evidence as to its correctness.*

*The fourth class consists of 'hosts of wicked spirits in the heavenlies.' The term 'spirits' is used in the gospels as synonymous with 'demons' (Matthew*

*8:16; Luke 9:42; and other places). That the Jews recognized the difference between the classes of unseen beings is clear from Acts 23:8-9, where the controversy between Pharisees and Sadducees over Paul is mentioned.*[42]

Another MacMillan quote about Satan's colleagues offers important insights especially at the end of this quotation:

*Demons are a class of beings which are distinct from angels, a fact recognized by the Jews (see Acts 23:8-9). Their origin is not given in the Bible, and various theories are held regarding it. One certainty is that they are disembodied spirits and seek to embody themselves in human beings or even in the bodies of animals (Luke 8:32). They thereby are enabled to gratify sensual instincts-the grosser forms of which are intemperance and impurity-through the organs of their victims. Often a possessed person, though normally self-controlled, manifests strange appetites utterly unknown previously.*[43]

> Demons are enabled to gratify sensual instincts-the grosser forms of intemperance and impurity-through the organs of their victims.

Michael Heiser would agree with MacMillan's assessment of the sensual focus of these demonic beings, citing the enigmatic passage Genesis 6:1-4 as an example when

*...the sons of God (ben elohim) saw that the daughters of men were beautiful; and they took wives for themselves, whomever they chose. Then the LORD said, "My Spirit shall not strive with man forever, because he also is flesh; nevertheless, his days shall be one hundred and twenty years."*

*The Nephilim were on the earth in those days, and also afterward, when the sons of God came in to the daughters of man, and they bore children to them.*

Heiser adds this insight:

---

42    MacMillan, pp. 113-115.

43    MacMillan, p. 95.

*The New Testament is silent on the origin of demons. There is no passage that describes a primeval rebellion before Eden where angels fell from grace and became demons. The origin of demons in Jewish texts outside the Bible (such as 1 Enoch) is attributed to the events of Genesis 6:1-4. When a Nephilim was killed in these texts, its disembodied spirit was considered a demon. These demons then roamed the earth to harass humans. The New Testament does not explicitly embrace this belief, though there are traces of the notion such as demon possession of humans (implying the effort to be re-embodied).*[44]

MacMillan continues his list:

*Finally, there are 'the hosts of wicked spirits in the heavenlies' — an innumerable body of demons, to whose close connection with mankind is due the grosser sins and deceptions, the stirring up of the animal passions and the incitement to all manner of sensual and sensuous desires. These are the beings that are present in the spiritist seance, impersonating and deceiving people of strong intelligence, like the well-known leaders connected with the cults today.*

*The 'kings of the earth upon the earth' comprise human world rulers and their subjects, all unregenerate men. An earthly ruler individually may be a Christian, but he is, by virtue of his office, a member of the great world system which has not yet come under the dominion of the King of kings. All-natural men are members by birth also in this system, and so must be 'delivered out of the power (exousia, authority) of darkness, and translated into the kingdom of his dear Son' (Colossians 1:13).*

*The seats of authority of these rebellious spiritual rulers are also in the heavenlies. From there they have dominated the human race since its fall. There they will remain until the divine 'purpose of the ages' is complete.*[45]

---

44    Heiser, *The Unseen Realm*, p. 325.

45    MacMillan, pp. 16-17.

## And the Future?

We have seen biblical truths about the past of the enemies of God from pre-creation days, and we have seen the ongoing hierarchy that continues to wage a futile campaign against God and His purpose to redeem His family. What about the future of the adversaries of God? We will see more about that in succeeding pages, but a glimpse is given by MacMillan, even as he stirs us to take our role in the warfare.

> *Slowly, believers are awaking to their high place of privilege in Christ and are assuming the responsibilities which it involves. The body of the man-child, who is to rule all nations with a rod of iron, is nearing completion. Born of the Church, but not itself the Church, the body consists of many members with widely differing offices. These members are out of every age and people. On its ascension to the throne of God, which now potentially it shares, the rebellious powers of the air which have so long resisted divine authority shall be fully and forever dispossessed of their seats to make room for the new incumbents.*[46]

This catalog of the dark side may seem intimidating to the would-be spiritual warrior or to the Christian who is plagued by demons. How much must I know to deal with the demonic? Neil Anderson provides this somewhat humorous illustration to help us focus on what is essential:

> *People's lives are like houses. Suppose a family hasn't taken the garbage out of their house for months, and they have spilled food and beverages without cleaning up. That will attract a lot of flies. To resolve this problem, I don't think it is necessary to study the flight patterns of the flies and determine their names and rank structure in the insect hierarchy. There may be some value in doing this which I am not aware of, but I don't think the answer is primarily found in gaining knowledge about and getting rid of the flies. Similarly, to "focus on the flies" in our lives is to allow the devil to set the agenda for us and distract us from the real issue — which is to get rid of the garbage. Repentance*

---

46    MacMillan, p. 53.

*and faith in God have been and will continue to be the answer in this present church age.*[47]

Of course, our purpose in describing these enemies of God is not merely to add to our theological and biblical knowledge. In a later chapter, we will examine how God enables His redeemed followers to work with Him in dispelling the powers of darkness. For now, we will continue to build up our courage knowing not only our identity in Christ and His provision of authority to us, as discussed in Chapter 3, but also the strategies of the twice-fallen enemy of God in the next chapter.

### Summary Thoughts from Chapter 6, Satan Exposed

- A hierarchy of rebels is identified in Scripture by various names.
- Demons are enabled to gratify sensual instincts — the grosser forms of which are intemperance and impurity.
- The hierarchy of satanic beings continues to wage a futile campaign against God and His purpose to redeem His family.

47    Anderson, *Bondage Breaker*, p. 254.

THE LION, THE CHURCH AND THE WARFARE

# 7

## SATAN'S STRATEGIES

God's enemy is a strategist, a schemer. That is why the Apostle Paul admonished his congregation at Ephesus to, *Put on the full armor of God, so that you can take your stand against the devil's schemes* (Ephesians 6:11). The Greek word for *schemes* is *methodeia*. So, it behooves God's people to know the methods, the strategies of Satan, including his limitations.

Satan's battle plan involves taking control of or influencing a person's mind, usually without the person knowing it. Sinful practices such as those mentioned in Scripture that involve occult practices have captured many minds to the control of the "angel of light,"[48] but more recent plagues, even epidemics, such as pornography, dark and evil video games, and mind-altering drugs, throw open wide the door for Satan to enter; and little do the subjects know of their subjugation. They think they are free, but truly they have become slaves to sin, as Paul documents in Romans 6:19-21.

*I am using an example from everyday life because of your human limitations. Just as you used to offer yourselves as slaves to impurity and to ever-increasing wickedness, so now offer yourselves as slaves to righteousness leading to holiness.*

---

48    Actually, Satan is not an angel of light. Second Corinthians 11:14 says Satan disguises *(meta schematizo)* himself as an angel of light.

*When you were slaves to sin, you were free from the control of righteousness. What benefit did you reap at that time from the things you are now ashamed of? Those things result in death!* (NIV)

Many of these people thus trapped profess interest in the work of the Lord and fellowship in the church. Just as demonized people gravitated to Jesus, their attraction to the church is like a moth to a lightbulb. Perhaps they know that church is the one place where deliverance should be most likely to come. But most churches fall far short of recognizing the devil in their midst, let alone knowing how to deal with such destructive forces.

> Many people trapped profess interest in the work of the Lord and fellowship in the church.

A story from a very credible source illustrates this in disturbing, graphic terms. Through an unexpected revelation from the Lord, perhaps a word of knowledge, a pastor — let's call him Pastor Bill — learned about a terrible act of sin perpetrated thirty years earlier by two young men on the altar of the sanctuary of their church. That information alarmed Pastor Bill so much that he contacted a man who had been an elder of that church at the time of the incident. The elder said he knew about the terrible act and was surprised that Pastor Bill knew about it. He said one of the young men confessed the sin and was forgiven by the congregation.

A few years later, they built a new sanctuary, turning the older part into a large narthex in which the platform area of the former church became an entryway. Despite increasing the capacity of the building threefold, the church stagnated at its former size, even though several good pastors had served there in those thirty years. Hearing this, Pastor Bill asked the elder if he knew if the present pastor was aware of the incident. He did not know, so Pastor Bill and the elder and his wife, after praying for wisdom, then decided that the former elder should call the present pastor and alert him to the situation.

To his relief and surprise, although the pastor had not heard of the sin, he received the truth and said that he and several other congregants often sensed a cool darkness as they walked through that part of the narthex. The elder asked him what became of the old altar. The pastor said it was no longer being used as the communion table but was off to the side of the front of the new sanctuary.

A few days after Pastor Bill and the elder spoke, the elder's wife called a friend, the wife of another former elder, who also had moved out of the state many years earlier, and told her about these events and conversations, whereupon the second elder's wife called the current pastor, whom she knew, and advised him to burn the old altar. He agreed, so he took the table to the parsonage, sawed it into pieces, and burned the pieces in his fireplace. He and his wife went to bed with the last piece of a table leg still burning, and the glass fireplace door firmly latched. The pastor said he always carefully checked before they retired for the night when they used the fireplace. The next morning, he went to work early and did not check the fireplace. His wife awoke a few hours later smelling smoke. She ran downstairs and saw the fireplace door open and the leg of the table out of the fireplace on fire and burning the carpet. Smoke was rapidly filling the parsonage. Firemen quickly came and extinguished the fire, but the entire interior of the first floor had to be restored.

There was more to this story told to me by the credible source. After the new sanctuary was built, classrooms on the second floor of the old building had been converted into an apartment for the sexton and his wife. This young couple had grown up in the church and were in Bible college. The sexton told one of the elders that many times he awoke with his wife coughing and choking. She said she felt hands around her neck each time. Across the hallway was another room that had a large closet. A few years earlier before the apartment was occupied, the people of the town were frantically searching for a young anorexic girl, whose father was the chief of police. One night, the pastor at that time saw a light in that upstairs area. He went to turn out the light and heard some strange noises coming from that closet. Opening the door, he was surprised to find the young girl who had made a nest filled with wrappers of junk food.

91

Hearing about this, Pastor Bill asked the elder if there was possibly a spirit of homosexuality or suicide evident in the church of the congregation. The elder then mentioned that ten years earlier, about the time both elders and wives moved out of the area, the youth pastor of the church committed suicide. Although most of the details had been kept out of the news, insiders knew that the youth pastor had been caught sexually abusing a young boy in the church and was about to be exposed by the boy's father.

All this sounds like so much bizarre fiction, but I am quite sure it is true. Of course, it raises the question about territorial spirits and demonic infestation through acts of sin. The reader may draw his or her own conclusions, but make no mistake. Satan hates the Church and all who want to be followers of Jesus. I checked some time ago about the health of that church and learned that the pastor at the time of the revelation of all this information had invited a well-known former missionary to come to help them cleanse the church building of any continuing demonic presence. Whether that was totally successful, I cannot say. The church still has not grown much, but there have been no recent manifestations of satanic presence, according to my source.

Incidents like these may not be that uncommon in local churches. MacMillan reports similar disturbances, such as this:

*In one of the cities of Canada, the pastor of an Alliance church said to the writer: 'There are about four different troubles going on all the time among my people. As soon as I get one straightened out, the devil has another ready to take its place.' Answer was made: 'Brother, you are right in your diagnosis of the source of your troubles, but you are wrong in your method of meeting them. What you are looking at are the coils of the old serpent through your congregation, and as you straighten out one kink, you may be sure that another will appear. Leave the coils alone, and go for the head; put your foot on that in the authority of the Lord; recognize the active agency of the enemy and conquer him; the coils will straighten out of themselves if he is dealt with.'* [49]

---

49    MacMillan, p. 64.

As we will see, Satan's strategies include deception, corruption, accusation, and a host of secrets which he does not want his subjects to discover.

## Satan's Deceptions

The primary attribute of Satan as a deceiver was manifested in his first encounter with humans in the Garden of Eden as he enticed Eve to disobey God's command not to eat of the tree of the knowledge of good and evil. God had told Adam, before Eve was created, that eating of that tree would result in death. Adam must have told Eve because she answered the tempter's question by saying they were forbidden from eating of that tree. Well, you know the rest of the story, and all humanity has suffered ever since.

By the way, any men who feel morally superior need to notice that Eve gave the fruit *also to her husband who was with her.* His sin was probably worse than hers, in that he was not deceived; he sinned with full understanding of what he was doing. As still is the case often with men, he [Adam] chose the woman over God. But the

> As still is the case often with men, he [Adam] chose the woman over God.

main point here is that Eve spoke truth by saying to God, *The serpent deceived me, and I ate* (Genesis 3:13).

Neil Anderson sees the devil's deception as his primary strategy for controlling people:

> If I tempted you, you would know it. If I accused you, you would know it. But if I deceived you, you wouldn't know it. If you knew you were being deceived, then you would no longer be deceived. Eve was deceived and she believed a lie. Deception has been the primary strategy of Satan from the beginning. That is why truth sets us free, and why Jesus prayed, "Sanctify them in the truth; Thy word is truth" (John 17:17). "Having girded [our] loins with truth" (Ephesians 6:14), we have available to us our first means of defense.
>
> There are three primary avenues through which Satan will attempt to dissuade you from God's truth and deceive you into believing his lies: self-deception, false

*prophets/ teachers, and deceiving spirits. We are vulnerable to Satan's lies if we fail to take every thought captive to the obedience of Christ (2 Corinthians 10:5).*[50]

Sometimes, the devil uses other humans as his agents to gain control, as MacMillan points out:

*Let it ever be held in mind that the authority committed to the believer is over the powers of the air and never over the fellowmen or their wills. He is called to bind the unseen forces but to deliver his brethren. **Satan's constant aim is the subjugation of the human will to himself;** God's purpose is the full liberation of the will that the freed spirit, through glad acquiescence in the divine will, may glorify his Creator. Human control of the will of another, as manifested in hypnotism, etc., is obtained through the use of occult powers latent in the soul and is as unlawful for the Christian as wizardry and necromancy, which are directly forbidden in the Word of God*[51] (emphasis mine).

We have all heard of the concept of mind-control; hypnotism is a form of mind control which apparently requires the consent and cooperation of the person being hypnotized. Maintaining control of our mind gives us a sense of autonomy and dignity which we believe is our right as a way to maintain our individuality. Unfortunately, we may not be as much in control as we think. In the case of unbelievers who voluntarily choose to defy God, the human mind finds itself cooperating with Satan's schemes, even if they do not know it. But, disobedient believers also give the devil a *foothold* (Ephesians 4:27). Anderson makes this point clear.

*Don't think that Satan is no longer interested in manipulating your mind in order to accomplish his purposes. Satan's perpetual aim is to infiltrate your thoughts with his thoughts and to promote his lie in the face of God's truth. He knows that if he can control your thoughts, he can control your life. That*

---

50    Anderson, *Bondage Breaker*, pp. 166-167.

51    MacMillan, pp. 42-43.

*is why Paul continues in the present tense with the statement, "And we are taking every thought captive to the obedience of Christ"* (2 Corinthians 10:5).[52]

Neil Anderson also notes that Satan's deceitful workings will continue to the very end of this age and are a "clear and present danger" to all humanity, including believers.

*In addition to deceiving ourselves and being deceived by false prophets and false teachers, we can pay attention to a deceiving spirit. "The Spirit explicitly states that in later times some will fall away from the faith, paying attention to deceitful spirits and doctrines of demons" (1 Timothy 4:1). John also cautioned us to test the spirits in order to unmask antichrists (1 John 2:18) and to distinguish the spirit of truth from the spirit of error (4:1-6). Satan's demonic forces are at work attempting to pollute your mind with lies in order to keep you from walking in the truth.*[53]

## Satan's Corruptions

MacMillan traces Satan's corruptions of mankind from the earliest cultures:

*The Old Testament introduces us to a multiplicity of gods. We find mankind from the earliest times adoring its deities and yielding itself in varieties of methods to worship. The philosophies underlying these forms of worship were sometimes noble and lofty in theory, but in practice the trend was to become unspeakably vile. Among the more cultured nations of antiquity, such as the Greeks and the Romans, the Eleusinian and the Bacchanalian mysteries were such that the apostle to the Gentiles says of them, 'Who being past feeling have given themselves over unto lasciviousness, to work all uncleanness with greediness,' and again, 'For it is a shame even to speak of those things which are done of them in secret' in the bosom of their societies (Ephesians 4:19; 5:12). And, in the latter part of the first chapter of his epistle to the*

---

52   Anderson, *Bondage Breaker*, p. 61.

53   Anderson, *Bondage Breaker*, p. 177.

*Romans, he exemplifies his statement by outlining the **descent from the knowledge of the true God to the indescribable abominations** which characterize most of the heathen religions.*[54]

In Romans Chapter 1, the Apostle Paul writes about stages of descent in which sinful humans abandon their image-of-God creation and descend into animalism.[55]

1. In verse 23, the descent begins with the worship of idols, in which mankind *exchanged the glory of the incorruptible God for an image in the form of corruptible man, and of birds, and four-footed animals, and crawling creatures.* Therefore, **God gave them over** *in the lusts of their hearts* (1:24) to become like the idols they sought after, for that is always the result and the curse of idolatry.

2. **God gave them over** in 1:26, 27 *to degrading passions*, as they descend below the level of the animals into the abominable sins of lesbianism and homosexuality, bringing on themselves *the due penalty of their error* – the corruption of their moral natures combined with the vile diseases which follow immorality and cause the deterioration of their physical beings.

3. The final stage of descent is seen in 1:28 in which **God gave them over** *to a depraved mind*, a morally hopeless state, where the whole mind and nature become corrupted and depraved as described in verses 29-32 by twenty-four foul attributes. Such is the downward path of Satan's successful corruption of humans, as the lusts of the flesh override all semblance of moral truth and spiritual life (emphasis mine).

---

54    MacMillan, pp. 103-104.

55    These thoughts from Romans 1 are similar to the four steps of "degeneration" in Ephesians 4, which we discuss in Chapter 10.

God's enemies must greatly enjoy the thought that modern man thinks idolatry does not exist in the West, and in cultures where it does exist, the idols are mere works of sculpture, not to be taken seriously. Tourists in Africa and Asia may even buy the little idols to take home as decorations. Such ignorance of the reality of the spiritual world is part of the arrogance that stems from "enlightenment" mentality.

> Ignorance of the reality of the spiritual world is part of the arrogance that stems from "enlightenment" mentality.

Reducing reality to what our five senses can comprehend conveniently exempts us from dealing with the fears and torments that the "poor primitive people" still endure. Perhaps Shakespeare had a more enlightened worldview when he had Hamlet say, *There are more things in heaven and earth, Horatio, than are dreamt of in your philosophy.*[56]

MacMillan continues to unfold Satan's strategies and his grip on a huge portion of humanity:

> *The worship of evil spirits, called generally animism, is frequently separated from visible and material representations of the objects of devotion.* **Demons may take as their abode huge old trees, rocks, caves, streams, etc., and cause the people to worship them there.** *What missionary has not come across altars reared at the foot of some ancient banyan tree, upon which sheaves of incense lifted smoky fingers in silent appeal to the dreaded spirits which inhabited it? Or, at the crossings of streams, inserted in the ground will be found a few spears of incense, renewed as one traveler after another seeks to propitiate the demon of the stream that he may be allowed to cross unmolested. Great is the fear of these water demons.*
>
> *To the heathen the presence of evil spirits is a terrible reality. The fear of the supernatural rests like a pall over the day and night. Someone has compared the native to the restive horse, ready to shy immediately at whatever unusual occurs about him. He lives in continual dread, overcome by the belief that multitudes of demons are ever at hand to do him harm*[57] (emphasis mine).

---

56   William Shakespeare, "Hamlet," Act 1, scene 5.

57   MacMillan, pp. 105-106.

**Satan's Accusations**

Besides deception and corruption, Satan also resorts to accusation to disarm and defeat God's people. I have met people who honestly believed they had "lost their salvation" by blaspheming the Holy Spirit. While this is not the place to go into a full exegesis of Mark 3:22-30, where Jesus raised the concept of blaspheming the Holy Spirit,[58] Satan has twisted this concept and accused some of God's children as blasphemers because of lesser sins than that of disbelief.

> *The devil is an accuser. He is like a prosecuting attorney deceptively seeking to discredit and discourage a witness on the stand. He points his slimy finger and says, "Aha! You've done it now! There's no hope for you. You've blasphemed the Holy Spirit!" Perhaps you have questioned some spiritual gift, anointed preacher, or apparent supernatural manifestation. Is that blaspheming the Holy Spirit? Of course not. In fact, it could be necessary discernment ... A Christian can grieve the Holy Spirit (Ephesians 4:30) and even quench the Holy Spirit (1 Thessalonians 5:19) — but neither of these is unpardonable.*[59]

> *Satan is called "the accuser of the brethren ... who accuses them before our God day and night" (Revelation 12:10). We have all heard his lying, hateful voice in our hearts and consciences. He never seems to let up on us. Many Christians are perpetually discouraged and defeated because they believe his persistent lies about them. And those who give in to his accusations end up being robbed of the freedom that God intends His people to enjoy.*[60]

Unfortunately, some Christians do the devil's work by accusing themselves. We need to know that if we are in Christ any image or thought

---

58  Basically, I align with many commentators who claim that the scribes' disbelief in Jesus as Messiah and ascribing His exorcism ministry to Satan was their blaspheming the Holy Spirit. The only sin that is unforgiveable is refusal to accept Jesus as Lord.

59  Anderson, *Bondage Breaker*, p. 163.

60  Anderson, *Bondage Breaker*, p. 152.

we have of our self that is not positive is unbiblical. Satan delights in eroding the confidence of God's people and encourages self-condemnation.

## Summary Thoughts from Chapter 7, Satan's Strategies

- Satan's battle plan involves taking control of or influencing a person's mind, usually without the person knowing it.
- Satan's strategies include deception, corruption, accusation, and a host of secrets which he does not want his subjects to discover.
- Ignorance of the reality of the spiritual world is part of the arrogance that stems from "enlightenment" mentality.

# 8

## SATAN'S SECRETS

Besides his deceptions, corruptions, and accusations, Satan has some secrets, even secrets about you that he does not want you to know. And one of those secrets is your identity in Christ.

### Secret #1: Because of Who You Are in Christ, You Are a Danger to Satan's Kingdom of Darkness

If you are a follower of Christ, you are already a graduate in God's army. You are not normal: You are meta-normal, or super normal. You are already eternal and endowed with His authority to represent Him in every area of your life. Paul tells us in Ephesians 2:6 that we are already *seated with Christ in the heavenly places,* and that all competing authorities have been placed under Christ's feet (Ephesians 1:22). So, even if you think you are the lowest part of the body of Christ, the feet, in Christ you still have authority over the enemy.

> Even if you think you are the lowest part of the body of Christ, the feet, you still have authority over the enemy.

So, don't ever let anyone, including the devil, tell you that you are less than who Christ says you are. You are forever Christ's chosen, adopted, and favored son or daughter with His credentials and empowerment to change the world. Your identity in Christ is far more powerful than you have imagined. If a voice inside you suggests you are inadequate, unworthy, or powerless, ignore it in Jesus' name. That voice is the lying, deceiving, accusing voice of Satan.

Satan also does not want you to know the potential of your impact for Christ. With the power of Christ, you can be the transformational leader in your family, in your church, in your work environment, and in the heavenly places. You do not need specialized combat training. You don't need to go to "Spiritual Warfare" graduate school. You merely need to believe what God says about you and to live a Christ-centered, Spirit-filled life. When you do so, you are a warrior. So, are you ready for this warfare? You need to be, because it is already raging, and, as we see in Chapter 9, your life is one of the battlegrounds.

But the great thing about this battle is that we already know the outcome — the war has been won already. Our continuing warfare is just to rescue some from the enemy, heal those he has hurt, and declare to the world that Christ, the rightful King, is coming again. Until He comes, we are to be alert to the enemy's strategies, including other secrets he does not want us to know.

### Secret #2: Satan Hates the Church

*A fact that is anew being forced upon the consciousness of the Church of Christ is that a great and aggressive warfare is being waged against her by unseen and powerful foes. The Scriptures have long revealed it, but few have given this warfare the attention which it requires. 'Our wrestling,' the apostle warns us, 'is not against flesh and blood, but against the principalities, against the world-rulers of this darkness, against the spiritual hosts of wickedness in the heavenlies' (Ephesians 6:12, ASV). In the life of the Christian assembly, in the purity of its doctrine, in the fellowship of its members and in their individual bodies and circumstances, subtle forces are working with keen understanding and masterful direction. The opposition is veiled, but it is real, and it is sometimes tremendous. Because its source is unrecognized, it is the more effective.* **The powers of evil are allowed often to have practically free course in groups of believers.** *Troubles that might be easily overcome, if rightly diagnosed, are laid to other causes, and because the remedy is not applied, the difficulties may increase until the very existence of the congregation is threatened* [61] (emphasis mine).

Of course, a church is just a collection of individuals, so Satan's success in infiltrating and infecting a church with his heinous spiritual viruses comes through corrupting individuals, even the people of God. How does he do this? Exactly the same way as he approached Eve: "Has God said ...?" or "Did God really say ...?" (NIV). Questioning or challenging the authority of God by making His requirements seem unreasonable so that we disobey Him enshrines our mind as our lord over God. The human mind is probably God's most advanced creation, but it is prone to the sin of arrogance, and when we obey the arrogant autonomy of our mind, the devil has us trapped.

MacMillan continues to press the point of God's total condemnation of every kind of work of the deceiver:

*When we turn to the Bible, we find it acknowledging the supernatural character of demonism in a number of passages. The Mosaic Law pronounced death against wizards and witches, not because their art was a mere pretense or imposture, but because it was a voluntary and real [communication] with evil spirits. The language of Scripture is too plain on this matter to be misunderstood. 'There shall not be found among you any one ... that useth divination, or an observer of times, or an enchanter or a witch, or a charmer; or a consulter with familiar spirits, or a wizard, or a necromancer. For all that do these things are an abomination unto the LORD' (Deuteronomy 18:10-12).* [62]

---

61    MacMillan, pp. 63-64.

62    MacMillan, p. 107.

Anderson amplifies these thoughts:

*God strictly forbade His covenant people from consulting any supernatural source other than Himself.... We do almost the opposite. People are channeling on TV and radio programs, and New Age teachers can propagate their world view while Christians can't. I read recently that more women consult with psychics or New Age practitioners than licensed professional counselors.*[63]

More women consult with psychics or New Age practitioners than licensed professional counselors.

*The craving for esoteric, "extra" knowledge in our culture was illustrated to me when two conferences, both open to the public, were held in Pasadena, California. One was a major world conference on international missions, and about 600 people attended. At the same time, a New Age conference was being conducted in the Pasadena Civic Center, and more than 40,000 people showed up.*[64]

*Satan's ultimate lie is that you are capable of being the god of your own life — and his ultimate bondage is the attempt to live as though his lie were truth. Satan is out to usurp God's place in your life. Every temptation is an endeavor by him to get you to live your life independent of God.*[65]

## Secret #3: Satan Uses Us Against Us

Sometimes we seem to be our own worst enemy, precisely because we cooperate with the devil's schemes. He is always eager to use the weaknesses of our flesh to imprison us in his vile clutches. We call these prisons "strongholds."

"Strongholds" *are fleshly patterns that were programmed into your mind when you learned to live your life independently of God. Your worldview*

---

63   Anderson, *Bondage Breaker*, pp. 127-128.

64   Anderson, *Bondage Breaker*, p. 127.

65   Anderson, *Bondage Breaker*, p. 42.

*was shaped by the environment you were raised in. But when you became a Christian, nobody pressed the "CLEAR" button. Your old fleshly habit patterns of thought weren't erased.*[66]

*In our natural state, we learned many ways to cope with life or defend ourselves which were not always mentally and emotionally healthy. Psychologists refer to these unhealthy patterns of living as defense mechanisms, and they are certainly not congruent with Christianity. For instance, many people have learned to lie in order to protect themselves. Other common defense mechanisms include:*

- *denial (conscious or subconscious refusal to face the truth)*
- *fantasy (escaping from the real world)*
- *emotional isolation (withdrawing to avoid rejection)*
- *regression (reverting to less threatening times)*
- *displacement (taking out frustrations on others)*
- *projection (blaming others)*
- *rationalization (making excuses for poor behavior)*

*Defense mechanisms are similar to what Paul calls strongholds. He writes, "Though we walk in the flesh, we do not war according to the flesh, for the weapons of our warfare are not of the flesh, but divinely powerful for the destruction of fortresses. We are destroying speculations and every lofty thing raised up against the knowledge of God, and we are taking every thought captive to the obedience of Christ" (2 Corinthians 10:3-5).*[67]

I have met many Christians who rely on their human logic to dismiss the possibility of Satan having control over a follower of Christ. Logic says that two beings cannot simultaneously occupy the same place, so, since Christians are inhabited by the Holy Spirit, no other spirit can also be in the Christian. By that logic, we must assume also that there is no room in us for our human spirit, thus depriving us of our human will and making

---

66   Anderson, *Bondage Breaker*, pp. 60-61.

67   Anderson, *Bondage Breaker*, p. 60.

us forever sinless. Nice thought, but discredited by our experience and by Scripture in many places. We continue to be a battlefield, and believers who are not walking in the light are being deceived and deceiving themselves, as the Apostle John wrote:

> *If we say that we have fellowship with Him and yet walk in the darkness, we lie and do not practice the truth; but if we walk in the Light as He Himself is in the Light, we have fellowship with one another, and the blood of Jesus His Son cleanses us from all sin. If we say that we have no sin, we are deceiving ourselves and the truth is not in us. If we confess our sins, He is faithful and righteous to forgive us our sins and to cleanse us from all unrighteousness. If we say that we have not sinned, we make Him a liar and His word is not in us.*

1 John 1:6-10

## Secret #4: Satan Works through Evil Spirits

Luke gives a helpful view into the personality and individuality of evil spirits. After Jesus cast out a demon which had rendered a man dumb, His detractors accused Him of casting out demons by the power of *Beelzebul, the ruler of the demons* (Luke 11:15). During the discussion of demons which followed, Jesus said:

> *When the unclean spirit goes out of a man, it passes through waterless places seeking rest, and not finding any, it says, "I will return to my house from which I came." And when it comes, it finds it swept and put in order. Then it goes and takes along seven other spirits more evil than itself, and they go in and live there; and the last state of that man becomes worse than the first.*

Luke 11:24-26

Anderson gleans several points of information about evil spirits from this passage:

- ***Demons can exist outside or inside humans.*** *Demons seem to be spirits which find a measure of rest in organic beings, preferring even swine over nothingness (Mark 5:12). These spirits may take territorial rights and associate with certain geographical locations which have been used for satanic purposes.*

- *They are able to travel at will. Being spiritual entities, demons are not subject to the barriers of the natural world. The walls of your church building do not establish it as sanctuary from demonic influence; only prayer and spiritual authority can do that. Remember, the only real sanctuary we have is our position "in Christ."*
- *They are able to communicate. It is obvious from Luke 11 that evil spirits can communicate with each other. They can also speak to humans through a human subject, such as they did through the Gadarene demoniac (Matthew 8:28-34). Such extreme cases reveal control of the central nervous system. A lesser degree of control comes from paying attention to deceiving spirits (1 Timothy 4:1).*[68]

In another context, Anderson writes about two ineffective ways and one effective way of responding to the attacks of demons:

Ø *... the most spiritually defeated Christians are those who pay attention to deceiving spirits (1 Timothy 4:1). They weakly give into the temptations and believe the lies and accusations. These Christians are defeated simply because they have been duped into believing God doesn't love them, or they will never be victorious Christians, or they are helpless victims of the past. ...*

> The most spiritually defeated Christians are those who pay attention to deceiving spirits. They weakly give into the temptations and believe the lies and accusations.

Ø *The second response is just as unproductive. Christians try to argue with the demons: "I am not ugly or stupid. I am a victorious Christian. That is not truth. I rebuke that lie." They think they are fighting the good fight, but in reality, those negative thoughts are still controlling them and setting the agenda. They are standing in the middle of the street shouting at the demons when they should be marching forward. ...*

---

68   Anderson, *Bondage Breaker*, pp. 116-117.

ø *The third response is this: We overcome the world, the flesh, and the devil by choosing the truth. We are not to believe evil spirits, nor are we to dialogue with them. We are instructed not to pay attention to them.*[69]

- ***Each one has a separate identity.*** *Notice the use of personal pronouns in Luke 11: "I will return to my house from which I came" (verse 24). We are dealing with thinking personalities as opposed to impersonal forces. That's why secular methods of research are not going to reveal their existence. Revelation alone is our authoritative source of the reality and personality of evil spirits.*
- ***They are able to remember and make plans.*** *The fact that they can leave a place, come back, remember their former state, and plan reentry with others shows their ability to think and plan.*
- ***They are able to evaluate and make decisions.*** *The fact that the evil spirit found its human target "swept and put in order" (verse 25) clearly indicates that it can evaluate its intended victim. Demons gain access to our lives through our points of vulnerability. Yet we are not to care what Satan thinks of us; we are to live our lives in a way that is pleasing to God (2 Corinthians 5:9).*
- ***They are able to combine forces.*** *In Luke 11 the one spirit joined with a group of seven others, making the victim's last state worse than his first. In the case of the Gadarene demoniac, the number of demons united for evil was "Legion" (Mark 5:9). I have heard many people identify a number of different voices in their mind, describing them as a committee.*
- ***They vary in degree of wickedness.*** *The first demon in Luke 11 brought back seven other spirits "more evil than itself" (verse 26). Jesus indicated a difference in the wickedness of spirits when*

---

69   Anderson, *Bondage Breaker*, p. 121.

*He said of one, "This kind cannot come out by anything but prayer" (Mark 9:29). The concept of variations of power and wickedness fits the hierarchy which Paul lists in Ephesians 6:12. I can personally attest that some cases are more difficult than others.*[70]

## Secret #5: Satan Cannot Own a Person

Another deception of Satan is that he can "possess" a person to the extent of ownership. In fact, the term "possession" may overstate Satan's ability, even if through evil spirits he is able to occupy a person.

*In his book* What Demons Can Do to Saints, *Dr. Merrill Unger wrote, "The demon enters ... as a squatter and not as an owner or a guest or as one who has a right there. But he comes in as an intruder and as an invader and enemy. But come he does if the door is opened by serious and protracted sin."*[71] *Satan knows he can never own you. But if he can deceive you into yielding control of your life in any way, he can impede your growth and destroy your witness for Christ.*[72]

Just as it is not always easy to remove squatters, evicting evil spirits can be taxing, as the nine disciples in the valley discovered as they were ineffective in casting out a demon from a young boy:

*And one of the crowd answered Him, "Teacher, I brought You my son, possessed with a spirit which makes him mute; and whenever it seizes him, it dashes him to the ground and he foams at the mouth, and grinds his teeth, and stiffens out. And I told your disciples to cast it out, and they could not do it."*

Mark 9:17-18

Jesus later told the disciples, *This kind cannot come out by anything but prayer* (verse 29). Eviction, or exorcism, occurs only when spiritual authority is

---

70    Anderson, *Bondage Breaker*, pp. 117-118.

71    Merrill F. Unger, *What Demons Can Do to Saints* (Chicago: Moody Press, 1977), p. 51.

72    Anderson, *Bondage Breaker*, p. 185.

exercised, and as in the episode in Mark 9, prayer is an essential part of gaining that authority.

## Secret # 6: Satan Can Use Music to Control People

Another Satanic secret is how the enemy can use the power of music to influence people. A twentieth-century example is how Adolf Hitler used music to educate, inspire, and incite young people in the *Hitlerjugend* (Hitler Youth) movement of the Nazi Party.

> *In the Nazi imagination, music had a unique significance and power to seduce and sway the masses. The party made widespread use of music in its publicity, and music featured prominently at rallies and other public events. Many propaganda songs were aimed at the youth, and the Hitlerjugend (Hitler Youth) developed an elaborate music program.*[73]

The connection between the demonic and music is even more clear in 1 Samuel 16:14-23 where David was asked to play his harp in King Saul's palace so that an evil spirit would depart from Saul. Music has tremendous power in influencing individuals and shaping cultures. And God's enemy knows that and uses music (and other media) to pervert people and cultures, as seen in this remark in *The Bondage Breaker*:

> *The Satanist I led to the Lord showed me numerous symbols on popular record albums indicating the groups' association with Satanism. He believed that about 85 percent of today's heavy metal and punk music groups are "owned" by Satanists.*[74]

Satan uses much of secular music to corrupt culture and especially young people.

Now, admittedly, music genres change and so do the devices to play music (record albums?), but the truth still applies — Satan uses much of secular music to corrupt culture and especially young people.

---

73    Holocaustmusic.ort.org.

74    Anderson, *Bondage Breaker*, pp. 131-132.

## Secret #7: Satan Has No Power

Although he appears as a powerful foe, one of Satan's nasty secrets is that he is not powerful. Satan is like an inflatable, a child's toy or a roadside advertisement, that is lifeless unless inflated by an outside source. Satan has

> Satan is like an inflatable, a child's toy or a tool that is lifeless unless inflated by an outside source.

no power; rather, he seizes on the law or principle of sin that works in us and deceives us. Again, remember, deception is his primary attribute. He wants us to believe that he is omnipotent, so he deceives us by using our sin against us. Paul reveals this truth in Romans 7.

> *I find then the principle that evil is present in me, the one who wants to do good. For I joyfully concur with the law of God in the inner man, but I see a different law in the members of my body, waging war against the law of my mind and making me a prisoner of the law of sin which is in my members.*
>
> Romans 7:21-23

Anderson asks,

> *Why, then, does the kingdom of darkness exert such negative influence in the world and in the lives of Christians? Because Satan has deceived the whole world, and therefore the whole world lies in the power of the evil one (1 John 5:19). Satan is not an equal power with God; he is a disarmed and defeated foe (Colossians 2:15). But if he can deceive you into believing that he has more power and authority than you do, you will live as if he does!*[75]

## Secret #8: Satan Is Defeated

The above quotes suggest another of Satan's secrets — he is a defeated foe. We know this because the ultimate fruit of sin is death, and death has been defeated with the resurrection of Jesus Christ. Satan can do nothing to reverse that great victory, but he can continue to deceive the world and keep it in the narrowness of the humanistic or naturalistic worldview. Through His resurrection, Jesus has disarmed the rulers and

---

75   Anderson, *Bondage Breaker*, p. 80.

authorities and made a public display of them, having triumphed over them (Colossians 2:15).

In the first century, while masses of people chose not to believe the resurrection of Jesus had occurred, many (over 500) had seen the resurrected Jesus, and their testimony fueled their zeal as evangelists throughout the Roman Empire, which spread the Christian church rapidly. Within a few centuries, the small Galilean group's credibility was so compelling that Christianity became the official religion of the empire.

Well, that was then, and this is now. No one who is alive today has seen the resurrected Jesus. But that was true also in the second century and beyond. So, what was the source of credibility of the succeeding generations of believers? What is the evidence of Satan's defeat? It is the corporate witness of the Church as well as the testimony of transformed people. From pagan to saint was a frequent experience, and one early church practice gives insight into their worldview. When Gentiles became Christians, it was common before they were baptized for them to be exorcised. Now, that is not a biblical prescription, but early church fathers assumed, correctly no doubt, that living outside any covenant commitment to God so polluted the Gentiles that Satan had not only a foothold but a stronghold in their lives.

In Section One: The War of the Ages, we have seen that the Bible's view of reality shows us to be participants in a war that involves much more than humanity and planet earth. History is merely the backdrop to the warfare between God and His enemy Satan who, with his co-rebels, is seeking to corrupt and eternally condemn all the good that God has created. In Chapters 5 and 6, we expounded significantly about Satan and his evil colleagues, known as demons, not to inspire fear but to give enemy intelligence. The Apostle Paul encouraged the Ephesian believers to stand firm against the *schemes*, the strategies of the devil (Ephesians 6:11). We move now to Section Two to consider the "Heavenly Hostilities," beginning with Chapter 9, "The Battleground," with which we are all too familiar.

## Summary Thoughts from Chapter 8, Satan's Secrets

- In his deceptions, Satan has secrets by which he tries to keep humans inept, impotent, and irrelevant to the spiritual warfare that rages around us.
- Even if you think you are the lowest part of the body of Christ, the feet, in Christ you still have authority over the enemy.
- Satan hates the Church; Satan uses us against us; Satan has no power; Satan is defeated; Satan works through evil spirits.
- Satan uses much of secular music to corrupt culture, and especially young people.

# SECTION TWO:
# HEAVENLY HOSTILITIES

# 9

## THE BATTLEGROUND

*It is the will of God as revealed in His Word that those who are oppressed of the devil should be set free. The Lord Jesus came 'to proclaim liberty to the captives, and the opening of the prison to them that are bound' (Isaiah 61:1, cp. Luke 4:18). The era in which we are living is 'the acceptable year of the Lord,' and it will not terminate until the Son of Man comes again to proclaim, 'the day of vengeance of our God' and to shut up in the prison house of the 'abyss' the rebel powers that have brought destruction and age long suffering to our race. During this period of grace, Christ's servants are commissioned to 'cast out devils' (Mark 16:17) as one of the 'signs' which follow 'them that believe.' The inference is that throughout the age there will be the need for this important ministry. History and experience confirm this inference.*[76]

A very destructive strategy of the devil occurred early in the twentieth century when European rationalists, posing as theologians, introduced the idea of *demythologizing* the Gospels. Led by men like New Testament scholar Rudolph Bultmann, this activity began with the premise that

---

76    MacMillan, pp. 170-171.

purported miracles have always been the unenlightened imaginations of primitive minds, propounding supernatural activities. They applied their "advanced, scientific methodology," even to Jesus, as merely superstition gone wild by people who desperately wanted to believe life is more than mere human, earthly existence. So, the biblical narratives that report miracles were viewed to be myth, much like Greek or Roman mythology. We won't go into the manifold reasons that demonstrate conclusively how wrong such demythologizers were, but we introduce the idea of demythologizing to use in a different way.

I believe we need to demythologize the prevalent view that demonic influence, whether possession, oppression, or influence,[77] will always be dramatic and demonstrable. Satan may be *a roaring lion seeking whom he may devour* (1 Peter 5:8) at times, but he is also a subtle serpent and an "angel of light" (2 Corinthians 11:14; see footnote 49). While Christians are not called on to be "ghost-busters" who find demons in every negative situation in life, the truth is that God's enemy is very eager to enter into the everyday life experiences of people who choose not to walk in the ways of truth and righteousness. One does not need to become a Satanist or join the occult to be fair prey for Satan. And that is why Jesus, Peter, John, Paul, James, and other voices in Scripture continually warn, admonish, and instruct people to submit to God and His ways.

> Christians are not called on to be "ghost-busters" who find demons in every negative situation in life.

Submission and resistance are two sides of the same coin which James expressed in this way: *Submit therefore to God. Resist the devil and he will flee from you* (James 4:7). Why are these two points linked like this?

*I have learned from personal experience if you try to resist the devil without first submitting to God, you will have a dogfight. On the other hand, you can submit to God without resisting the devil and stay in bondage.*[78]

---

77  The Bible does not differentiate between levels of demonic activity by different terminology. The Greek word that describes demonic presence or power in a person's life may best be translated "demonized."

78  Anderson, *Bondage Breaker*, p. 258.

Another myth is the idea that we can go our own way in life without negative consequences. Our own way is called "the flesh" or the "sinful nature," part of the devil's threefold pathway to hell — the world, the flesh, and the devil. There is no neutral ground. Either we worship and submit to God, or by default we remain in the enemy's camp into which we were born having inherited the sinful nature of our first parents. The Good News, however, is that God is *not wishing for any to perish, but for all to come to repentance* (2 Peter 3:9).

> *People who are caught up in the sin-confess-sin-confess cycle eventually begin to lose hope that they can experience any real victory over sin. Sheer willpower can't keep them from repeating the sin they just confessed, and Satan pours on the condemnation. Self-control seems like an illusion, and the Christian life is one of unending ups and downs.*

> *God will enable us to overcome this sin cycle of defeat. "My little children, I am writing these things to you that you may not sin. And if anyone sins, we have an Advocate with the Father, Jesus Christ the righteous" (1 John 2:1).*[79]

So, the battle is on — the fight for your soul. You are the Battleground. We may like to think of ourselves as Warriors, but more than that, each of us is a battlefield of the war. And that thought draws us back to the Ephesians, a war-torn people whose instructions from Paul are totally relevant for us today. Now, we have noted that Professor MacMillan, in referring to "heathens" and "pagans," wrote with terminology that would not be politically correct today. Those terms, however, accurately describe people, regardless of how civilized, sophisticated, educated, and advanced they may be, if they are not living in submission to the authority of God. The Apostle Paul used the term "Gentiles" because prior to Christianity, the non-Jews were *without God and without hope* (Ephesians 2:12).

---

[79] Anderson, *Bondage Breaker*, p. 149.

## A Demonized City

We may see in Paul's letter to the Ephesians[80] how Christians are to respond to the spiritual warfare that is in us and around us. We begin by looking more closely at Paul's immediate audience. Who were these early believers and what was their city like? How were they not only in a battlefield, but also part of it?

The Christian church in Ephesus was pastored by Paul from the years 52 to 55 A.D. Paul's special relationship with the believers at Ephesus is evident in the narrative found in Acts 19, and even more so in the latter half of Acts 20. Ephesus might rightly claim to have been the site of the first Christian seminary. Acts 19:8-10 indicates that Paul used his years in Ephesus to train some disciples who went out and evangelized the entire province of Asia (western Turkey). Paul wrote this letter nearly a decade later, probably during his last imprisonment in Rome in 62 or 63 A.D., when he was able to write more reflectively.

Ephesus itself was a busy commercial city in today's southwestern Turkey. We do not know a great deal about the church, although it seems that Timothy became the leading pastor or bishop of the church at Ephesus. When Christianity was introduced there, Ephesus was a very superstitious and spiritually pluralistic environment.

Analysis of the brief letter indicates that Paul wrote Ephesians to give to the Church a summary statement of Christian theology and ethics, namely, that by God's sovereign decree He is gathering a community of people, redeemed in Christ Jesus, who is head of this body. A deeper look in the first and last chapters of Ephesians reveals the spiritual worldview backdrop underlying all the other issues in the letter. The Ephesian church was clearly one of the battlegrounds of the warfare waged by God and His

---

80　While some early manuscripts do not designate the letter to a specific church, and while there is internal evidence that would suggest it may have been a cyclical letter like Colossians was intended to be, there is enough internal and historical evidence to affirm that Paul's primary audience was the church at Ephesus, which by the time of the writing may have been under the pastoral oversight of Timothy, Paul's son in the Lord.

archenemy Satan. And more than that, the Ephesian believers were enlisted into that war to demonstrate to the enemy that God's intended purpose at creation of entering into a pure and loving relationship with free moral agents does and will succeed as people of the Church reflect God's nature in all their relationships.

There are two prominent ideas in the letter that give us an enlightened and inspired vantage point for understanding our role in the cosmic warfare, as we saw in Chapter 8:

1) You are not who you think you are (hint: if you are in Christ, you are far better and more than you imagine);

> You are not who you think you are. If you are in Christ, you are far better and more than you imagine.

2) By growing in spiritual maturity, you will be able powerfully to impact every relationship in your life.

Neil Anderson, in his prominent counseling ministry, has observed:
*One of the most common attitudes I have discovered in Christians — even among pastors, Christian leaders, and their wives and children — is a deep-seated sense of self-deprecation. I've heard them say, "I'm not important, I'm not qualified, I'm no good." I'm amazed at how many Christians are paralyzed in their witness and productivity by thoughts and feelings of inferiority and worthlessness.*

*Next to temptation, perhaps the most frequent and insistent attack from Satan to which we are vulnerable is accusation. By faith we have entered into an eternal relationship with Jesus Christ. As a result, we are dead to sin and alive to God, and we now sit with Christ in the heavenlies. In Christ we are important, we are qualified, we are loved. Satan can do absolutely nothing to alter our position in Christ and our worth to God. But he can render us virtually inoperative if he can deceive us into listening to and believing his insidious lies accusing us of being of little value to God or other people.*[81]

---

81    Anderson, *Bondage Breaker*, p. 151.

The dark power that deceives, accuses, and paralyzes people today had his way with thousands of people in biblical days, none more under his spell than the Ephesians. Ephesus was:

- A pagan city with a few weak Christians, who later received the fullness of the Holy Spirit – Acts 19:1-10
- A city plagued by false religion and demonism – Acts 19:11-20
- A city exploited by commercial interests – Acts 19:23-34

If ever a church-plant should have failed, it was Ephesus. The account in Acts 19 of Paul in Ephesus is headline stuff: "Religious Fanatics Threaten Economy" or "Riot Breaks Out Over New Cult." Not exactly the way you want to launch a new church plant! Here are highlights of Pastor Paul's exciting new church planting effort:

Some Jews were trying to cast out evil spirits, but one time a man with an evil spirit leaped on them, overpowered them, and attacked them with such violence that they fled, naked and beaten up. Because demons were responding to the name of Jesus as Paul ministered in Ephesus, among both Jews and Greeks alike, *a solemn fear descended on the city, and the name of the Lord Jesus was greatly honored* (Acts 19:17), so many became believers. They confessed their sinful ways, and those who had been practicing sorcery brought their incantation books and burned them at a public bonfire. So, the message about the Lord spread widely and had a powerful effect on the citizens of Ephesus. From this we deduce two important ideas:

1. The Ephesians certainly had an open worldview, including the reality of spiritual beings that could harass human beings. Today, demonic beings, including the devil, are largely considered to be part of the mythology of the Christian unenlightened worldview. But such "enlightened" people are blind to realities beyond their five senses. Quite likely, a visit to a country like Haiti, India, or Nigeria, as reported below, would open their eyes. In Uganda recently I heard this comment,

"In Africa, we have a supernatural worldview; America has a superficial worldview."

2.   Another observation from the text in Acts 19 is that people in the grip of demonic power often want deliverance and can find it only in the name of Jesus. Even the Jewish young men, the sons of Sceva, were using the name of Jesus.

Catherine Booth, wife of William Booth, the founder of the Salvation Army, wrote,

*Many do not recognize the fact as they ought, that Satan has got men fast asleep in sin and that it is his great desire to keep them so. He does not care what we do if he can do that. We may sing songs about the sweet by and by, preach sermons and say prayers until doomsday, and he [Satan] will never concern himself about us, if we don't wake anybody up. But if we awake the sleeping sinner he will gnash on us with his teeth. This is our work — to wake people up.*[82]

We may sing songs, preach sermons and say prayers until doomsday, and he [Satan] will never concern himself about us, if we don't wake anybody up.

## A god From Heaven?

The story goes on in Acts 19:23-41 to show that serious trouble was about to break out because of *the Way*. A silversmith named Demetrius got angry because his large idol manufacturing business which made shrines of the Greek goddess Artemis was being threatened because so many were turning to Christ and abandoning their pagan religion. He stirred up the citizens of Ephesus, and they had a two-hour riot in the amphitheater, shouting, "Great is Artemis of the Ephesians!" Eventually, the mayor of the city quieted them and suggested that Demetrius and the craftsmen could lodge formal legal charges.

Talk about a battlefield! The battle was not really Paul vs. Demetrius, but about the gospel of Jesus Christ vs. the cult of Artemis.

---

82   Found in AZ Quotes on the internet.

Why were the ancient people so adamant about their god? Consider this information from a long scholarly article: *The Worship of Meteorites* by Professor Hubert A. Newton.

> The image, which was the central object in this temple, was said to have fallen from heaven.

*I propose to speak briefly of one more meteorite whose worship has had a world-wide fame: the image of the Ephesian Artemis. This worship had its centre at Ephesus, but was widely extended along the shores of the Mediterranean. Temple after temple was built on the same site at Ephesus, each superior to the preceding, until the structure was reckoned one of the Seven Wonders of the World. As a temple, it became the theatre of a most elaborate religious ceremonial. ... The image, which was the central object in this temple, was said to have fallen from heaven. Copies of it in all sizes and forms were made of gold, of silver, of bronze, of stone and of wood, by Ephesian artificers, and were supplied by them to markets in all lands. What a lifelike picture is given us in the 19th chapter of the Acts of the Apostles, of the excited crowd of Ephesians, urged on by the silversmiths, who made for sale the silver shrines of the goddess, and who saw that their craft was in danger if men learned to regard Artemis as no real divinity, and to despise the image that fell down from the sky.*[83] [84]

Let's not think too ill of these pagan worshippers. Twenty-first-century educated people "worship" far less heavenly idols in elaborate temples called auditoriums, arenas, and stadiums every week. These "religions" are also funded by commercial interests, like those televised Super Bowl ads that cost in the millions of dollars.

---

83    Hubert A. Newton, *The Worship of Meteorites*, Meteoritehistory.info, from a lecture delivered in New Haven, CT. The original article appeared in the American Journal of Science. This e-text version is from that reprinted in Nature, August 12th, 1897 Volume 56, number 1450.

84    Besides giving us insight into the religion of Artemis, this is amazing secular testimony to the veracity of the book of Acts.

What a great contrast there is between these idol-driven worldviews and the theistic worldview presented in the letter Paul addressed to the believers in Ephesus. But that was the environment into which the church at Ephesus was birthed. Truly, it was "enemy-occupied territory," such as described by C. S. Lewis:

> *Enemy-occupied territory — that is what the world is.*
> *Christianity is the story of how the rightful king has landed,*
> *you might say landed in disguise,*
> *And is calling us all to take part in a great campaign of sabotage.*[85]

## Living in Sin City

We told the story of Acts 19 to show the context of godlessness where Satan seemed to have total dominance. And yet, in that demonically infested environment, Paul planted a church which would itself become a battleground that required the new believers to live in the truth and purity of the gospel that insulates the soul from the attacks of the devil. Toward the end of Ephesians Paul tells his readers to put on spiritual armor, but because we are not just warriors, but also the battleground, we are admonished in Ephesians 4:17-32 how to live, even in "Sin City":

> *So I tell you this and insist on it in the Lord, that you must no longer live as the Gentiles do, in the futility of their thinking. They are darkened in their understanding and separated from the life of God because of the ignorance that is in them due to the hardening of their hearts. Having lost all sensitivity, they have given themselves over to sensuality so as to indulge in every kind of impurity, with a continual lust for more.*
>
> *You, however, did not come to know Christ that way. Surely you heard of him and were taught in him in accordance with the truth that is in Jesus. You were taught, with regard to your former way of life, to put off your old self, which is being corrupted by its deceitful desires; to be made new in the attitude of your*

---

85    C. S. Lewis, *The Meaning of Christmas.* For the rest of the poem, see Addendum 4.

*minds; and to put on the new self, created to be like God in true righteousness and holiness.*

*Therefore, each of you must put off falsehood and speak truthfully to his neighbor, for we are all members of one body. In your anger do not sin: Do not let the sun go down while you are still angry, and do not give the devil a foothold. He who has been stealing must steal no longer, but must work, doing something useful with his own hands, that he may have something to share with those in need.*

*Do not let any unwholesome talk come out of your mouths, but only what is helpful for building others up according to their needs, that it may benefit those who listen. And do not grieve the Holy Spirit of God, with whom you were sealed for the day of redemption. Get rid of all bitterness, rage and anger, brawling and slander, along with every form of malice. Be kind and compassionate to one another, forgiving each other, just as in Christ God forgave you.*

Ephesians 4, then, begins with a plea for unity of the Spirit, growth and maturity, and stability in belief. And now, Paul injects the thought that these Christians should also walk in purity! We would think that this idea would just be assumed as old business. So, why does Paul write about such majestic concepts as equipping the saints to be ministers to build up the body of Christ and attaining to the maturity of the fullness of Christ, only now to treat his readers as spiritual infants, barely a notch above paganism? Chapter 10 looks at this very question.

## Summary Thoughts from Chapter 9, The Battleground

- Demonic influence will not always be dramatic and demonstrable. The Bible does not differentiate between levels of demonic activity by different terminology. The Greek word that describes demonic presence or power in a person's life may best be translated "demonized."

- You are not who you think you are; if you are in Christ, you are far better and more than you imagine.
- Twenty-first-century educated people "worship" far less heavenly idols in elaborate temples called auditoriums, arenas, and stadiums every week.

# 10

## WALKING IN SIN CITY

In the fourth chapter of his letter to the Ephesians, Paul has taken his readers to lofty theological thought, writing about such majestic concepts as equipping the saints to be ministers to build up the body of Christ and attaining to the maturity of the fullness of Christ. But then he treats his readers as spiritual infants, barely a notch above paganism. Why does he descend to this level? The answer is that, like us, the Ephesian believers lived in a decadent society and were prone to spiritual attack. The cult of Artemis glorified the sensual life. Immorality was the norm; purity was virtually a foreign concept. And, even for those who might admire the ethical life, such as the Jews — and even they were unable to live according to the Law (Romans 7:14-23) — these Gentiles would not be able to escape the enticements of their immoral culture without knowing the ways of God and appropriating the ability He provides those who seriously seek to follow Him.

### Walking in Purity

Despite the decadent society we live in, walking in purity is possible as we are renewed in the spirit of our mind. Our mind must undergo radical transformation and then we will have power for purity which comes from

God. Notice the contrast between the unconverted mind and the converted mind. It is the contrast between degeneration and regeneration. This passage shows the strong connection between the life of the mind and a person's morality. The battleground is really the battle for our mind, as we quoted earlier in Chapter 7.

> Our mind must undergo radical transformation and then we will have power for purity which comes from God.

*Don't think that Satan is no longer interested in manipulating your mind in order to accomplish his purposes. Satan's perpetual aim is to infiltrate your thoughts with his thoughts and to promote his lie in the face of God's truth. He knows that if he can control your thoughts, he can control your life.*[86]

One of Satan's modern-day traps is the abundance of graphic and easily accessed pornography.

John Piper, founder and teacher of desiringGod.org and chancellor of Bethlehem College & Seminary, discusses the neurological, addictive impact of pornography in his October 2013 blog "Pornography: The New Narcotic." Just as cocaine acts as a stimulant that releases dopamine in the brain, causing a "high" and subsequent cravings for more and stronger doses, so, it has been proven, pornography does the same. Piper quotes Morgan Bennett,

*... internet pornography does more than just spike the level of dopamine in the brain for a pleasure sensation. It literally changes the physical matter within the brain so that the new neurological pathways require pornographic material in order to trigger the desired reward sensation.*[87]

The human mind is the gateway to the soul, and often the human eye is the gateway to the mind, as we see from the first human sin when Eve

---

86    Anderson, *Bondage Breaker*, p. 61.

87    John Piper, quoting Morgan Bennett, "The New Narcotic," October 9, 2013, https://www.thepublicdiscourse.com/wp-content/uploads/2018/07/WIS-PD-Wordmark-FULL-Website.png.

*saw* *that the tree was good for food, and that it was a delight to the eyes* (Genesis 3:6, emphasis mine).

We might tend to think of our mind as a neutral field on which all sorts of games might be played, but a better image is a mountain slope down which are many pathways. Some are pleasant, scenic paths that are healthy and life-giving. Others lead to cliffs which lead to death. The human mind is very susceptible to what we expose to it. That is why the psalmist said,

*How can a young person stay on the path of purity? By living according to your word.*

*I seek you with all my heart; do not let me stray from your commands.*

*I have hidden your word in my heart that I might not sin against you.*

Psalm 119:9-11, NIV

The lure of the flesh is certainly not a new problem, although the word "pornography"[88] may be new. Jesus was a realist about this as He cautioned the disciples,

*… I say to you that everyone who looks at a woman with lust for her has already committed adultery with her in his heart.*

Matthew 5:28

The first written book of the Bible dealt with this battle for the mind, and the eyes being the doorway to sin. In his last discourse, Job, still advocating for his innocence, said,

*I made a covenant with my eyes not to look lustfully at a young woman.*

Job 31:1

John Stott, in his commentary on Ephesians, also demonstrates the battleground of the mind:

---

88   From Greek, *porneia*, occurring 26 times in the Greek concordance of the NASB, used primarily to refer to illicit sexual activity, such as in Acts 15:20, 29; Romans 1:29; 1 Corinthians 6:12ff, 7:2; 2 Corinthians 12:21; Ephesians 5:3; Colossians 3:5; 1 Thessalonians 4:3.

*What is immediately noteworthy is the apostle's emphasis on the intellectual factor in everybody's way of life. While describing pagans he draws attention to the futility of their minds, adds that they are darkened in their understanding and attributes their alienation from God to the ignorance that is in them. He thus refers to their empty minds, darkened understanding and inward ignorance, as a result of which the head becomes callous, licentious and insatiably unclean. In contrast to them the believer has "learned" Christ, "heard" him, been "taught" in him, all according to the "truth" which is in Jesus. Over against the darkness and ignorance of the heathen, Paul thus sets the truth of Christ which the Christians had learned. Scripture bears an unwavering testimony to the power of ignorance and error to corrupt. And the power of truth to liberate, ennoble and refine.*[89]

Paul notes that the Gentiles normally walk in *the futility of their mind* (Ephesians 4:17-19). When Paul uses the word *mind*, it is evident that his thinking was greatly influenced by the Hebrew view of the human being which sees unity of personhood. The human soul, by Jewish way of thinking, is not partitioned with cognitive (intellectual) faculties on one side and emotive (emotional) faculties on the other. The Old Testament speaks of having an *understanding heart* and of the *desires of the understanding*. Hebrew thought recognized that there is much feeling in our thoughts and an element of intelligence in our feelings. Charles Hodge notes, *The idea that the heart may be depraved and the intellect unaffected is as incongruous as that one part of the soul should be happy and another miserable, or one faculty saved and another lost.*[90]

By referring to the futility of pagan thinking Paul used a word that connotes worthless or empty thinking. It is totally profitless and of no value. Worse, it is easily susceptible to arrogance, which is like an on-ramp

---

89    John Stott, *God's New Society* (Downers Grove, IL: InterVarsity Press, 1979), pp. 175-176.

90    Charles Hodge, *Commentary on the Epistle to the Ephesians* (New York: Robert Carter and Brothers, 1860), pp. 249-250.

for the enemy. Man-made religions, that is, those belief systems in which humans depend on their good works to justify themselves, are examples of how prone we are to self-sufficiency and self-deception.

**Degeneration**

There are two developmental processes that are possible for human beings, and every person is in one of these processes. One is growing down; the other is growing up. The first is the process of degeneration of the mind. The second is maturing spiritually.

Degeneration of mind begins with **obstinacy**, insistence on hanging onto our right to live as we choose and be who we choose to be. Paul calls it *the hardening of their heart* (Ephesians 4:18). This is similar to the ideas expressed in Romans 1:18, 21, and 28; by their stubbornness, people *suppress the truth*, and *although they know God they do not honor him as God* and *they do not acknowledge Him*. Here we see most clearly the sinfulness of the Adamic nature. While we may have inherited our futile mind from the fall, each individual has the opportunity either to direct his or her mind God-ward and with a softened heart accept God's leadership, or to deny the futility of his or her mind and insist on its supposed inherent worth.

Obstinacy leads to stage two in the process of degeneration, namely, **darkness**. In Ephesians 4:18 Paul refers to the fact that *they are darkened in their understanding* and also to *the ignorance that is in them*. Likewise, in Romans 1:21, Paul writes that, for those outside of Christ, *they became futile in their speculations and their foolish heart was darkened.*

This darkness is exactly opposite of what Paul prayed for the Ephesians: *that the eyes of your heart may be enlightened.* The most damning condition of a dark mind that has never been penetrated by light is the person's unawareness that there is such a thing as light.

> The most damning condition of a dark mind that has never been penetrated by light is the person's unawareness that there is such a thing as light.

Imagine trying to describe to a person born totally blind the nature of light and the sense of sight; it would be virtually impossible. A mind that remains in darkness does not even know what it is missing, as Paul writes in verse 18, as well as in 1 Corinthians 2:14:

*But the natural man does not receive the things of the Spirit of God, for they are foolishness to him; nor can he know them, because they are spiritually discerned.*

1 Corinthians 2:14, NKJV

The third stage in this process of degeneration is **judgment**. Verse 18 of Ephesians 4 says *they are alienated from the life of God*. As we saw earlier, Romans 1:24, 26, and 28 say three times *God gave them up*. The mind that refuses to come to the light — that stubbornly insists on its right of remaining independent of God — has no inheritance in God who is light. The only option for God is to keep that person in darkness, separated from Him and His glory. God will not force His light on anyone who prefers the darkness of spiritual blindness.

The fourth and final stage of degeneration is total **moral recklessness**. Ephesians 4:19 indicates that these pagans, having lost all (moral) sensitivity, have *given themselves over to sensuality so as to indulge every kind of impurity with a continual lust for more* — similar to Romans 1:24, 26-31 where Paul indicates God gave them up to *impurity, dishonorable passions, shameless acts, improper conduct, and all manner of wickedness.*

> Individuals and nations which do not honor God or seek to walk in His ways move from obstinacy to darkness to spiritual judgment to moral recklessness.

The process of moral degeneracy occurs in individuals and in societies that are dominated by sin and sinful leaders. Individuals and nations which do not honor God or seek to walk in His ways move from obstinacy to darkness to spiritual judgment to moral recklessness. This occurs even while people are trying to retain a veneer of respectability through various religious practices.

Charles Hodge gives this insightful thought:

*Men in their folly think that morality may be preserved without religion, and even that morality is religion; but reason, experience and scripture all prove that if men do not love and fear God, they give themselves up to vice in some form, usually immorality or greed. A twofold reason: 1) the nature of the soul — it has no independent source of goodness in itself, so that if it turns from*

*God it sinks into pollution. 2) The punitive justice of God — He abandons those who abandon Him — Romans 1:24.*[91]

The result of degeneration is threefold. People become so hard-hearted that they are not even aware they are sinning and do not believe there is such a thing as sin. They also become indecently sensual, so dominated by sin that shame is lost and decency is forgotten. In fact, they even flaunt their sensual lifestyle. Third, they become insatiably lustful, so much at the mercy of their desires that they do not care whom they injure or destroy as long as their lusts are satisfied. They become Satan's playground: their lust may be for money, sex, or power. This is the picture of the person who stubbornly rejects the light of God.

## Growing Up

The second possible developmental process is spiritual maturing. In 1 John 2, John points out the three-fold levels of Christian growth. Neil Anderson lays it out brilliantly.

*First John 2:12-14 describes three levels of Christian growth in relation to sin. The first level is compared to "little children" (verse 12). Little children in the faith are characterized by having their sins forgiven and possessing knowledge of God. In other words, they are in the family of God and have overcome the penalty of sin, but they are not yet mature in Christ.*

*The second level is "young men" (verses 13, 14), so characterized because they have overcome the evil one. These are maturing believers who are strong because the Word of God abides in them. They know the truth and have overcome the power of sin. They are no longer in bondage to uncontrollable habits, and they have resolved the personal and spiritual conflicts which keep many Christians from experiencing freedom in Christ. They are experiencing their freedom in Christ and they know how to stay free.*

---

91 Charles Hodge, *Systematic Theology*, Peabody, MA (Hendrickson Publishers, 1981 edition), p. 255.

*The third level is "fathers" (verses 13, 14), those who have developed a deep personal knowledge of God and a deep personal relationship with their heavenly Father.*[92]

Aside from John's strictly masculine terminology, it is clear that there are levels or stages of Christian growth, which move from a focus on dealing successfully with sin (being freed from the penalty of sin) to appropriating the truth of God's Word for power over sin, to a depth of personal relationship with the eternal God. The biblical and theological term for this maturing process is *sanctification*, a term used eight times in the New Testament. Romans 6 and 1 Thessalonians 4 are key chapters that expound on sanctification. As we mature in our faith, the focus is less on us and more on Him. While, to some extent, we remain part of the battleground, increasingly we become the spiritual warriors God intends us to be.

## Summary Thoughts from Chapter 10, Walking in Sin City

- The mind that refuses to come to the light — that stubbornly insists on its right of remaining independent of God — has no inheritance in God who is light.
- Individuals and nations which do not honor God or seek to walk in His ways move from obstinacy to darkness to spiritual judgment to moral recklessness.
- Sanctification is a process of spiritual maturing that leads us from being "little children" to "young men" to "fathers."

---

92   Anderson, *Bondage Breaker*, pp. 138-139.

# 11

## UNEXPECTED BATTLEFIELDS

Attacking us in the area of personal behavior is an obvious strategy of Satan. We all struggle with the "flesh," which includes our sexuality, our self-image, our pride, our autonomy, and our desire for human approval (popularity). But is that the crux of spiritual warfare?

What comes into your mind when you think about spiritual warfare? Besides thinking about our personal battles, those whose worldview includes a spiritual realm would quite likely think about a dramatic encounter with a demon-possessed person. Such cases in the New Testament might cause us to believe that Satan's only warfare strategy is to inhabit and torture humans. However, the warfare between the kingdom of God and the kingdom of darkness is not an intermittent, contained war; it rages intensely all the time, everywhere. Some of Satan's best work is to promote discord, anger and strife in our homes and work environments. He is intent on destroying relationships, and usually he does it without us even knowing he is the source. He loves to corrupt people toward eternal condemnation, the same judgment he knows awaits him.

In Ephesians, Paul's blueprint for successful godly living, it is evident that spiritual warfare includes many other fronts than the heavenly realms and the souls of some troubled people. The Apostle Peter knew that *the devil prowls around like a roaring lion looking for someone to devour* (1 Peter 5:8). And, Satan doesn't prowl only in nightclubs, theaters, dark alleys, red-light districts, and casinos. He prowls in our homes, our neighborhoods, our schools, our churches, the marketplace, and he is all over the internet.

> Satan doesn't prowl only in nightclubs, theaters, dark alleys, red-light districts.

In Chapter 20, The Battle Plan, we consider how to wage effective warfare in several ways, but in this chapter, we want also to look at some of the unexpected places of daily living where we need to be on the alert.

## Domestic Conflicts

### Your Family

If God's people are going to represent his kingdom well, primary relationships must be handled properly, including parent/child relationships and boss/worker relationships. Satan loves to sabotage relationships by creating conflicts so that people lose their focus on God and the joy that comes from being in right relation to Him and others.

In Ephesians 6, Paul suggests that the kingdom of God can be seen in proper parent/child relationships (verses 1-4). Each Christian family ought to be a microcosm of the ideals of the kingdom of God where all relationships are healthy.

The family is the most basic of all human institutions. If the principles of the kingdom of God are not seen at the family level, then the family has a makeover project to do. But when husband and wife love and respect each other, and when they discipline their children in love, and when children submit to Christ and their parents, and Jesus is honored and in His rightful place as Lord of a family, their example represents the kingdom of God, even in the midst of sin-city. It may be more important to have a well-disciplined Christ-centered family in every neighborhood than to have a Bible study in every neighborhood. The modeling done by a Christian family is a powerful evidence of the reality of Christ and His kingdom.

Notice that Paul directly addressed the children (*Children, obey your parents* ...), assuming they would be present in the assembly of believers when the letter would be read. Offering programs geared especially for children and youth is a fairly modern practice of the Church, and is usually a good feature. Parents and church leaders want to provide programs that minister to the special needs of the kids. But the concern is also to ensure that the kids will not get turned off to church by having to sit through "boring" adult sermons.

I believe that the Church needs to do a lot more than keeping the interest of the young people. The Church needs to challenge the young people. A church that tries to compete with the world by entertaining the kids is going to lose out. I suspect the enemy is quite satisfied when all the church does is entertain the young people. The church should provide what only the church can provide: a challenge to change the world. This challenge needs to be communicated directly to the young people from the pulpit and reinforced by the parents. The twelve apostles were likely in their teens and twenties when Jesus called them to follow Him, and their parents, such as Zebedee, father of James and John, released them.

Throughout history, young people have always been the world-changers. For example, the famous Welsh Revival of 1904 was sparked by Evan Roberts, who was 26 at the time. His life of disciplined prayer and passionate evangelistic preaching reached hundreds of thousands of people, beginning with the mine workers. The story was reported that, so thoroughly were the workers converted, that their coal-cart donkeys couldn't understand their cleaned-up language. That revival spilled across the Atlantic to New York and then to Azusa Street in Los Angeles. There the modern Pentecostal movement began under William Seymour, only 36 at the time.

We know that child rebellion is very destructive in the life of a nation. Eli's sons provide a sad illustration of this idea. First Samuel 2 describes them as being *worthless men who did not know the Lord* (verse 12). Verses 22-25 describe how evil they were. Taking advantage of Eli's advanced years and his position as a priest, these two sons seduced women into sexual misconduct even at the place of worship. The text also indicts Eli as an indulgent father. Thus, we see in this example the destructiveness of an undisciplined family.

After his short message to the children in Ephesians, Paul tells the fathers how they ought to conduct themselves as parents. The emphasis is on self-control, gentleness and patience as educators. Biblically, the father is the final authority of discipline in the family. And in that role, he needs to be cautious not to exasperate or frustrate his children. Many fathers overplay their hand of authority, causing their children to rebel actively or passively. Sometimes when the wife senses that the father is not using his authority properly, she steps in to usurp her husband's role. This situation can cause even greater damage. Why are fathers so critically important to their children? As we consider spiritual warfare, fathers have the role of being the protector; they are the covering over their family.

Colossians 3:21 is a parallel verse to Ephesians 6:4. In Colossians Paul admonishes the fathers not to exasperate their children to the point that they lose heart. This might be done in several ways. Harsh authoritarianism certainly causes children to become exasperated. Endless teasing or undermining of ability is another unfortunate tactic used by fathers trying to control their children. Sometimes fathers expect too much of their children too soon, pushing them to excel in areas where they either are not gifted or not yet mature enough for success.

### His Mansion
Several years ago, I received a call from the director of His Mansion, a retreat and rehabilitation center in New England. The young people who go there are struggling with addiction or abuse. In that community the young people find safety and hope. As they work, study, worship, and live together, gradually they begin to experience love — many of them for the first time.

The director told me something I'll never forget, "I have worked with hundreds of severely troubled kids for over twenty years now, and I've never met one, not one, who had a good experience with his or her dad. A father is the most significant figure in anyone's life, and these kids all hate their fathers."

Very few things I've heard have affected me like that statement. Knowing how deep was my bond to my father, who was a great dad, I'd never thought about the likelihood that every kid's father plays such an important role in his or her life.

The process of raising children is one of making disciples. When Paul encourages fathers to train and instruct children in the ways of the Lord, he is really admonishing them to make disciples of their children. The biblical character qualities of discipleship are the very qualities which need to be built in the lives of all family members.[93] As all family members become disciples of Jesus Christ, we will be modeling the kingdom of God and insulating ourselves against the ravages of the devil. Short of this, we expose our family members to the fiery darts of the wicked one (Ephesians 6:16).

**Your Work**

Another relationship discussed by Paul in Ephesians 6 is that of the master and slave. By giving moral guidance in Ephesians 6:5-8 to slaves and masters Paul was not endorsing that economy or social system; he was called to be an apostle of the gospel of Jesus Christ, a gospel which would lead to social reform, which would lead to the overthrow of the long entrenched evil of slavery. Paul was well aware that slavery is a great evil, not only because his own Jewish people had been slaves in Egypt for four hundred years, but also because he saw it continuing in the current Roman Empire. In the first century, the majority of Gentile Christians were slaves. In time, God would lead people like William Wilberforce in England and Abraham Lincoln in the United States to take a strong Christian stance against slavery.

Today we live in a society in which slavery has been outlawed, so we might think that this is an irrelevant section of scripture. However, this text is relevant to contemporary boss and worker relationships.

---

93  My book *Follow Me: The Disciple-making Strategy of Jesus* (Orlando: Xulon Press, 2013) and companion *The Follow Me Group Guide* focus on the fifteen character qualities in the Gospel of Luke which Jesus taught His disciples.

Paul admonishes workers to be obedient to their *earthly masters*, his way of indicating he knew that ultimately the master of Christian workers is Jesus Christ. Nevertheless, he encourages workers to *respect and fear* their bosses as if they are working for Christ Himself. He also tells them to work *with sincerity of heart*, which rules out ulterior motives and hypocrisy and emphasizes singleness of heart, which will result in faithful and steadfast service.

Paul warned about working only when being watched. The motivation for such selfless and sincere service, even to an unbelieving employer, is that the Lord Himself will be the rewarder of the person who serves in this way.

In our day of depersonalized management and advocacy of worker's rights, some of these principles may need to be brought back to the center stage in order for us to demonstrate kingdom qualities. Whether in the factory, the business office, or any other work setting, Christians who serve wholeheartedly, seeking to please their supervisors rather than just take home a pay package, will be seen to be exceptional and valuable, even causing some to wonder what makes us tick.

Surprisingly, some Christians were slave owners. Paul admonishes the *masters* to treat their slaves with the greatest respect. Applying this principle to managers or bosses today, we see that Paul would expect mutual respect to be demonstrated.

Hierarchy of position for Paul is really more a distinction of responsibilities than of privilege or value. Three principles are provided for the Christian boss.

- First, they are to *treat your slaves in the same way*. This means they are to give respect if they hope to receive it. They are to have a servant's heart even for their slaves if they expect that in return. In other words, masters or bosses are to be like Jesus as He is described in John 13:12-17. After washing twelve pairs of feet Jesus said, *I have set you an example that you should do as I have done for you* (verse 15). Imagine having Christ as part of your staff under your supervision. How would you treat Him if He were under your employment?

No doubt there would be the same discomfort that Peter expressed when Jesus began to wash his feet.

- Second, Paul warns bosses to stop using threats as a way of managing their employees. Any management consultant today would recommend the same. The best way to get effective and high-quality service from a worker is through encouragement rather than through threats. Paul forbids masters to act as though they own their slaves (which, in fact, they did in Roman society). He encourages them to lead from love, not from fear. He admonishes them not to abuse their authority *since you know that he who is both their Master and yours is in heaven.* Slave and master, worker and boss, who are Christians have only one Master.

- The third principle outlined by Paul for effective management of workers is to remember that workers and bosses are really equals before God. There is no partiality or favoritism with God, so when bosses treat their workers with condescension, they find themselves to be at odds with God — a situation no right-thinking human would ever want.

If workers are to serve their bosses as though the boss were Christ, fair turn-around demands that their bosses be like Christ would be as a boss. There are ample illustrations of His conduct with His disciples on which to pattern Christ-like leadership in the office, marketplace, or any other venue of work.

The centrality of the person of Christ is seen by the fact that Christ is mentioned in each of the five verses (5-9) where Paul discusses this relationship. Workers are to obey as they would obey **Christ** (verse 5) and to behave as servants **of Christ** (verse 6). They are to render service **as to the Lord** (verse 7) and they know they will receive their reward **from the Lord** (verse 8). Masters are reminded that the **Lord is Master** of slave and owner (verse 9). This Christ-centeredness changes the perspective of the worker altogether. He is no longer merely a cog in the machine or a tool in the process; rather he now sees himself as a disciple serving the true master.

The key concept is that of brotherhood. Paul's letter to Philemon, the owner of the runaway-but-converted slave Onesimus, was revolutionary in this regard. The most humane of all secular writers, even those who sought liberation of slaves, would have stopped short of calling a slave *brother*. Paul, however, admonished Philemon to receive Onesimus back *no longer as a slave but more than a slave, as a beloved brother* (Philemon 6).

This is entirely consistent with Paul's comment to the Colossians that *in Christ there is … neither slave nor free, but Christ is all, and is in all* (Colossians 3:11). Similarly, in Galatians 3, *You are all sons of God through faith in Christ Jesus … there is neither … slave nor free … for you are all one in Christ Jesus* (Galatians 3:26, 28).

These principles which united masters and slaves as brothers would eventually lead to the radical change of institutions in Christian societies. It is tragic that the change was such a long time in coming. Nevertheless, today these principles can lead to a radical change in employer/employee relationships. If Christians are to usher in God's new society and be sign posts of the kingdom of God, the deepest of relationships must be redeemed to reflect the most ultimate human relationships – brothers and sisters within the family of God. In heaven there will be no husbands and wives, no fathers and mothers, no sons and daughters, and no employers and employees. We will all be brothers and sisters. Learning to live that way appropriately on earth will enable us to point toward God's forever family in the kingdom. The centrality of Christ in the marketplaces where Christians work also is a "Keep Out" sign to the devil, who loves to corrupt the commercial world.

Satan's corrupting agenda is responsible for the cosmic warfare waged in the heavenlies and on earth and for the clashing cultures we see on earth in the home, in the marketplace and in every setting where human relationships should be loving. But his seeds of hate are sown everywhere, holding people captive in his kingdom of darkness even though most people are not aware of his chains. God calls upon His children to join Him in emancipating the captives, and to that topic we now turn.

## Summary Thoughts from Chapter 11, Unexpected Battlefields

- Satan loves to destroy relationships because it distracts people from their focus on God.
- The warfare between the kingdom of God and the kingdom of darkness rages intensely all the time, everywhere.
- Some of Satan's best work is to promote discord, anger and strife in our homes and work environments.
- Paul's instruction for the master/slave relationship, as unfortunate as it was, provides some good principles for employer/employee relationships.

# 12

## RECLAIMING THE CAPTIVES

**Apostle Paul (of Nigeria)**

Far from being just theology, the following true-life story introduced me to the power of darkness that imprisons a culture in poverty, disease, and sin.

Some years ago, a young man from Nigeria came to the USA hoping to meet me. He had found my name on a brochure, and he sensed the Lord telling him he should seek me out for mentoring. His name was Apostle Paul Taiwu Adenuga. A bit skeptical, eventually I accepted his invitation to hold an evangelistic and revival series in Lagos. I took three young men with me.

During the ten days in Nigeria, we witnessed amazing things that made us feel like we were living in the book of Acts. On our second day, we traveled to two different towns and met with two kings. One was the Regent of Olata of Ota, and his chiefs. I gave a four-point message from the Sermon on the Mount on the choices Jesus gives us (the road we will travel, the fruit we will eat, the foundation we build on, and the master we will serve). The message was well received by the chiefs, and then the Regent took about twenty minutes and repeated almost everything I said in all four points and elaborated on why they were important. We were amazed. Then he, the Queen, and the chiefs did an amazing thing — they knelt before us and asked that we pray for them.

At the second town, we met with King Onlogbo of Ilogboland. We arrived a few hours earlier than they anticipated, which led to a small controversy because only ten of his chiefs were there. He said we were the first white missionaries in 120 years to visit that village. Back in the 1880s, a Catholic priest went there, but he was rejected. According to the king, since then, that village has "had a curse" on it. The king asked me to give a message and to lift the curse. On the spot, the Lord gave me a message about the curse of the serpent, but the promise that the Messiah would stomp on the head of the serpent and destroy the curse of sin. Then I prayed for God to lift the curse and bring the light of the gospel to the people. (The king followed up by coming to the first three nights of the crusade in Lagos, traveling a two-hour drive each way. He heard the gospel very clearly each night, but we were not sure whether he believed.)

> According to the king that village has "had a curse" on it. The king asked me to give a message and to lift the curse.

We got back to Lagos just in time to go to the crusade. As we arrived, several thousand people were already there worshipping. A special section of several hundred choir members was to the left of the platform; to the right were several hundred pastors, and behind the platform were many intercessors, who throughout the week waged spiritual warfare. Apostle Paul preached on Acts 3:19; his theme was repentance. After his sermon, he left the platform and went onto the field, microphone in hand, and for nearly ten minutes walked back and forth in front of the crowd, looking upward and shouting. Then he called people up to the front to be delivered from spiritual bondage. In particular, he asked the Holy Spirit to fall on two witches he sensed were in the crowd of about 5000 people. We were amazed by the boldness of Paul. He said that these two women had washed their private parts and cooked their husbands' meals in the blood (in a superstitious effort to block their husbands from marrying other wives, as polygamy is rather common there). Eventually, two women came forward and confessed their sins.

Later at the crusade I announced the theme of the week: "That I May Know Him" (Philippians 3:10) and then preached on "Knowing Jesus as My Savior." During the service my friend Lonnie shared his testimony, and later he had a strong vision of a huge snake coiled over the congregation. It uncoiled and then exploded. After I preached, about 250 people responded to the altar call. The team then ministered to the people for a while. Later, Apostle Paul prayed for the fire of God to come on demonized people, and we experienced a crazy event of ushers carrying to the front about forty people that had been "slain in the spirit." Most just lay still and quiet; others thrashed around, but none cried out. Some actually vomited out the oppression. Paul did everything he could to avoid sensationalism, but to deal with the problems. Whether in deliverance or praying for healing, he would not allow anyone to touch the people, but merely to pray. None of us had ever seen such a display of spiritual authority at work.

The next day I asked Paul what was going on as he was shouting into the heavenlies before the invitation. He acted surprised by my naïve question, and answered, "Spiritual warfare, calling on God to break through enemy strongholds and release the people." I knew then that the spiritual world these Nigerians live in is very real to them, and we have so much to learn.

## Doing Battle

Perhaps you cannot imagine yourself contending in warfare like this. Neither could the Israelites, as the younger generation of those who escaped Egypt were preparing to go into Canaan. The nations they were to dispossess were fearsome, having *horses and chariots and people more numerous than you* (Deuteronomy 20:1), but Moses encouraged them with these words:

> ... *do not be afraid of them; for the Lord your God, who brought you up from the land of Egypt, is with you. Now it shall come about that when you are approaching the battle, the priest shall come near and speak to the people. And he shall say to them, "Hear, O Israel, you are approaching the battle against your enemies today. Do not be fainthearted. Do not be afraid, or panic,*

*or tremble before them, for the Lord your God is the one who goes with you, to fight for you against your enemies to save you."*

Deuteronomy 20:1-4

> King Onlogbo wanted me to come back and pray with him to receive Jesus.

The day after we got home from Africa, I received a call from Apostle Paul saying King Onlogbo wanted me to come back and pray with him to receive Jesus. I could not go, so I sent Lonnie and his wife, who a few days later called me with the king on the line to tell me he had received the Lord.

Some lasting impressions I gained from these and other incredible experiences in Nigeria that I wrote in my journal:

1. It was a week of profound sense of the presence of God and, at the same time, unrelenting spiritual warfare; more like New Testament times than anything I had ever experienced. We knew we were on the battleground.

2. Spiritual warfare is really real, and God has given His children much authority.

3. While God continues to use signs and wonders, it is still the Word of God that transforms people. The so-called third world has much to teach us and we have much to teach them.

4. Learning to "exegete" a culture is crucial to effective communication, but love is the universal language God will always bless. Working with a team of anointed ministers is so helpful and effective — even biblical! There is amazing power in the name of Jesus Christ, if one truly knows and trusts Him.

The clash of worldviews could not have been greater than between my daily life in New York and my experiences in Nigeria. Which worldview is right, or closer to reality? Neil Anderson discloses the worldview that he believes is closer to the biblical worldview:

*The Christian worldview perceives life through the grid of Scripture, not through culture or experience. And Scripture clearly teaches that supernatural, spiritual forces are at work in the world. For example, approximately one-fourth of all the healings recorded in the Gospel of Mark were actually deliverances. The woman whom Jesus healed in Luke 13:11-12 had been the victim of a "sickness caused by a spirit" for 18 years.*[94]

*Over the last four decades people in the West have begun to think there is more to life than what science can explain and what they can discern through their five physical senses. On the surface this new hunger may sound encouraging to those of us with a Christian worldview, but in fact many of the same people who are disillusioned with the materialistic world are also disillusioned with established religion. Instead of turning to Christ and His church, they are filling their spiritual void with old-fashioned occultism dressed in the modern garb of parapsychology, holistic health, Eastern mysticism, and the numerous cults marching under the banner of the New Age movement.*[95]

The "captives" we are to rescue are found in all earthly cultures. Reclaiming them for Christ is not merely moral reformation, but spiritual transformation. In the ministry of spiritual emancipation that leads to transformation, we can expect to see in ourselves and others some remarkable "make-overs," which the first-century Apostle Paul delineates in Ephesians 4.

## Spiritual Transformation

### Knowing Christ

In Ephesians 4:20-24, Paul reminded the Ephesians of the direction they had been headed and the consequences they had been spared by their new life of regeneration in Christ. The starting point of regeneration is moral education. But this does not mean learning the right rules of behavior;

---

94   Anderson, *Bondage Breaker*, p. 33.

95   Anderson, *Bondage Breaker*, p. 35.

rather, as Paul states in verse 20, this education requires that *one come to know Christ*. Christ Himself is the content of the teaching. The education is moral because it is impossible to know Christ without being changed.

Verse 21 literally says, *You have heard him*. Stott says, *When sound Biblical moral instruction is being given, it may be said that Christ is teaching about Christ.*[96]

> Christ is the classroom, the teacher, and the subject of moral education.

Furthermore, the text says, *You were taught in him*, that is, Christ is the context and the atmosphere of the teaching. We may then properly say that Christ is the classroom, the teacher, and the subject of moral education. Why is this important? Only He has the authority to dispel the powers of darkness and eradicate the sinful nature so that we may be transformed into His likeness. Satan responds to no other name.

Referring to Christ, the Apostle writes in Philippians 2:9-11:

*Therefore God also has highly exalted Him and given Him the name which is above every name, that at the name of Jesus every knee should bow, of those in heaven, and of those on earth, and of those under the earth, and that every tongue should confess that Jesus Christ is Lord, to the glory of God the Father* (NKJV).

Presumably, Satan is included in this promise, which will be his ultimate humiliation.

### Identifying with Christ

In first-century Ephesus and Rome, and in twenty-first-century Africa, America, and the entire world, the powers of darkness were and are intent on plunging the planet into the darkness described in Genesis 1:2, the watery wasteland Satan and his tribe inhabited before God said, *Let there be light*. God's enemy is also intent on keeping God's creatures in spiritual darkness. God's answer, of course, has been to send *the light of the world* to enlighten every person with the knowledge of God — not just theological knowledge, but personal knowledge.

---

96   Stott, p. 179.

The Apostle Paul — the first-century one — was not content just to know Christ; he also wanted to know His resurrection power because only as people experience His power will they be able to be transformed. Nothing less than full identification with Christ should be our goal.

*It is the duty and privilege of every Christian to understand and enter into the divine desire for our perfecting and to claim the place with Christ, both in His cross and resurrection and ascension, that the Father has appointed. God has reckoned each believer in His Son to have died with Him at Calvary. 'Know ye not,' demands Paul (Romans 6:3ff), 'that so many of us as were baptized into Christ were baptized into his death?' Alas, it is a truth of which very few who claim the saving grace of our Lord have any practical knowledge, but it is of vital importance.* **All of our growth into the stature of the risen son of Man depends upon our identification with Him.** *'Our old man,' the apostle goes on to say (6:6), 'was crucified with him, that the body of sin might be annulled' (its power over us destroyed completely and forever). We enter into the experience of this through faith: 'Likewise reckon ye also yourselves to be dead indeed unto sin, but alive unto God through Jesus Christ our Lord' (6:11). Then, as we positively present ourselves unto God as alive from the dead and withdraw our members from the demands of sin, we shall find ourselves through the action of the Holy Spirit, who carries out within us the action of faith, realizing the truth of the promise (6:14), 'Sin shall not have dominion over you'*[97] (emphasis mine).

## Being Regenerated

We saw the process of degeneration in Chapter 10. The process of regeneration is threefold. First, we ***put off the old self***, which is being corrupted by its deceitful desires; second, we put on the new self, which is created to be like God in true righteousness and holiness; and third, we become renewed in the attitude of our mind. The first two parts of the process, putting off the old self and putting on the new self, are found in the aorist tense in Paul's writing (Ephesians 4:22 and 24), indicating

---

97    MacMillan, pp. 74-75.

a simple action of a total repudiation of our fallen nature. It is like an exchange of clothes which occurs as one activity.

*Putting on the new self* is illustrated in this story: On a trip to Italy we found ourselves traveling with a woman who was working through some serious grief. After twelve years of tending to her husband who was battling but succumbed to cancer, she booked her trip to find some relief from oppressive surroundings and get some badly needed mental and emotional rest. But only a few days before departure, her younger brother who had been fighting drug addiction, had a fatal heart attack while riding his motorcycle. Needless to say, she was fragile and in great need of ministry. Compounding her hurts was a very insensitive response from a priest and church that she had joined to please her husband.

The Lord had arranged it so that out of the twenty-one members in the tour group, only she, my wife and I had scheduled a two-day extension in Venice. We had been building a relationship with her and strongly sensed she would respond to the Lord's love as we expressed it. On the morning of our last day in Italy, a conversation led to her wanting to pray to receive Christ as her Savior and Lord. I asked if she wanted to pray, and she said she wanted me to lead her. I told her that I could say the words, but the Lord was looking at her heart. So, I began a very simple prayer of repentance and paused; she followed with a very heartfelt, sincere and humble begging of the Lord for forgiveness. Then, after each sentence I offered, each time she embellished my words with beautiful phrases that revealed depth of understanding of what she was doing. I was amazed at her grasp of the exchanged life she was inviting and receiving. Her repentance and regeneration were real. Four months after returning, we received a very sweet email telling that she was attending a Grief Share group in a church we recommended, and she was exulting in her new life in Christ.

The third part of the process, *being renewed* in the attitude of our mind, was written in the present tense indicating a continuing activity. The thought here is parallel to Paul's idea in Romans 12:2, *Be transformed by the renewing of your mind*. The result of this process is that we become truly like God in righteousness and holiness (verse 24). So much can be said about transformation because this is really the goal of the gospel for everyone.

Neil Anderson provides a very practical understanding of the challenge and nature of a renewed or transformed mind beginning with three scriptures.

> *He rescued us from the domain of darkness and transferred us to the kingdom of His beloved Son, in whom we have redemption, the forgiveness of sins* (Colossians 1:13, 14*).*

> *If anyone is in Christ, he is a new creature; the old things passed away; behold, new things have come* (2 Corinthians 5:17). *For you have died and your life is hidden with Christ in God* (Colossians 3:3).

> *"If those verses are true, then how come I still struggle with the same thoughts and feelings I did before I became a Christian?" I suspect that every honest Christian has asked that question or at least thought about it. There is a very logical reason why you still think, feel, and too often act as you did before you were born again.*

> *During those early and formative years of your life you had neither the presence of God in your life nor the knowledge of His ways. Consequently, you learned to live your life independent of God. This learned independence from God is a major characteristic of what Scripture calls the flesh. When you became a new creation in Christ, nobody pushed the delete button in your memory bank. Everything you learned before Christ (and all the feelings that go with it) is still recorded in your memory. That is why Paul said, 'Do not conform any longer to the pattern of this world but be transformed by the renewing of your mind' (Romans 12:2 NIV). Even as believers we can still be conformed to the wrong material.*[98]

---

98   Anderson, *Bondage Breaker*, pp. 59-60.

*What was learned has to be unlearned. If you have been trained wrong, can you be retrained? If you believed a lie, can you renounce that lie and choose to believe the truth? Can your mind be reprogrammed? That is what repentance is: a change of mind. We are transformed by the renewing of our minds. We can be transformed because we have the mind of Christ within us and because the Holy Spirit will lead us into all truth. But the world system we were raised in and our independent flesh patterns are not the only enemies of our sanctification. Even though we are new creatures in Christ, we still battle the world, the flesh, and the devil.*[99]

> We can be transformed because we have the mind of Christ within us and because the Holy Spirit will lead us into all truth.

## Summary Thoughts from Chapter 12, Reclaiming the Captives

- All of our growth into the stature of the risen Son of Man depends upon our identification with Him.
- As new creatures, we are God's children who take on His qualities in direct contrast and rebuke to the enemy.

---

99    Anderson, *Bondage Breaker*, p. 61.

# 13

## GOD-LIKE LIVING

Because the Church as a whole is called to spiritual unity and maturity, Paul insists that every individual in the church must stop living like a pagan. In fact, he affirms that those in the church should all aspire to a God-like life of righteousness and holiness. Primary among the attributes of God is his tri-unity, which we call the Trinity. The fellowship between the three Persons of the Godhead — Father, Son, and Holy Spirit — is the model of Christian unity and fellowship, and it is our strength in spiritual warfare.

In Ephesians 4:25-32, Paul describes the God-like life. Living like God in true righteousness and holiness entails truthful talking (4:25), righteous reactions (4:26), generous working and giving (4:28), edifying speech (4:29), and loving behavior (4:32) — five ways Christians are to change. These changes are not merely "Christian cosmetics" — masking who we really are so that the church and the world will admire us. They are not options for those who want to be deep, committed Christians. No, those ideas miss the point of the battleground — that our exchange of identity in Christ is to be evident by our truly being *new creatures in Christ* (2 Corinthians 5:17). And as new creatures, we are God's children who take on His qualities in direct contrast and rebuke to the enemy.

Spiritual warfare really begins here — living in Christ in unity as transformed beings.

> *Therefore each of you must put off falsehood and speak truthfully to your neighbor, for we are all members of one body. "In your anger do not sin": Do not let the sun go down while you are still angry, and do not give the devil a foothold. Anyone who has been stealing must steal no longer, but must work, doing something useful with their own hands, that they may have something to share with those in need. Do not let any unwholesome talk come out of your mouths but only what is helpful for building others up according to their needs, that it may benefit those who listen. And do not grieve the Holy Spirit of God, with whom you were sealed for the day of redemption. Get rid of all bitterness, rage and anger, brawling and slander, along with every form of malice. And be kind and compassionate to one another, forgiving each other, just as in Christ God forgave you.*

Ephesians 4:25-32, NIV

> Spiritual warfare really begins here — living in Christ in unity as transformed beings.

Each of the five transformations in Ephesians 4 contains a negative, a positive, and a motivation. Each one concerns relationships with other people. If we are to be God-like in righteousness and holiness, we must do it in a social context. It is impossible to be holy in a vacuum. God calls us to community based on His own nature. Jesus expressed this beautifully in John 17:21, *That all of them may be one, Father, just as You are in Me and I am in You.* The organic unity of the Trinity is the model for the Church.

### New Mouth

If you are going to grow up, if you want to be renewed and put on the new self, here is where to begin — stop telling lies and start telling the truth (verse 25). The negative is *put off falsehood*. The positive is *speak truthfully*. The motivation is *we are all members of one body*. The verb Paul uses for the negative part of this injunction is *lay aside*, or *put off*, much like one would do with a garment. The clothes which must be removed by Christians are described by the word *pseudo*, the Greek word for lies. Anything false is to be put off. During college and graduate school years I worked a job where a uniform was required. Leaving work, I would lay aside or put off those clothes and put on the clothes of a student again — the clothes that more truly represented who I was.

In contrast, we are to speak truthfully, that is, as followers of Jesus we should be known as honest, reliable people whose word can always be trusted. The reason for this is that *we are members of one another*. A lie is a stab into the very vitals of Christ because fellowship is built on trust and trust is built on truth. Falsehood undermines fellowship. When we lie, we

> A lie is a stab into the very vitals of Christ because fellowship is built on trust and trust is built on truth.

necessarily hurt ourselves. This is like the title of an article written by a George Washington University professor: "How Come Every Time I Get Stabbed in the Back, My Fingerprints Are on the Knife?"[100]

Lying is also the character of Satan. Jesus told the Pharisees that they were like their father the devil who is a liar (John 8:44). When we lie, whether blatant falsifying of truth, exaggeration, or spinning the truth ("white lies?"), we are playing into the devil's hand. In fact, we are playing his hand.

Why is it that believers sometimes speak or live lies? Perhaps the most common reason is that we want people to think of us other than we really are. We want to enhance our image or reputation. Ananias and Sapphira were guilty of this. As a statement to the early Church that we must be a community of truth and trust, God severely judged Ananias and Sapphira by striking them dead (Acts 5). Such a dramatic judgment surely indicates the importance God places on honesty and truthfulness in the life of the Church. The first part of the spiritual armor to be put on is the belt of truth, indicating that truth is foundational to all other protective parts of

---

100  Jerry B. Harvey, "How Come Every Time I Get Stabbed in the Back, My Fingerprints Are on the Knife?" from *The Abilene Paradox and Other Meditations on Management* (San Francisco: Jossey-Bass, 1999).

our armor — righteousness, peace, faith, and salvation, while the sword of
the Spirit, the Word of God, is our source of truth and our only offensive
armament (Ephesians 6:14-17).

Some believers who would never think about lying to someone else
are guilty of lying to themselves. They adopt a false sense of their identity,
either by exaggeration or pseudo-humility. I think the latter is a greater
problem among Christians who refuse to walk in the anointing of their
spiritual gift and feed their insecurity by telling themselves they are no
good, as Neil Anderson suggested above.

Proverbs 6:16-19 lists six things, even seven, which are an abomination
to the Lord. The list concludes with *a false witness who utters lies and one who
spreads strife among brothers.* So, first in the list of five ways Christians are to
change is gaining a new mouth.

**New Emotions**

The second area of change is our emotions. Paul exhorts the believers,
*in your anger do not sin.* That is, we are to not lose our temper but to ensure
that our anger is righteous. The negative here is that we are to not sin even
when we are angry. The positive is that we may be righteously angry. The
motive is *do not give the devil a foothold.*

Scripture allows Christians to be angry. But anger must always be holy
anger, as we see in the life of Jesus on a number of occasions. For example,
in Mark 3:5 Jesus *looked around at them in anger,*
referring to people who were watching to see
whether or not He would heal a man on the
sabbath. He also demonstrated that holy wrath
in cleansing the temple. Righteous anger is never focused on one's own
rights. Hodge rightly states, *Anger if mingled with holy affections or in a holy mind
is virtuous; if mingled with malice it is sinful.*[101]

Righteous anger is never focused on one's own rights.

Just to make sure that Christians understand the limitations of anger,
Paul uses three qualifying negatives: 1) do not sin, 2) do not let the sun

101   Hodge, p. 270.

go down on your anger, and 3) do not give the devil an opportunity. The first of these needs no explanation. The second requires Christians to keep daily accounts with other Christians. The third implies that the devil loves to exploit anger to break fellowship between Christians. He steps into the cracked relationships exposed by our anger.

At the first church I pastored, the elders and I were quite sure something was holding back the full blessing of God. As we sought the Lord, one of the brothers hesitantly mentioned that a former elder, still a member of the church but very withdrawn, had a vendetta against another member who owed him money. Clearly, the indebted member was in the wrong, and always had good intentions, so he said, as we confronted him to pay the debt. But, sensing his insincerity, we decided to appeal to the former elder to forgive him his debt, as the Lord's Prayer admonishes. He said it wasn't a matter of money — he was well-off; rather, he was angry not only at his debtor, but at us elders for not publicly exposing and expelling the other brother and his family from the church. Clearly, the devil had penetrated the life of the congregation because of unresolved sin and anger. I wish I had access to MacMillan's wisdom in those days, but we were not alert to the real source of the problem. MacMillan would have counseled us:

> *The conflicts in our churches, in which neither party will give way, and which lower the spiritual power of the assembly, may be controlled by prayer and authority directed against those evil principalities and powers, whose working foments and continues the trouble. Individual lives, taken in the snare of the devil, depressed and hopeless, may be restored to their place of assurance, peace and joy in God. Attacks on physical health, on social relationships and on financial matters may often be traced to unseen workings and thus overcome in the name of the Lord.*[102]

Why do Christians often get unrighteously angry? The predominant reason is that we believe our rights have been violated. An example of this is found in 2 Samuel 13 and 14 in the story of three of David's children,

---

[102] MacMillan, p. 77.

Absalom, Amnon, and Tamar. Was Absalom's anger over Amnon's raping his sister Tamar righteous or unrighteous? Certainly, he had reason to have righteous anger, but it became unrighteous because he harbored it for two years until in bitterness of soul he sought revenge, rather than restoration, and murdered his half-brother Amnon. Ecclesiastes 7:9 says, *Don't be hasty in your spirit to be angry, for anger resides in the bosom of fools.*

## New Hands

Third, Paul states in verse 29 that Christians are not to steal but to work *doing something useful with their own hands*. The negative is don't steal. Interestingly Paul says, *He who has been stealing must steal no longer.* The inference is that a number of the Ephesian believers had been thieves. The positive is *work with your own hands*. The motive is that the believer *may have something to share with those in need.*

The word for steal is the Greek *klepto*, from which we get kleptomania – habitual thievery. The eighth commandment, *Do not steal*, was given wide application. It referred to stealing property, tax evasion, customs dodging, oppressing workers with unfair pay, giving poor service, stealing time from work, and robbing God. It might also apply to slander, that is, stealing someone's reputation. Christian economics starts with a converted thief and teaches him how to work to support himself so that soon he will be eager to be generous. Only Christ can transform a burglar into a benefactor.

Why do Christians sometimes steal? Greed or material insecurity may cause a person to steal. Zacchaeus (Luke 19) became wealthy by extorting others for his own financial benefit. When he met Jesus, he gained new hands; that is, rather than using his cunning to take money from others, he found ways to become generous.

Think for a moment about a sponge. It can take in and hold much liquid, or it can give out that liquid. By its nature a sponge absorbs liquid; to give it out the sponge must be squeezed or it must be sopping full. Sometimes people appear to be generous when they are being squeezed, when pressure is on them to give. How far better when people give because they are so full they cannot contain anything more, not full financially, but full of the love of a generous God. That is the ideal of Christian charity and living a God-like life.

## New Speech

The fourth injunction for change is similar to the first one in that it applies to our speech. Paul says, *Do not let any unwholesome talk come out of your mouths* (verse 29). This is the negative. Do not speak evil. The positive is to edify people by speaking *only what is helpful for building others up according to their needs.* The motivation is not to grieve the Holy Spirit (verse 30).

The word used for evil is the Greek word *sapros*, often used to refer to rotten trees and fruit. This word occurs in Matthew 7:17-18 and Matthew 12:33, where the texts refer to a bad tree and bad fruit. When Jesus spoke about bad trees and bad fruit, He was referring to the speech of people: *But I tell you men will have to give an account on the day of judgment for every careless word they have spoken. For by your words you will be acquitted and by your words you will be condemned* (Matthew 12:36, 37).

James 3:1-12 deals with the terror of the tongue as the Apostle gives eight metaphors for the tongue: a horse's bit, a ship's rudder, a spark of fire, wild animals, deadly poison, a spring of water, a fig tree, and a grape vine. James teaches that the power of the tongue is

> Eight metaphors for the tongue: a horse's bit, a ship's rudder, a spark of fire, wild animals, deadly poison, a spring of water, a fig tree, and a grape vine.

all out of proportion to its small size. All of these images are apt, but the spark of fire stands out because in our day we often hear of raging fires that destroy whole communities and hundreds of acres of forest because of one small spark, perhaps from a lit cigarette carelessly thrown by a smoker. Sometimes, inappropriate comments can cause a huge blaze of resentment, even among believers.

Paul is telling the Ephesians that Christians are to edify others, that is, to build them up and encourage them, specifically *according to the need of the moment.* This demands sensitivity which comes only as we are filled with God's Spirit.

Job was a good example of edifying others, as testified by Eliphaz, the Temanite: *Behold you have admonished many and you have strengthened weak hands. Your words have helped the tottering to stand and you have strengthened feeble knees* (Job 4:1-4). No wonder Satan wanted to bring Job down!

Why do Christians sometimes speak unwholesomely? Perhaps the most frequent reason is that we see other humans as competitors rather than as colleagues. We see them as our rivals rather than as brothers and sisters. I was in a planning session with about thirty key leaders in a church one time when a member innocently made a comment about the kitchen. Off in a huff of hurt with a hurtful comment went one of the church officers. Apparently, the comment touched a raw nerve. It was a spark that potentially could have lit up the whole church. Thankfully, reason and maturity kicked in and the hurt member returned.

What happens when we speak unwholesomely? The Holy Spirit is grieved. The word for grief expresses a human emotion meaning to cause pain, sorrow or distress. Certainly, the Holy Spirit can be grieved because He is a person, not an it. When believers hurt other believers by intemperate tongues, the Holy Spirit is distressed.

*As a temple is sacred and everything that profanes is an offense to God, so the indwelling of the Holy Spirit in the people of God is made the reason why we should treat them with reverence, as this apostle teaches when he says, 'Do you not know that you are a temple of God, and that the Spirit of God dwells in you? If any man destroys the temple of God, God will destroy him, for the temple of God is holy and that is what you are.' To pollute therefore the souls of believers by suggesting irreligious or impure thoughts to them is a profanation of the temple of God and an offense to the Holy Spirit.*[103]

Paul uses a lovely phrase, accurately rendered, that (you) may give grace to those who hear you. The implication is that we may use language as a gift to others.

In verse 29 Paul uses a lovely phrase, accurately rendered, *that (you) may give grace to those who hear you.* The implication is that we may use language as a gift to others. This is

103   Hodge, p. 264.

affirmed by Proverbs 12:18, *There is one whose rash words are like sword thrusts, but the tongue of the wise brings healing.* So, the Apostle Paul calls on Christians to be people with renewed tongues.

### New Heart

In the previous four injunctions from Ephesians 4, Paul affirms that transformation is seen as we gain a new mouth, new emotions, new hands, and new speech. Perhaps most important is gaining a new heart. Only a heart transformation can change us from being unkind to being compassionate and loving. Only a changed heart recognizes that because God has forgiven us we have no right to hold anything over anyone else.

A transformed Christian cannot be unkind or bitter but rather is kind and loving (verses 31, 32). The negative here includes six unpleasant attitudes: bitterness, rage, anger, brawling, slander, and malice. The positive is that we are to be kind, tenderhearted and forgiving. The motive is that *in Christ God forgave you.*

*Bitterness* refers to having a sour spirit. *Rage* is passionate wrath. *Anger* speaks of subtle hostility. *Brawling* is loud quarreling. *Slander* defames others. And *malice* wishes for or plots evil against someone. These are all destructive, ungodly attitudes and/or actions. Rather, Paul insists that Christians be *kind.* The word here means that we are to be tenderhearted and compassionate.

Joseph of the Old Testament was such an individual. He was able to forgive his mean-spirited brothers because behind their malice he could see the sovereign purposes of God. He told them, *You intended to harm me, but God intended it for good* (Genesis 50:20).

Why do Christians sometimes wish evil on others? Perhaps ego insecurity is the primary reason. To be kind, compassionate and forgiving we must be secure and other-person centered. We need to be able to forgive without being asked for forgiveness.

The Lord's Prayer is a prayer about forgiveness. The phrase, *forgive us our debts,* **as we also have forgiven** *our debtors* (Matthew 6:12; emphasis added) is a bold prayer asking God to extend His forgiveness of us in proportion to the forgiveness we offer to others. How many people say that prayer every week without understanding what they are saying!

In Ephesians 4:25-32, therefore, we find five negative attributes of a person caught up in degeneration which need to be supplanted by five positive attributes which describe a person in the process of transformation. Lies must be replaced by truth. Unholy anger must be replaced by righteous anger. Stealing must be replaced by generosity. Unwholesome talk must be replaced by edifying speech. And unkindness must be replaced by compassion.

The negatives in Ephesians 4 express the influence and presence of evil powers. An important part of spiritual warfare is giving no foothold to the devil, but rather to "live as Jesus lived, love as Jesus loved, and serve as Jesus served" — the motto of a church in my area. Living like this is made possible because of our Commanding Officer, known by many names, including Lord Sabbaoth, the God of Heaven's Armies, whom we meet in the next chapter.

### Summary Thoughts from Chapter 13, God-like Living

- A lie is a stab into the very vitals of Christ because fellowship is built on trust and trust is built on truth.
- Righteous anger is never focused on one's own rights.
- Spiritual warfare really begins here — living in Christ in unity as transformed beings.

# 14

## THE COMMANDING OFFICER

While there are many differing worldviews of the realities we experience on planet earth, including some that deny the existence of the realms and beings we have considered in the previous chapters, one thing all humans can agree on, and that is the presence of evil and suffering. Both natural evil, such as earthquakes, floods, and hurricanes, and moral evil caused by humans, such as murder, rape and theft, affect humans around the world. The biblical worldview being expressed in this book attributes all evil and suffering, ultimately, to the sin brought into the world by Satan and ratified by our first parents who disobeyed God.

Sin, the deliberate defiance of God's authority, infects the entire world. Even creation has been subjected to the fall, and groans awaiting release from its *slavery to corruption* (Romans 8:21). Natural evil was never intended by God, whose creation of Paradise has been interrupted by the present dimension of sin and the spiritual warfare that engulfs us. Moral evil, of course, was not intended by God, but was made possible by the free will God gave His earthly family.

The warfare in the heavenlies and on earth between God and Satan is truly a matter of life and death. Romans 3:23 says *the wages of sin is death, but the free gift of God is eternal life in Christ Jesus our Lord*. This same Jesus has already conquered death through His resurrection and is now in the process of *bringing many sons and daughters to glory* (Hebrews 2:10). While we meet Him in Scripture as Jesus of Nazareth, in His resurrected and glorified existence, Jesus is the conquering Savior, the Hero, the Victor, and to Him we now turn our attention.

### His Super-cosmic Preeminence

Although He is our commanding officer and the victor in the spiritual war that is in the mop-up stages prior to the enemy's final destruction, Jesus Christ is far more than a warrior. We need to see this battle for planet earth and its occupants in the larger context of who Christ is.[104]

The second person of the Godhead has eternally been part of the Trinity quite apart from His relation to us. Jesus Christ has eternally existed as part of the Godhead, known to us as the Son. Only of late, with the creation and dawning of time, space, and matter, including human life, has He fulfilled His role as Jesus (meaning Savior) and Christ (Messiah). We get hints of His other existence and functions which are, let us say, extra-terrestrial, meaning beyond this earth. Jesus Christ is God's agent for all things pertaining to our planet and this creation.

> Jesus Christ is God's agent for all things pertaining to our planet and this creation.

Consider these functions based on references and allusions in the Bible:

- His own references to His pre-earthly presence with the Father:

---

104　See David Bryant, *Christ Is Now* (New Providence Publishers, Inc.: New Providence, NJ, 2017). Bryant, founder of Concerts of Prayer International and of Proclaim Hope, released in 2017 a 600-page epic work called *Christ Is Now*, a magnificent volume calling for a "Christological reformation." In the book, Bryant examines seven dimensions of Christ as He relates to us, using seven prepositions: who Christ is TO us, FOR us, OVER us, BEFORE us, WITHIN us, THROUGH us, and UPON us. It's a rich study in which we see the person and ministry of Christ primarily in relation to us.

*And now, Father, glorify me in your presence with the glory I had with you before the world began.*

John 17:5

*Father, I want those you have given me to be with me where I am and to see my glory, the glory you have given me because you loved me before the creation of the world.*

John 17:24

• His role in relation to the universe and creation:
*In the beginning was the Word, and the Word was with God, and the Word was God. He was with God in the beginning. Through him all things were made; without him nothing was made that has been made.*

John 1:1, 2

The Word is revealed in John 1:17 as Jesus Christ, and in verse 18 as *the one and only Son, who is himself God and is in closest relationship with the Father. For in him all things were created: things in heaven and on earth, visible and invisible, whether thrones or powers or rulers or authorities; all things have been created through him and for him. He is before all things, and in him all things hold together.*

Colossians 1:16, 17

*...in these last days he has spoken to us by his Son, whom he appointed heir of all things, and through whom also he made the universe.*

Hebrews 1:2

*He who descended is the very one who ascended higher than all the heavens, in order to fill the whole universe.*

Ephesians 4:10

• His current heavenly position and various activities and functions:

*...[Jesus Christ] has gone into heaven and is at God's right hand — with angels, authorities and powers in submission to him.*

1 Peter 3:22

*Therefore God exalted him to the highest place and gave him the name that is above every name, that at the name of Jesus every knee should bow, in heaven and on earth and under the earth.*

Philippians 2:9-10

Psalm 110:1, the Old Testament passage most often quoted in the New Testament, also presents the super-cosmic Christ, as David refers to Him as "my Lord": *The LORD (Yehovah) says to my Lord (Adonai): "Sit at my right hand until I make your enemies a footstool for your feet."*

Psalm 2:4 shows the "LORD and His anointed" to be scoffing at the arrogance of earthly rulers: *The One enthroned in heaven laughs; the Lord scoffs at them.* This messianic psalm depicts the presence of the Christ enthroned with/as God observing the affairs of mankind on earth.

*Now the main point of what we are saying is this: We do have such a high priest, who sat down at the right hand of the throne of the Majesty in heaven, and who serves in the sanctuary, the true tabernacle set up by the Lord, not by a mere human being.*

Hebrews 8:1, 2

*Therefore, since we have a great high priest who has ascended into heaven, Jesus the Son of God, let us hold firmly to the faith we profess.*

Hebrews 4:14

- His authority over non-human beings is seen in several passages:

*That power is the same as the mighty strength he exerted when he raised Christ from the dead and seated him at his right hand in the heavenly realms, far above all rule and authority, power and dominion, and every name that is invoked, not only in the present age but also in the one to come. And God*

*placed all things under his feet and appointed him to be head over everything
for the church.*

Ephesians 1:19-22

*The seventh angel sounded his trumpet, and there were loud voices in heaven,
which said:*
>*"The kingdom of the world has become
>The kingdom of our Lord and of his Messiah,
>And he will reign for ever and ever."*

Revelation 11:15

*Then the end will come, when he hands over the kingdom to God the Father
after he has destroyed all dominion, authority and power.*

1 Corinthians 15:24

All this is to say that our Commanding Officer, Jesus Christ, is and
always has been the Son of God, and He is totally consequential. In every
regard, the Godhead has delegated to Jesus Christ all that pertains to
everything on planet earth and beyond, as history will eventually roll up
into eternity.

## Our Supreme Commander

Every war is fought by a hierarchy of soldiers. Their rank is usually
evident by insignia on their sleeve or medals on their chest. It is always clear
who the superior officer is in any group of soldiers. The Commander-in-
Chief of the winning side of the spiritual war in which we are involved is
known by some distinctive markings gained in battle: wounds on His hands
and feet, gash from a spear on one of His sides, and scars on His forehead.

His name, of course, is Jesus Christ. His coming was predicted from
the earliest days[105] and amplified often in the Old Testament, Isaiah 53
providing the clearest insights about His appearance. Another surprising
source, who also lived in the 6th century B.C., referred to Him. Records

---

105   See Genesis 3:15.

show that Gautama Buddha began his ministry in 531 B.C. He always claimed he was but a mere man and recognized the problem of sin for himself and all mankind. The Buddhist Scriptures of Cambodia contain a prophecy regarding a "Holy One" to come, who would lead people away from the old way and introduce a new way:

*When Buddha was traveling and living in this world, there was an old Brahman priest who wore white robes who asked the Buddha, "How will all men and all Brahman continue in their merit-making so as to escape the results of sin?" Buddha went on to explain that even the most extreme number of prayers and acts of benevolence would not suffice. The old Brahman priest asked further, "What are we all to do to be saved?" Buddha went on to explain there was no way this could be done. He said, "I have given up my high position and entered the priesthood. I considered that even though I am good, I would have only a very small amount of merit at the end of the year. If I was given the same amount of merit for 100,000 epochs and live 10 more lifetimes, I would not be saved from sin's results even once."*

Buddha answered him, "The Holy One who will keep the world in the future will be like this: in the palm of his hands and in the flat of his feet will be the design of a disk, in his side will be a stab wound; and his forehead will have many marks like scars."

*The Old Brahman priest asked further, "So what should we all do?" The Buddha answered, "Keep on making merit and look for another Holy One who will come and help the world and all of you in the future." Then the old Brahman priest asked, "What will the characteristics of the Holy One be like?" The Buddha answered him, "The Holy One who will keep the world in the future will be like this: in the palm of his hands and in the flat of his feet will be the design of a disk, in his side will be a stab wound; and his forehead will have many marks like scars."*[106]

---

106 Permission was given to copy these Buddhist Scriptures from Wat Phra Sing Chiang Mai Province by Phra Sriwisutthiwong in Bangkok, Thailand. "It is guaranteed that this copy is accurate according to the original, that there is no error in transmission, which is in the book of the district headman, the religious encyclopedia volume 23, book #29. This inquiry was made on October 13, 1954 A.D. [Buddhist era 2497]."

Our Commander is no stranger to battle. One of His Hebrew names is *YHWH Tsebha'oth*, translated as Lord Sabaoth, the Lord of Hosts. The hosts are the heavenly armies who engage in battle with Him. At times, their warfare is on earth, as seen in 2 Kings 6:8-23; other times they fight in the *epouranios* (heavenly realms), such as in Daniel 10:12-14. But make no mistake, the Commander does not need the help of an army. By the word of His mouth He is able to, and will, vanquish the entire regiment of all wickedness.

Revelation 19:11-16 reveals truths about the Commander, written in apocalyptic language, telling about His names, His appearance, and His functions:

- His Names
    1. Faithful and true
    2. No one knows
    3. The Word of God (rational principle of the universe)
    4. King of kings and Lord of lords

- His Appearance
    1. Eyes of fire
    2. Head with crowns
    3. Clothing dripped in blood (He overcame not by shedding blood of others, but his own.)
    4. Mouth with sword (see 19:21)

- His Functions
    1. To judge and make war justly
    2. To strike down the nations
    3. To rule the nations
    4. To invoke the wrath of God

**The Commander Messiah**

Above, we mentioned that Psalm 110 is the most frequently quoted Old Testament passage in the New Testament. Besides its very evident messianic meaning, Psalm 110 also shows that part of the role of the Messiah is to be a warrior. This is consistent, of course, with the insight that Jesus Christ is the primary agent of the Godhead for all things pertaining to earth. Since the psalm is only seven verses, it is good to see it in its entirety, and note the emphases in bold, as these passages reveal the Messiah's role in spiritual warfare.

> *1 The LORD said to my Lord,*
> *"Sit in the place of honor at my right hand*
> ***until I humble your enemies,***
> *making them a footstool under your feet."*
> *2 The LORD will extend your powerful kingdom from Jerusalem;*
> ***you will rule over your enemies.***
> *3 **When you go to war,***
> *your people will serve you willingly.*
> *You are arrayed in holy garments,*
> *and your strength will be renewed each day like the morning dew.*
> *4 The LORD has taken an oath and will not break his vow:*
> *"You are a priest forever in the order of Melchizedek."*
> *5 The Lord stands at your right hand to protect you.*
> *He will strike down many kings when his anger erupts.*
> *6 He will **punish the nations***
> *and fill their lands with corpses;*
> *he will shatter heads over the whole earth.*
> *7 But he himself will be refreshed from brooks along the way.*
> ***He will be victorious.***
>
> Psalm 110, NLT (emphasis mine)

The three direct quotes of Psalm 110 in the New Testament emphasize, not only His messianic role, but also His warrior role.[107]

---

107    Direct Quotes: Matthew 22:43-45 [=Mark 12:35-37; Luke 20:41-44]; Acts 2:33-36; Hebrews 1:13.
Allusions: Matthew 26:63-64 [=Mark 14:61-62; Luke 22:67-69; cf. Daniel 7:13]; Mark 16:19; Acts 5:30-31; 7:55-56; Romans 8:34; 1 Corinthians 15:24-25; Ephesians 1:20, 22; 2:6; Colossians 3:1; Hebrews 1:3b; 8:1b; 10:12-13; 12:2; 1 Peter 3:21b-22; Revelation 3:21. See http://www.hebrew-streams.org/works/texts/ps110-list.html.

Now, it's important to know that *Jesus Christ is the same yesterday, today, and forever* (Hebrews 13:8). But He has been manifested in several forms:

- The Pre-existent Jesus appeared to Old Testament people.
- The Incarnate Jesus, known as the Christ (Messiah) and the Son of God, lived 33 years, mostly in Galilee.
- The Resurrected Jesus Christ appeared over 40 days to over 500 people, before ascending.
- The Ascended, Glorified Christ is seated at the right hand of the Throne of God and will return.

Everything about this Jesus Christ is heroic and supernatural:

1. His life fulfilled hundreds of prophecies.
2. His birth was supernatural.
3. His life was sinlessly impeccable.
4. His teachings are unparalleled and God-inspired.
5. His mighty miracles were incontestable.
6. His passion and crucifixion were majestic and strategic.
7. His resurrection was unimaginable, yet irrefutable.
8. His resurrected body and ascension were spectacular and widely witnessed.
9. His ongoing revelations and witness through signs and wonders are conclusive proof that He lives and reigns.

If you don't believe these truths, you cannot really claim to be a Christian. Worse, you will one day be forced to your knees before Him to try to explain why you have lived in rebellion and disbelief. And you will have no excuse because that Jesus Christ, God the Son, is the central figure of all history, and demands that all men everywhere repent and believe. The key moment of all history was the resurrection of Jesus. That event fulfilled the prophesied plan of God.

> The key moment of all history was the resurrection of Jesus.

Failure to believe it and receive its blessings by coming under His saving protection leaves one exposed to sharing in the future of Satan, the enemy of God.

As important for our salvation and central to God's plan of redemption as was the resurrection of Christ, His ascension and enthronement in heaven are seen by MacMillan to be the capstone of the victory as our Captain is placed well beyond the adversary's access, from which He will orchestrate the final campaign.

*Having been thus raised from among the dead, Christ Jesus was exalted by God to His own right hand in the heavenlies. Then was seen the reason of such mighty working. The resurrection had been opposed by the tremendous 'powers of the air': 'all principality, and power, and might, and dominion, and every name that is named, not only in this world [aion, age] but also in that which is to come' (Ephesians 1:21). The evil forces of the 'age to come' had been arrayed against the purpose of God. They had, however, been baffled and overthrown, and the risen Lord had been enthroned 'far above' them, ruling with the authority of the Most High.*[108]

Neil Anderson, also citing the same truths from Ephesians, gives the implications for Christ's followers. Not only is our resurrection secured, but our authority with Him over spiritual powers that seek to harass and dominate human beings.

*Paul wants us to see that when Christ was raised from the dead (1:20), those of us who have believed in Him were also resurrected from our condition of spiritual death and made alive "together with Christ" (2:5-6). The resurrection of Christ from the tomb and our resurrection from spiritual death happened at the same time. It's only logical that the head (Christ) and the body (His church) should be raised together.*

*Furthermore, when God seated Christ at His right hand and conferred on Him authority (Ephesians 1:20-21), He also seated us at His right hand (2:6) because we are "together with Christ" (2:5). The moment you receive*

---

108   MacMillan, p. 10.

*Christ, you are seated with Him in the heavenlies. Your identity as a child of God and your authority over spiritual powers are not things you* **are** *receiving or* **will** *receive at some time in the future; you have them right now. You are a spiritually alive child of God right* **now**. *You are seated with Christ in the heavenlies* **right now**. *You have the power and authority over the kingdom of darkness and to do His will* **right now.** [109]

> Your identity as a child of God and your authority over spiritual powers are not things you are receiving or will receive at some time in the future; you have them right now.

## Summary Thoughts from Chapter 14, The Commanding Officer

- Jesus Christ is God's agent for all things pertaining to our planet and this creation.
- The Buddhist Scriptures of Cambodia contain a prophecy regarding a "Holy One" to come.
- The key moment of all history was the resurrection of Jesus.
- Your identity as a child of God and your authority over spiritual powers are not things you **are** receiving or **will** receive at some time in the future; you have them **right now.**

---

109   Anderson, *Bondage Breaker*, pp. 83-84.

# 15

## ADOPTED AND DRAFTED

### First- and Twenty-first Century Trauma

As we saw in Chapter 7, Paul's letter to the Ephesians was addressed to a church born in conflict and under satanic control. Thus, continuing to consider the Commanding Officer and His authority, let us return to Ephesus to learn more about the Ephesian church and Paul's emphases in writing to them.

Acts 19 gives some clues about the challenge of being a Christian church in the city of Ephesus. Not only was there an inadequate theological foundation (verses 1-7), and not only did the believers face Jewish cynicism about the truth claims about the kingdom (verse 9), but the city was filled with demonism, superstition, and idolatry. Verses 11-16 reveal the problem of demonism. Jewish exorcists were trying to deal with the problems, but Paul's success and their failure were notable, resulting in the whole citizenry being awed by the power of God and the name of Jesus. The superstition which fueled demonic activity was pervasive, but many who practiced "magic" became believers and brought their paraphernalia to be burned (Acts 19:19).

Intensifying the problems of superstition and demonism was the false religion of the goddess Artemis. This goddess, also known as Diana, was the Ephesian jewel. Artemis was the mother goddess of Asia Minor, considered to be "the mother of gods and men."[110] The temple erected to her worship in Ephesus was one of the seven wonders of the ancient world and measured 400 feet by 200 feet. The image of Diana was a multi-breasted female, embodying the nourishing capacity of nature. The image itself was considered to have descended from heaven. As we saw in Chapter 9, Professor Newton speculated that the actual statue may have been a meteorite. Outstanding biblical commentator Professor F. F. Bruce agrees with that possibility.[111]

For many who lived in the province of Asia, Artemis was the core of religion, the center of life. The statue was valued so highly in Ephesus that a huge public demonstration broke out because the ministry of the Christians was beginning to cut into the financial profit of the silversmiths who crafted the idols. Their fear was that *our trade will lose its good name, [and] that the temple of the great goddess Artemis will be discredited, and the goddess herself, who is worshiped throughout the province of Asia and the world, will be robbed of her divine majesty* (Acts 19:27). The mob's chant "Great is Artemis of the Ephesians" lasted over two hours, and order was restored by a city clerk who reassured the crowd that the goddess' stronghold on the culture was not in jeopardy.

Against this dark spiritual backdrop, Paul's letter to the Ephesians contains a very high Christology, and since many of the church members were fresh out of pagan superstition and belief in Artemis, the letter provided pastoral counsel on spiritual warfare (Ephesians 6). Paul taught them about their identity in Christ (Chapter 2); and the dramatic difference between their "walk" as Gentiles without Christ and their new walk in Christ is given in most graphic terms (Chapters 4 and 5). Knowing that the young church was vulnerable to the powerful influence of the idolatry around

---

110    F.F. Bruce, *The Book of Acts* in *The New International Commentary on the New Testament* (Grand Rapids, MI: Wm. B. Eerdmans Publishing Co., 1954), p. 397.

111    Bruce, p. 398, footnote 53.

them, Paul insisted on unity in the body and training for the leaders so they would be able to lead all others into full spiritual maturity (Chapter 4).

If I'm reading our country aright today, a majority of citizens, and especially Christians, are frightened and frustrated about being shoved around by worldviews and social agendas that are hostile to Christian faith. The response of many is anger and expressions of outrage. As a result, Christians are being stereotyped as nasty, intolerant, unloving bigots — "haters". And the news media love to portray us that way. But is that how Commander Jesus wants us to be viewed? I think not.

How can we stand firmly for truth and be loving, magnetic representatives for Christ in the midst of a hostile world? Paul challenged the Ephesian Christians, as a minority group in a pagan culture, to live positively and redemptively in order to continue the ministry of our Commander, King Jesus, in building the kingdom of God.

To reach such a culture, Paul wants believers to know we are already victors in the cultural and spiritual war because of who the winning warrior is — He is Jesus Christ, our Commanding Officer. No other person, strategy or plan is needed. Without any doubt, for the Apostle Paul, God's provision of Christ for the Church was His one and only strategy for undoing the damning effects of Satan in the world. That Jesus Christ is God's champion for the world and our Commander-in-Chief is the greatest blessing the world has experienced.

## His Commanding Provisions

While Paul's letters often address church issues in an attempt to help God's people experience the fullness of the blessings of Christ, the central solution to all human problems is Jesus Christ. That is why Paul began the letter to the Ephesians by showing seven blessings that center on Christ. These provisions from God are confidence-builders that enable the followers of Christ to stand firm against the enemy's onslaughts. While spiritual warfare and demonic forces can frighten even the saints, the blessings and provisions from our Father and His Son, our Commander, should give us full confidence to stand firm against the deceptive schemes of the devil. Let us notice how He has prepared us.

The first two blessings mentioned in Ephesians 1 **come from the Father**. He *has* **chosen** *and predestined us to be* **adopted** *as His sons and daughters.* Central to these acts is the person of Christ, God's provision for this wonderful relationship. This special relationship demonstrates the intensity of God in pursuing us and waging war against our enemy. God does not view us just as soldiers in warfare, but also as sons and daughters whom He dearly loves. Scripture makes it clear that we are adopted, but because we are in spiritual warfare, we are also drafted to be warriors.

> He wants to display His power through transformed creatures who were corrupted by Satan — transformed so thoroughly that He trusts us to wage warfare with Him.

We might wonder why the loving Father and our Commander wouldn't just fight the battle without subjecting His children to the trauma of war. That answer lies only in His mind, but from many biblical narratives we may assume that He wants to display His power through transformed creatures who were corrupted by Satan — transformed so thoroughly that He trusts us to wage warfare with Him through His provision of power. In doing so, we, His children, grow in maturity and demonstrate our kingdom citizenship, and especially our special relation to Him as chosen and adopted into the divine family.

What does it mean to be His children? A wonderful couple who were leaders in the first church I pastored were not able to conceive their own children biologically, so they adopted a little girl and a little boy. All who knew the four of them saw something very special — adopted children who functioned with such security and confidence that we knew their parents had invested and instilled in them a very deep love. When I talked with these young people, they rightly observed that with biological children, the parents have to take what they get. In their case, they knew they had been chosen and adopted; thus, they felt special and their parents made sure they knew that.

The Greek word Paul used to describe being chosen in Christ (Ephesians 1:4) is the word for election. A careful study of the word *exelexato* indicates that the word does not imply rejection of what is not chosen but the will to show favor, kindness, and love to what has been chosen.[112]

The word used here is also found in John 15:16, *I have chosen you.* When a man proposes to a woman, he chooses her to be his wife and in so doing others are not chosen, but the focus of the choice is based on the love for the one chosen, not as a rejection of all others leading to the choice by the process of elimination. The choice is based on love. And even though it may be viewed as favoritism, that is the prerogative of the lover.

This choice came from the gracious disposition of God the Father who was not under any compulsion to extend favor or to establish a loving relationship with His creation. We do not understand His motivation for restoring the fallen creation. Certainly, it came not from any need on His part as though He were lonely, bored, or in any way compelled to create or restore a fallen creation. But, we don't need to understand our adoption in order to enjoy it.

**Spiritual Blessings**

The remaining five spiritual blessings for which Paul gives praise to God in Ephesians 1:7-14 are described as **coming from Christ.** These verses show the centrality of Jesus Christ in God's plan and relationship with us.

- *He is so rich in kindness and grace that he purchased our freedom with the blood of his Son and **forgave our sins** (verse 7).*
- *He has **showered his kindness** on us, along with all wisdom and understanding (verse 8).*
- *God has now **revealed to us his mysterious plan** regarding Christ, a plan to fulfill his own good pleasure. And this is the plan: At the right time he will bring everything together under*

---

112 Another Greek word, *airetidzo* might have been used by Paul but was not. That word refers to choosing something by reason of its suitability, such as in Matthew 12:18, *behold my servant whom I have chosen.*

*the authority of Christ — everything in heaven and on earth* (verses 9, 10).

- *Furthermore, because we are united with Christ, we have received an **inheritance** from God, for he chose us in advance, and he makes everything work out according to his plan (verse 11).*
- *The Spirit is God's **guarantee** that he will give us the inheritance he promised and that he has purchased us to be his own people. He did this so we would praise and glorify him (verse 14).*

Ephesians 1:7-14, NLT (emphasis mine)

These magnificent blessings are not for us alone. These truths are like army boot camp indoctrination facts. When one joins the military, the first job of the officers in charge is to get civilians to think like soldiers. Mental reconditioning is a key part of training. And so it is for those whom Christ has called to serve in spiritual warfare. We must know how our Commanding Officer has prepared and equipped us to serve with Him. We close this chapter with MacMillan's comments on our response to the provisions God has given for this warfare.

*It is not enough that the divine Fullness outpours unstinted supplies; there must be a receptive heart and attitude on our part. A bottle may be submerged in the waters of a fountain. But if the cork is not removed, the holder may wait indefinitely and at last carry it away empty. In accord with this simile, multitudes of truly spiritual believers are, as it were, immersed in the omnipotence of God; it presses them on every side. There is a longing for its experience and a belief that it should be theirs and a readiness to receive, these things being the Witness of their spirits to the truth which the Holy Ghost has unfolded in the Word. Yet, because their minds have been 'holden' as they have read the Word, the simplicity and the glory of this truth have not dawned upon them. Do we not need, indeed, continually to pray with deep heart-humility that 'the eyes of [our] mind may be enlightened' (Ephesians 1:18)?[113]*

---

113   MacMillan, p. 32.

## Summary Thoughts from Chapter 15, Adopted and Drafted

- God's provision of Christ for the Church was His one and only strategy for undoing the damning effects of Satan in the world.
- Paul insisted on unity in the body and training for the leaders so they would be able to lead all others into full spiritual maturity (Chapter 4).
- God wants to display His power through transformed creatures who were corrupted by Satan — transformed so thoroughly that He trusts us to wage warfare.

# 16

## THE ETERNAL STRATEGIC PLAN

A recent popular theme in the organizational world is "Start with Why," pioneered by Simon Sinek. That is really the right question when pondering the purposes of God. In biblical studies, so many people get caught up with when, how, where, who, and what questions; **why?** is really the most important.

We might rightly wonder what God's great plan is. Why did the God of eternity create a universe which is seemingly such a vast wasteland? Why has He bothered to create a world with the potential to spawn rebels? Surely this speck of dust we call earth cannot meet some psychological need of Almighty God. So, what was His point? Discovering this mystery helps us grasp the significance of our Commander.

As we humans learn more about the vastness of the universe, our earth seems to become smaller and more insignificant. Does our presence as humans dignify it in some way? Does life as we know it give the earth a privileged status in the eyes of the Creator?

The Hubble Space Telescope has given us new eyes to behold the universe. Nearly every month new reports come from the most recent sightings of that marvelous explorer. The current estimate, as of 2019, is that there are about **two trillion galaxies**, having an average of 100 million stars.[114] Placing this super eye in the sky was a great achievement that enhances our knowledge and understanding about the universe.

Having recently read the account of Babel in Genesis 11, however, I was reminded how easily man's arrogance pushes his scientific and technological drive. If there is any "take-away" from these empirical astronomical calculations, it should be for us to be humbled before such truly awesome findings. Unfortunately, in our arrogance and pride, we tend to congratulate ourselves for being so brilliant for discovering what many astrophysicists believe is a 14-billion-year-old universe. The irony of this is that such findings should make us feel smaller, as David seemed to feel: *When I look at the night sky and see the work of your fingers — the moon and stars you set in place — what are mere mortals that you should think about them, human beings that you should care for them?* (Psalm 8:3, 4). Fortunately, David came to a more positive conclusion about humanity, as he continued his psalm: *You have made them a little lower than the angels and crowned them with glory and honor* (Psalm 8:5).

Musing on this existential thought, I gained an insight from one of the parables:

*Again, the Kingdom of Heaven is like a merchant on the lookout for choice pearls. When he discovered a pearl of great value, he sold everything he owned and bought it!*

Matthew 13:45, 46, NLT

The correct interpretation of the parable, undoubtedly, focuses on the great worth of the kingdom, and we would probably assume the merchant is a person looking for riches. The thought came to me, however, that the earth is like the pearl of great value. Many other pearls are out there, but God has chosen to invest in this one, to purchase it for His Son. Christ was sent to planet earth to rescue us from the kingdom of darkness. He purchased this pearl called the kingdom of God at the price of His own blood.

---

114  Internet article in SPACE.com by Elizabeth Howell, "How Many Stars Are in the Universe?" May 17, 2017.

THE ETERNAL STRATEGIC PLAN

## God's Objective

Let us go back to the question of "Why?" Answering the *why* question is the ultimate obsession of mankind. Not only philosophers, but artists, scientists, and indeed all thinkers are committed to the task of explaining why there is something rather than nothing. As part of creation, mankind has the distinct disadvantage of operating from within that which we examine. We are unable to obtain a fully objective vantage point for examining our existence. On the other hand, we have the paradox of being given minds which cannot be satisfied until that meaning becomes clear.

Certainly, God must have a grand eternal plan. We saw in Chapter 5 that:

> *His intent was that now, through the church, the manifold wisdom of God should be made known to the rulers and authorities in the heavenly realms according to his eternal purpose which he accomplished in Christ Jesus our Lord.*

> Ephesians 3:9-11, NIV

In essence, the *why* of the creation, of planet earth, and of humanity is really a subplot to an extraterrestrial, and maybe even extra-universal, purpose that is being fulfilled in the heavenly realms. We know only what is in this theater, on this stage, and in this drama, and act. Scripture hints that there is far more on God's agenda than we perceive or has been clearly revealed.

In the world of business and commerce a highly valued strategy is summed up by three letters, MBO, which stand for "management by objective." The key idea of MBO is to plan, execute, and review our work according to specific measurable objectives or goals. Planning our work and working our plan may well be an example of our being created in the image of God, for God is a planner. He is the ultimate, effective executive. He is a creative self-starter, based on His vision, and has developed a carefully calculated plan. He made adequate preparations and provision for His plan. He knows how to delegate authority within the Godhead, and He is achieving the objectives He set out when He created the plan.

Strategic planning begins with values. In the for-profit world, the value is primarily financial reward. In the not-for-profit world, the value will likely be humanitarian. We might wonder, does God value that would cause Him to create the universe, the world and physical and spiritual life? I believe we get our best clue from Jesus, and that clue comes from the first word of the Lord's Prayer. Jesus told the disciples, *When you pray, say: 'Abba'* (Luke 11:2; emphasis mine). *Abba* means "Father," and it was a fairly radical directive Jesus gave the disciples to call God "Father." Jewish people in the days of Jesus, and still today in Orthodox communities, do not say or write the name of God. However, Jesus was inviting the disciples into an intimate relationship with God.

The implication is that God, the Creator God, wants to be a Father. God wanted a family. He is a relational Being. We see that in the Trinity, and we see it in His lavish love for humanity. *God so loves the world* (John 3:16) and a host of other scriptures testify to God's great love for people. That's the big **why**. But it raises a question:

Why would God choose to have a family of fallible, self-willed, sinful humans? That would seem to be a faulty plan. But, we are not God; His ways are not our ways. His plan is called a mystery (Ephesians 1:9) because it is incomprehensible to mankind. The Greek word *musterion*[115] refers not to a puzzle or something difficult to understand, but to something kept secret and incomprehensible to the person who is not initiated into its meaning.

**Mystery Revealed**

Imagine, for example, bringing a man who knew nothing about Christianity into a communion service. He would witness what would seem to be a very bizarre ceremony. Why would people eat small crumbs of crackers or bread and drink barely half a swallow of juice or wine? Certainly, hunger and thirst would not be satisfied. There must be some other reason for these strange activities. To the uninformed this would be a mystery. To

---

115   W. E. Vine, *Vine's Complete Expository Dictionary* (Nashville: Thomas Nelson Publishers, 1996), p. 424.

a Christian, however, the mystery has been entirely solved. We have been brought into the meaning of the mystery and it makes entirely good sense to us.

Knowing the intention of God's ultimate purpose, namely, *to bring everything together under the authority of Christ — everything in heaven and on earth* (Ephesians 1:10), is a great spiritual blessing because it satisfies the natural curiosity God has put in humans as part of our rationality. As rational creatures, humans have a built-in need to have a worldview or an intellectual framework. We need to know how we fit in with the world around us. Philosophy is the pursuit of an understanding of reality. From the early eastern and pre-Socratic western philosophers down through the centuries to our present-day philosophers, there has been a great longing to provide an adequate explanation for existence.

Only one source outside of creation exists, namely, the Creator, who because of His own good pleasure has chosen to reveal the mystery of His purpose for creation, and He has given us an objective point of view about the nature of reality in His Word, which explains the mystery to the believer. Those who are chosen, adopted and redeemed are blessed by being informed about the mystery of God's purposes. We are not told why God chose to bring together all creation in Christ, but we are told that is the intention of God, and He is fulfilling His purposes for both humankind and the rebellious fallen beings here on planet earth through His one plan — providing a Champion Warrior, His Son, our Commander Savior. His victory has been achieved for the salvation of repentant humans through His crucifixion, and it has been achieved over the satanic, demonic world through His resurrection and the defeat of death, the consequence of our own sin and fallenness.

Our Commander has been given full authority to fulfill God's purpose, as He told His first disciples, *I have been given all authority in heaven and on earth* (Matthew 28:18, NLT).

> Our Commander has been given full authority to fulfill God's purpose.

MacMillan points out that Christ's authority is over *all principality, and power, and might, and dominion* (Ephesians 1:21).

*The great princes and authorities are subject to Him. So are the lesser ones; He is far above all 'might' (dunameos, a word usually used in the New Testatment of spiritual power). This refers to that working of satanic energy which is becoming increasingly manifest, directed as it is against the bodies and minds of the children of God.*[116]

Believers also share in their Commander's authority:

*As we meditate on the completeness of His authority, let us remember that He is there as the Representative of redeemed humanity (Hebrews 2:5-9). And may 'the eyes of [our] understanding be enlightened' (Ephesians 1:18) by the Holy Spirit so that we may believe, without any doubt or shrinking, that the wisdom and will of the Father have made us sharers of this same authority, and that He verily intends that we should exercise it day by day in growing comprehension and apprehension.*[117]

**Seated in Honor**

In Chapter 14 we cited many verses that depict Jesus at the right hand of God. Our emphasis there was His positioning, and here we see that He is not seated alone and His attention is very much on the world to which He will return, as MacMillan reports:

*When the Master foregathered with eleven on the Galilean mountain, at some time during the forty days of His manifestation after His passion, He said to them: 'All authority is given unto me in heaven and in earth' (Matthew 28:18). His formal assumption of that authority took place when He sat down 'on the right hand of the throne of the Majesty in the heavens' (Hebrews 8:1). The right hand of the throne of God is the center of power of the whole universe, and the exercising of the power of the throne was committed unto the ascended Lord. He is still there in full possession of His rights, awaiting the Father's time when His enemies shall be made the footstool of His feet.*

---

116  MacMillan, p. 22.

117  MacMillan, p. 21.

THE ETERNAL STRATEGIC PLAN

*The elevation of His people with Him to the heavenlies has no other meaning than that they are made sharers, potentially for the present, of the authority which is His. They are made to sit with Him; that is, they share His throne. To share a throne means without question to partake of the authority which it represents. Indeed, they have been thus elevated in the plan of God for this very purpose, that they may even now exercise, to the extent of their spiritual apprehension, authority over the powers of the air and over the conditions which those powers have brought about on the earth and are still creating through their ceaseless manipulations of the minds and circumstances of mankind.*[118]

*That there may be no misunderstanding of the Holy Spirit's meaning in this presentation of the truth of the elevation of the Lord's people with their Head, He gives it a second time in Ephesians 2:4-6. They are made to sit with Christ 'in the heavenlies.' Christ's seat is at the right hand of God. His people, therefore, occupy 'with him' the same august position. This honor is not to a chosen few, but is the portion of all those who share the resurrection of the Son of God. It is the birthright of every true believer, of every born again child of God.*[119]

Sitting may seem like a strange posture for waging battle, but He is the Commanding Officer. That means He commands others, and we who live under His authority are the ones He equips and empowers for the battle. But, strangely enough, we also sit with Him in the heavenlies, as Neil Anderson reminds us. Remember, *we wrestle not against flesh and blood.* This is not an earthly war.

*It is the eternal purpose of God to make His wisdom known through the church to "the rulers and authorities in heavenly places." When it comes to fulfilling this purpose, how is the church doing? Some are still asking, "What rulers and authorities?" How are we going to fulfill our calling in the world*

118   MacMillan, pp. 13-14.

119   MacMillan, pp. 12-13.

*if we don't believe what God says about the kingdom of darkness? Some are pleading, "O God, please help us! The devil is roaring at us!" And God responds, "I've done all I'm going to do. I defeated and disarmed Satan at the cross. I conferred all authority on you in Christ. Now open your eyes. Realize who you are and start living accordingly."*[120]

## Jesus in the Heavenlies — His Ascension

Let's examine more intently the very truth of Jesus' current residence in the heavenlies. One of the most important truths in Scripture, but often overlooked, is the ascension of Jesus — equally as or more important for us than Christmas and even Easter. The ascension of Jesus is an absolutely critical part of the gospel. Let me explain.

The incarnation without the crucifixion was interesting, but insignificant. Even being virgin-born, by itself, would not have allowed Jesus to give us forgiveness of sin and access to God.

The resurrection without the ascension, while good for Jesus, would have been meaningless for us.

The crucifixion without the resurrection was a depressing defeat. Thousands died on crosses during Roman cruelty. Had Jesus died as a totally innocent victim without being resurrected, it would have meant a victory for Satan and no provision for our resurrection or eternal life. But even more, the resurrection without the ascension, while good for Jesus, would have been meaningless for us. What would have become of a resurrected Jesus? Would He have lived perpetually ageless on the earth? What would His standing have been in the Godhead, still separated from the Father?

David Bryant, founder of Concerts of Prayer, International, wrote a six-part blog in 2018 about the ascension:

*Is it not evident that, despite the Resurrection, if there had been no Ascension we would be lost? If the Father had not been fully satisfied with all his Son did for us wouldn't it all be rendered null and void? Would we not be forever*

---

120   Anderson, *Bondage Breaker*, p. 85.

*undone, without help and without hope, if Jesus had not entered heaven on our behalf, celebrated with hymns of victory?*

- *If Christ had not ascended for us, where else could we go to find the Father's welcoming arms?*
- *There would be no high priest to represent us and intercede for us at the throne.*
- *We would be stripped of free, clean access into God's presence. There would be no one preparing a home for our eternal dwelling.*
- *Our lives, as well as the whole universe, would be without a mediator to symphonize all things with the will of God.*
- *Pentecost would have been permanently postponed, and so believers would remain forever devoid of the Spirit's indwelling power.*
- *The promises meant to be Jesus' inheritance, to be shared with all who belong to him, would be locked up and shelved.*
- *Above all, Jesus' very best gift, his saving efforts for us, would be stuck in the past, as it were — where he was last seen, visiting with disciples after exiting the tomb, but left at the fringes of history.*[121]

The ascension of Jesus is not some little side theological issue, a PS or after-thought to the gospel. It was central to the plan of God and the teaching of the early church. Jesus' earthly ministry, including His crucifixion and resurrection, was just a prelude to His greater purpose of bringing many sons and daughters to glory, starting with the divine Son of God.

Forty days on earth after His resurrection — this was His favorite day, the one He looked forward to most from the day He was born on earth, the day He would rejoin the Father. Imagine the party in heaven as He ascended!!!

---

121    David Bryant, "What If Jesus Had Never Sat Down on Heaven's Throne?" — ChristNOW; https://christnow.com > Blogs, May 10, 2017.

What does the Bible tell us about this vastly uncelebrated event, the ascension of Jesus — uncelebrated on earth, but greatly celebrated in heaven?

*In my first book I told you, Theophilus, about everything Jesus began to do and teach until the day he was taken up to heaven* (a historical event, not myth or fantasy) *after giving his chosen apostles further instructions through the Holy Spirit.*

*During the forty days after his crucifixion, he appeared to the apostles from time to time, and he proved to them in many ways* ("infallible proofs") *that he was actually alive. And he talked to them about the Kingdom of God.*

*Once when he was eating* (eating — not a ghost or phantom) *with them, he commanded them,*

*"Do not leave Jerusalem until the Father sends you the gift he promised, as I told you before. John baptized with water, but in just a few days you will be baptized with the Holy Spirit."*

*So when the apostles were with Jesus, they kept asking him, "Lord, has the time come for you to free Israel and restore our kingdom?"*

*He replied, "The Father alone has the authority to set those dates and times, and they are not for you to know. But you will receive power when the Holy Spirit comes upon you. And you will be my witnesses, telling people about me everywhere — in Jerusalem, throughout Judea, in Samaria, and to the ends of the earth."*

*After saying this, he was taken up into a cloud while they were watching, and they could no longer see him. As they strained to see him rising into heaven, two white-robed men suddenly stood among them. "Men of Galilee," they said, "why are you standing here staring into heaven? Jesus has been taken from you into heaven, but someday he will return from heaven in the same way you saw him go!"*

*Then the apostles returned to Jerusalem from the Mount of Olives, a distance of half a mile.*

Acts 1:1-12, NLT

Those are the logistics of the ascension, but what else does the Bible say about the ascended Jesus? What did Jesus Himself say about it?

To the Sanhedrin He said, *But from now on the Son of Man will be seated in the place of power at God's right hand* (Luke 22:69, NLT).

There — they had Him. He had just committed blasphemy, and it was blasphemy, unless it really happened. Is the Son of Man seated in the place of power at God's right hand?

## Summary Thoughts from Chapter 16, The Eternal Strategic Plan

- God chose to bring together all creation in Christ, and He is fulfilling His purposes for both humankind and the rebellious fallen beings here on planet earth.
- Our Commander has been given full authority to fulfill God's purpose, as He told His first disciples, *I have been given all authority in heaven and on earth.*
- The resurrection without the ascension, while good for Jesus, would have been meaningless for us.

# 17

## THE COMMANDER'S POSITION AND PURPOSES

### The Commander's Position

Now we want to look at our Commander's position of power — where He is now — and what He is doing. Mark 16:19 declares that *when the Lord Jesus had finished talking with them, he was taken up into heaven and sat down in the place of honor at God's right hand* (NLT, and ensuing verses in this chapter).

Biblically, the "right hand" was the place of privilege and trust. In medieval days, we are told, enemies were seated to the left of the king or prince, who would have a sword hidden in his cloak for easy access to his right hand, if he were a right-handed king.

In Acts 2:33, Peter at Pentecost declared, *Now he is exalted to the place of highest honor in heaven, at God's right hand.*

Acts 5:30, 31 reports that Peter said to chief priests, *The God of our ancestors raised Jesus from the dead after you killed him by hanging him on a cross. Then God put him in the place of honor at his right hand as Prince and Savior.*

In Acts 7:55, 56, Stephen, while being stoned to death ... *full of the Holy Spirit, gazed steadily into heaven and saw the glory of God, and he saw Jesus standing in the place of honor at God's right hand. And he told them, "Look, I see the heavens opened and the Son of Man standing in the place of honor at God's right hand!"* The other reports tell of Jesus sitting; why is He standing here? Perhaps to welcome and receive Stephen.

Paul also tells about Christ's position, as in Romans 8:34, *Who then will condemn us? No one — for Christ Jesus died for us and was raised to life for us, and he is sitting in the place of honor at God's right hand, pleading for us.*

And, in Colossians 3:1, *Since you have been raised to new life with Christ, set your sights on the realities of heaven, where Christ sits in the place of honor at God's right hand.*

Citing Ephesians 1:20, MacMillan also highlights this truth of Christ's authoritative positioning:

> *We notice, first of all, that, the Risen Christ has been 'made to sit.' The act of sitting indicates that, for the time being, certain aspects of His work are in abeyance. Later, the Lord will again 'rise up to the prey.' But just now, with 'all authority' delivered unto Him, He is awaiting the Father's time, and meanwhile exercising the powers placed in His hands for the working out of the redemption purchased from mankind on Calvary.*[122]

Hebrews, likewise, shows the positioning of the Son of God:

1:3 - *The Son radiates God's own glory and expresses the very character of God, and he sustains everything by the mighty power of his command. When he had cleansed us from our sins, he sat down in the place of honor at the right hand of the majestic God in heaven.*

10:12 - *But our High Priest offered himself to God as a single sacrifice for sins, good for all time. Then he sat down in the place of honor at God's right hand.*

12:2b - *Because of the joy awaiting him, he endured the cross, disregarding its shame. Now he is seated in the place of honor beside God's throne.*

And Peter affirms Christ's positioning in 1 Peter 3:22 - *Now Christ has gone to heaven. He is seated in the place of honor next to God, and all the angels and authorities and powers accept his authority (have been subjected to him — NASB).*

---

122  MacMillan, pp. 21-22.

THE COMMANDER'S POSITION AND PURPOSES

How did Mark, Matthew, Luke, Peter, Paul, and the writer of Hebrews know this? Besides being inspired by the Holy Spirit in their writing, no doubt they were familiar with Psalm 110:1:

*The LORD says to my Lord:* (literally, *Yahweh says to Adonai*)
*"Sit at My right hand*
*Until I make Your enemies a footstool for your feet."*

As noted earlier, this is the most frequently quoted Old Testament verse in the New Testament (5 times): Matthew 22:44, Mark 12:36, Luke 20:42, Acts 2:34 and Hebrews 1:13.

What does it mean? Proof of His being the Messiah — son of David — son of God. That was the point Jesus was making when He asked the Pharisees,

*"What do you think about the Messiah, whose son is He?" They said to Him, "The son of David." He said to them, "Then how does David in the Spirit call Him 'Lord,' saying, 'THE LORD SAID TO MY LORD, "SIT AT MY RIGHT HAND, UNTIL I PUT YOUR ENEMIES BENEATH YOUR FEET?" If David then calls Him 'Lord,' how is He his son?" No one was able to answer Him a word, nor did anyone dare from that day on to ask Him another question.*

Matthew 22:42-46, NASB

Do you get this? David the writer is referring not to himself, but to *my Lord*. David writes, *The Lord, Yahweh, God the Father, says to my Lord, Adonai, sit at my right hand.* God didn't invite David to sit at His right hand. He invited David's Lord, the Messiah, who was not just the son of David, but the Son of God.

## The Commander's Purposes

But what does that have to do with us? Why is it important for us to know where Jesus is? Is it just a nice ending to a gripping story, a feel-good story, that goodness triumphed over evil? Modern people might be prone to ask, "So, Jesus, what have you done for me lately?" Let's look at His

Is it just a nice ending to a gripping story, a feel-good story that goodness triumphed over evil?

purposes for being ascended and in heaven.

First, He is **preparing a place** for His followers. In John 14:1-3, after predicting that Peter would deny Him, Jesus said to the disciples,

> *Don't let your hearts be troubled. Trust in God, and trust also in me. There is more than enough room in my Father's home. If this were not so, I would have told you. I am going to prepare a place for you. When everything is ready, I will come and get you, so that you will always be with me where I am.*

Can you visualize this? Probably not. But that does not stop us from living with this reality. Jesus wants us to be with Him eternally. He is preparing a place for us. He wants all His family to be together, and He is getting ready for it. Positioned at the Father's right hand, no doubt He is commanding the angels, His *ministering spirits* as they are called in Hebrews 1:14, to construct our heavenly homes to be places of superior hospitality, beauty, and comfort — beyond anything imaginable on earth.

Second, as He is preparing a place for us, He is also **building His Church.** Jesus told Peter, *And I tell you that you are Peter, and on this rock I will build my church, and the gates of Hades will not overcome it* (Matthew 16:18). Whether Jesus meant Peter was the rock or Peter's confession of Jesus being the Messiah was the rock is not important here. What is important is that, seated at the right hand of God in the heavenlies, Jesus is fulfilling His purpose of building His Church. Furthermore, the gates of hades[123] will not prevail against it.

> *It may seem a strange statement to many Christians, but it is nevertheless a profound spiritual truth that the authority of the risen Head at the right*

---

123  *Hades* refers to the place of the dead. It is not hell; that is *Gehenna. Hades* is the Greek word for the concept of the Hebrew term *sheol*, the place of disembodied spirits awaiting the resurrection (unto eternal life or judgment).

*hand of the throne of the Majesty in the heavens is planned to reach its full development and manifestation through His Body. The Son of God became incarnate not merely that He might save men from their sins, but also that He might bring man to that place of dominion over the works of God, which was planned in the counsels of eternity (Psalm 8:6). Today, the inspired writer tells us (Hebrews 2:9), 'we see Jesus': holding in trust for redeemed mankind all that the race has lost through sin. Our Lord has Himself taken the Headship and is forming for Himself a Body through which He will fulfill the original divine purpose.*[124]

That is a promise that continues. Jesus is building His Church, which is a great encouragement in the face of opposition and persecution. Whatever happens, we can be confident in the promise that Jesus is building His Church. Not even death can destroy the work of God, and Jesus said this to Peter before the crucifixion and resurrection.

Third, one way in which Jesus builds His Church is by **equipping His people**. In Ephesians 4:11-12, Paul wrote that Christ gave *apostles, prophets, evangelists, pastors, and teachers to equip the saints for the work of ministry, for building up the body.* He equips believers by giving to the Church people who are gifted as overseers, preachers, evangelists, Bible teachers, and shepherds who prepare us to do the ministry of building the Church.

The five-fold gifts to the body equip believers to do the work of ministry by:

- Expanding the kingdom by planting and overseeing churches - Apostles
- Declaring God's Word and His will through preaching - Prophets
- Telling and showing the gospel to lead people to salvation - Evangelists
- Shepherding the local church, protecting and caring for the people - Pastors

---

124   MacMillan, p. 60.

- Explaining and applying scripture for Christian growth - Teachers

Fourth, Jesus is **exercising His divine authority** in the *epouranios,* the heavenly realms, which are inhabited by unseen rulers and authorities, according to Ephesians 3:10.

_____
Jesus is exercising His divine authority in the epouranios, the heavenly realms, which are inhabited by unseen rulers and authorities.
_____

What is He doing there? Paul reveals this in Ephesians 1:19-23:

> I also pray that you will understand the incredible greatness of God's power for us who believe him. This is the same mighty power that raised Christ from the dead and seated him in the place of honor at God's right hand in the heavenly realm (epouranios). Now he is far above any ruler or authority or power or leader or anything else — not only in this world but also in the world to come. God has put all things under the authority of Christ and has made him head over all things for the benefit of the church. And the church is his body; it is made full and complete by Christ, who fills all things everywhere with himself.

Jesus is positioned at the Father's right hand in the heavenlies as the authority over all powers that seek to tear down the Church. In fact, He is building up the true Church. Earthly churches fail as they do not submit to His obedience, but He is preparing for and protecting the called-out ones (*ecclesia)* who will join Him. That final number is still being filled. The main point here is that Christ is reigning in heaven for you now, and you have full access to His authority if you are His follower. But the question is, Are we using His privileged position and power?

A few years ago, I awoke in the middle of the night with the room spinning around me. Thinking it was the tail end of a dream, I began to get up to go into the bathroom, but I couldn't stand. I had no balance, and the room continued to spin. My wife was awakened, and since she had had an episode of vertigo, she suggested that I was likely falling to vertigo — literally. In her case, she could hardly be upright for nearly a week. Lying back down, I had a strong sensation that this was not merely a physical problem, but that I was under attack from God's enemy, Satan. Taking the authority I know I have in Jesus, I rebuked whatever power was trying to sideline me. I claimed the power of the blood of Jesus and reminded the devil of my identity in Christ. At that, I stood up, the room stopped spinning, and I walked into the bathroom, returned, slept peacefully, and was never bothered again. Christ's power in the heavenlies prevails for us.

Fifth, besides being seated in the place of authority, the Scripture says He is **interceding and advocating** for us. Hebrews 7:23-26 declares,

> *There were many priests under the old system, for death prevented them from remaining in office. But because Jesus lives forever, his priesthood lasts forever. Therefore he is able, once and forever, to save those who come to God through him. He lives forever to intercede with God on their behalf. He is the kind of high priest we need because he is holy and blameless, unstained by sin. He has been set apart from sinners and has been given the highest place of honor in heaven.*

Who is he praying for? Those who come to God through Him. How is He praying? Interceding with God on our behalf as a holy and blameless high priest.

As our intercessor, Jesus is the only mediator we need, the only One the Father will accept. If you are trying to pray through any other being, you are wasting your time. Jesus ever lives to represent your concerns in heaven. Worse than wasting your time, you are committing idolatry by putting someone else in the place of the Son of God. Do not let false religious teachings jeopardize your standing as a child of God. You are invited directly into His presence through the mediation of your Savior and High Priest. There is no other Savior (Acts 4:12), and no other priest is needed or effective in representing you to God.

So, to sum up, what is the ascended, glorified Christ doing in heaven for us today?

- He is preparing a place for us.
- He is building His church, the whole global Church.
- He is equipping His people for mature ministry.

- He is exercising His divine authority against evil forces for us.
- He is interceding and advocating for us.

But more than anything, I believe Jesus is sitting on the edge of His seat next to the throne, just waiting to hear the Father say, "Go, go get your bride, the Church. Go, bring all our family together."

The ascension of Jesus and His positioning at the right hand of the Father guarantee His return, His second coming. What does that mean for us? Exactly what it meant for the Thessalonians to whom Paul wrote these comforting words in 1 Thessalonians 4:13-18:

> *And now, dear brothers and sisters, we want you to know what will happen to the believers who have died so you will not grieve like people who have no hope. For since we believe that Jesus died and was raised to life again, we also believe that when Jesus returns, God will bring back with him the believers who have died. We tell you this directly from the Lord: We who are still living when the Lord returns will not meet him ahead of those who have died. For the Lord himself will come down from heaven with a commanding shout, with the voice of the archangel, and with the trumpet call of God. First, the Christians who have died will rise from their graves. Then, together with them, we who are still alive and remain on the earth will be caught up in the clouds to meet the Lord in the air. Then we will be with the Lord forever. So encourage each other with these words.*

In Chapter 5 we have seen the adversary, Satan, and in Chapter 14, the Commanding Officer, we have seen Jesus Christ. The irony of this warfare is that the warriors and the battlefield are the same, the very people Christ came to rescue. In Chapter 9, we observed that the battleground is not a field or any place at all; it is the human race, which God's enemy has dominated since sin entered God's creation. We move, now, to consider the Warriors, the people of God, known collectively as the Church, which the Commanding Officer is using to humiliate His enemy by rescuing those who will be with Him forever.

## Summary Thoughts from Chapter 17, The Commander's Position and Purposes

- Seated at the right hand of God in the heavenlies, Jesus is fulfilling His purpose of building His Church. Furthermore, the gates of hades will not prevail against it.
- Jesus is exercising His divine authority in the *epouranios*, the heavenly realms, which are inhabited by unseen rulers and authorities.
- The ascension of Jesus and His positioning at the right hand of the Father guarantee His return.

# 18

## THE WARRIORS

Just as Jesus was both the sacrificing high priest and the sacrifice to atone for our sins,[125] a similar paradox is that the battleground, the human family, and especially the Church (Chapter 9) are also the warriors in the battle. The premise of this book is that the Church is at war; God's people are engaged with Him in rescuing Satan's captives and destroying the works of darkness and the source of spiritual darkness, God's enemy, Satan. Therefore, we are spiritual warriors. While the battle truly is the Lord's, who as Commanding Officer has already won the war, the adversary's resistance continues. Does Christ need us to fight His battle? Absolutely not. However, part of His strategy is to use as His warriors the very ones Satan is trying to contain in his dark kingdom and future.

We have seen in Chapter 13 some of the qualities that God has provided for His people. Our focus there was on our value to Him, which prompted Him to sacrifice His Son on the field of battle. For some reason, God decided we are worth fighting for, and He has waged that battle in Christ. However, the warfare is not over because God's purpose in bringing many sons and daughters to glory (Hebrews 2:10) has not been completed. Not

---

125   See Hebrews 10:12.

only are we the embattled ones He is fighting for, we are also participants in the warfare.

We may not see ourselves to be qualified warriors until we understand these truths from 2 Corinthians 10:4-5: ... *the weapons of our warfare are not of the flesh, but divinely powerful for the destruction of fortresses.* To serve as warriors in Christ's army, *We demolish arguments and every proud thing that is raised up against the knowledge of God, and we take every thought captive to obey Christ.*

How are we trained to do this since the enemy is a formidable foe who holds captive the minds of men and women whose lack of knowledge of God keeps them imprisoned? What the devil has not taken into account is what Christ has done to strengthen and equip His earthly army.

## The Warriors' Identity: Ephesians 1-3

In his effort to alert the Ephesian believers to their many advantages, Paul began his letter by describing what God had already done for them to make them who they really had become.

> As you grow in spiritual maturity, you will powerfully impact every relationship in your life and nullify Satan's influence.

As we mentioned in Chapter 9, there are two prominent ideas in Ephesians: 1) You are not who you think you are; in Christ, you are far better and more than you imagine; 2) As you grow in spiritual maturity, you will powerfully impact every relationship in your life and nullify Satan's influence.

You might be thinking, "Who am I, to think that I am or could be a spiritual warrior? I am just an ordinary Christian trying to live a good life and please God." Wrong, wrong, wrong. No Christian is ordinary. Being in Christ automatically makes you extraordinary.

Neil Anderson observes, *Every defeated Christian I have worked with has had one thing in common. None of them have known who they were in Christ or have understood what it means to be a child of God.*[126]

---

126  Anderson, *Bondage Breaker*, p. 46.

Understanding that we are extraordinary because we are in Christ is, of course, a matter of belief. A person who does not believe what Scripture clearly says about our identity and our placement in Him will never become a spiritual warrior. Because so few Christians seem to believe and appropriate their identity in Christ which qualifies them as spiritual warriors, along with MacMillan, I'd like to take us back to Ephesians 1 to point out **the relationship between our belief in who we are in Christ and our ability to exercise the authority He provides.**

*Few comprehend the primary thought of 'belief.' It has a twofold meaning, fraught with deep significance. In it are combined two old Anglo-Saxon words: 'be,' to live or exist; and 'lifan,' which conveys the thought of accordance. Thus to believe means to literally 'to live in accordance with' anything. We are accustomed to consider 'belief' as simply mental acquiescence with some particular truth. But its root leads us to action; that which the mind accepts, the will must obey. We do not truly believe, therefore, unless our conviction is manifested in our life. Thus understood, 'belief' stands on a par with its great synonym 'faith,' which in its deeper sense means not only to have trust in a person but to manifest that trust by practical committal.*

*Do we believe that God 'hath quickened us together with Christ and hath raised us up together, and made us sit together in heavenly places in Christ Jesus' (Ephesians 2:5-6)? If we do, our reaction to it will be a fervent: 'Lord, I accept Thy gracious word. I believe that Thou hast thus wrought for me. In humble faith I do now take my seat in the heavenly places in Christ Jesus at Thy right hand. Teach me how to fulfill this sacred ministry, how to exercise the authority which Thou hast entrusted to me. Train me day by day that I may attain to the full stature of the perfect man in Christ, so that in me Thy purpose of the ages may be fulfilled. Amen.'*

*If we are walking in the Spirit our normal life is in the heavenlies. To secure the consciousness of this, there must be the daily acceptance of the fact. Let us, morning by morning, as one of our first acts of worship, take our seat with*

*Christ (as suggested in the previous paragraph) and return thanks to God for all that it implies. Let us often remind ourselves that we are seated far above all the powers of the air, and that they are in subjection to us. As our faith learns to use the Name and the Authority of Jesus, we shall find the spiritual forces yielding obedience in ways that will surprise us. As we continue to abide closely in Him, our prayers for the advancement of the kingdom will become less and less the uttering of petitions and will increasingly manifest the exercise of a spiritual authority that recognizes no national boundaries, but fearlessly binds the forces of darkness in any part of the world.*[127]

> As our faith learns to use the Name and the Authority of Jesus, we shall find the spiritual forces yielding obedience in ways that will surprise us.

Satan greatly underestimates God's people who through the power of their testimony and the blood of the Lamb (Revelation 12:11) overcome *the great dragon — the ancient serpent, who is called the devil and Satan* (Revelation 12:9). Besides the "heavenly host" of angels the Lord Sabbaoth commands, His redeemed people are also spiritual warriors. He equips them for battle primarily by transforming them (us) by His Spirit to be His *workmanship* (NASB) (*handiwork* — NIV, *masterpiece* — NLT). The word *poiema* occurs only in Romans 1:20 and Ephesians 2:10, and refers to *that which has been made; a work of God as creator.*[128] As His *handiwork*, we are *created in Christ Jesus for good works* (Ephesians 2:10), which includes His warfare work.

**Who we are (His *handiwork*) is more important than what we do** as warriors. That is why Paul went to elaborate efforts explaining to the Ephesians their identity and God's provisions for them in Ephesians 1-5 before he introduced them to the spiritual armor in Chapter 6. And, so in this chapter, our focus is not on the warfare, but on the warrior. In Chapter 20 we will look at the battle plan.

---

127  MacMillan, pp. 32-34.

128  Thayer's Greek Lexicon, Electronic Database Copyright © 2002, 2003, 2006, 2011 by Biblesoft, Inc.

God's "new society," as John Stott calls the Church, are people God has called and blessed in every imaginable way as part of His strategy for displaying the "manifold wisdom" of His eternal plan to bring together His whole family in heaven and on earth. In order to help us understand God's plan and participate in it fully, Paul prayed that three inner workings would occur in us, activated by all three Persons of the Godhead. Paul prayed in Ephesians 3 that God would:

1. Empower us with inner strength through the Spirit - 3:16
2. Make His home in our hearts, through Christ, and help us truly grasp the unlimited dimensions of His love - 3:17, 18
3. Completely fill us up to all the fullness of God - 3:19

Then, Paul assures us in Ephesians 3:20, 23 that God's ability to answer this prayer is matched by His willingness to do it. Here is the confidence that we need as warriors. God is:

- Able
- Able to do what we ask
- Able to do what we ask or imagine
- Able to do all that we ask or imagine
- Able to do more than all that we ask or imagine
- Able to do immeasurably more than all that we ask or imagine
- Able to do immeasurably more than all that we ask or imagine according to his power that is at work within us.[129]

## Selected Warriors

You may not think of yourself as a warrior, but if you are in Christ, you need to understand that you have willingly signed up to receive His salvation, but before you had that opportunity you were already selected by God. And those He has chosen are to be not only His special possession as family members of the King, but also chosen to fight with Him the battle

---

129   Stott, *God's New Society*, pp. 139-140.

of the ages. But, fear not, He will not leave you abandoned in the battle. You are destined to win because He has already won. Our job is to declare the victory and help others join the ranks of the victorious Christ and the others He has rescued. But often, those still in darkness have a difficult time believing that God would choose them. No doubt that was a problem with the believers in Ephesus also.

> Our job is to declare the victory and help others join the ranks of the victorious Christ and the others He has rescued.

As we have already seen from Acts 19, Ephesus was a pagan city with a few weak Christians, who later received the fullness of the Holy Spirit — verses 1-10. It was a city plagued by false religion and demonism — verses 11-20, a city exploited by commercial interests — verses 23-34.

To reach such a culture, Paul wants believers (them and us) to know we are chosen in Christ to display His character, as he wrote in Ephesians 1:3-6 (NIV):

> *Praise be to the God and Father of our Lord Jesus Christ, who has blessed us in the heavenly realms with every spiritual blessing in Christ. For he chose us in him before the creation of the world to be holy and blameless in his sight. In love, he predestined us for adoption to sonship through Jesus Christ, in accordance with his pleasure and will — to the praise of his glorious grace, which he has freely given us in the One he loves.*

You have been chosen, we might say "drafted," except that you have also volunteered. The Greek word Paul used to describe being chosen in Christ is the word for *election.*

The one chosen is really the Christ. The believers who are in Christ are chosen because of their position in Him, not because of their merit over others. The identity of Christ extends to all those who are in Him, and therefore their relation to God the Father is the same as the relation of the Son to the Father. It is impossible to overestimate the significance of the two words, *in Christ* in Pauline theology. In fact, in Ephesians 1:1-14 the phrase *in Christ* occurs nine times. This little phrase has a powerful meaning because it speaks of the incorporated status of believers in the second Adam. Romans 5 teaches that all people are either in the first Adam or in the second Adam, who is Christ Jesus. Truly we believers in Christ are princes and princesses in the King's royal family.

However, should we be tempted to think that our election is based on our merit, Paul indicates that the choosing occurred before the creation of the world. This implies an eternal plan, one which began before time, when the Father granted to the Son a kingdom consisting of the redeemed parts of creation. Charles Hodge shares this important insight, *From eternity the whole scheme of redemption with all its details and in all its results lay matured in the divine mind; hence everything is certain. There is no possibility of failure or of any change of purpose.*[130]

Romans 8:29-30 indicates that the election is over. The verbs are all in the past tense, moving from God's foreknowledge to predestination to election to justification to glorification. God's choice of you is final and completed; while the drama will still continue to play out, the election is over. So, if you are in Christ through repentance and humble trust in His death as payment for your sins, and if you believe in His resurrection and confess your faith, you are His forever.

## Chosen for Holiness

You might wonder why He has chosen you. Why has God bothered to provide this special relationship for humans with Himself? Surely, humans do not make up for anything God lacks. One of His attributes is aseity, or self-sufficiency. Why did God bother to create a material world in the first place, and once humans rebelled against Him, why did He bother to restore it (us) rather than destroying the whole material world? I believe His reason predates creation and human history, as we described in Chapters 1 and 16. His eternal plan was and is to have a family of sons and daughters who love and fellowship with Him, participating in His holy attributes. For that

---

130   Hodge, p. 32.

reason, after our fall from holiness, He sent His uncreated, eternal Son to redeem us from the fall and impute His holiness to us. That assignment is still being fulfilled.

Perhaps it's like a father who decides to give his son a mechanically sophisticated car. But the computer malfunctions, so the father decides to scrap the car. The son says, "No, wait, I can fix it by repairing the corrupted computer." He chooses the right parts, restores the car to operate as it was intended, and achieves the father's original purpose. In this illustration and in the heavenlies, the father and son are in total agreement.

Through the inspiration of Scripture Paul pulls back the veil somewhat, supporting this reason for creation by saying that those chosen in Christ should be *holy and blameless* before Him, or in His sight. *Holy* refers to being separate. It also includes being altogether without any moral imperfection or sin. *Blameless* is frequently used to describe a sacrifice which was perfect. Of course, none of us meets these standards. That is why it is essential that we are in Christ, who meets the requirements fully and perfectly. We can be sure that these qualities are a rebuke to God's enemy who was anything but holy and blameless. We are like God's trophies, evidences of Christ's victory.

> We are like God's trophies, evidences of Christ's victory.

For the believer, the sovereign choice of God to extend His grace by incorporating people in His beloved Son should be a source of great confidence — because it is based on the righteousness of the Son — and a source of great humility to be eternally included in the divine family.

Our election gives to the believer a certain guarded security. It is certainly not a license to sin, as indicated by Romans 6:1, 15. Paul asked the question, *Shall we go on sinning because we are under grace?* Then he expressed scorn for those who would even ask such question. While committing sin is certainly a possibility for those who are chosen, Paul's appeal to basic rightness and justice, in view of all that election has benefitted the believer, expresses the shamefulness of continuing to sin.

The prophet Amos warned his audience not to relish the privilege of being chosen because, if they failed in their responsibility, they would continue to be chosen but chosen for punishment.

*You only have I chosen of all the families of the earth;*
*Therefore, I will punish you for all your sins.*

Amos 3:2

God brings under His corrective disciplines those believers who choose to walk in sin and disobedience, wanting to bring them to repentance and restored fellowship because not only are they hurting themselves, they bring reproach on His cause and add fuel to the enemy's cause.

Peter continues this theme by indicating that election really is a call to radical character change. *Therefore my brothers be all the more eager to make your calling and election sure. For if you do these things, you will never fall* ... (2 Peter 1:10).

The same theme is found in Paul's letter to the Colossians, *Therefore as God's chosen people, holy and dearly loved, clothe yourselves with compassion, kindness, humility, gentleness and patience* (Colossians 3:12). An example of these implications is the special responsibility put on an athlete who is chosen to represent his or her country in the Olympics. Great privilege attends that choice, but great expectations and responsibility come with that privilege.

Paul used the military metaphor as he encouraged Timothy's warriors, the people in the church at Ephesus where Timothy was pastor:

*No soldier in active service entangles himself in the affairs of everyday life, **so that he may please the one who enlisted him** as a soldier.*

2 Timothy 2:4, emphasis added

In other words, pleasing our Commanding Officer by being in Him holy and blameless means not going spiritually AWOL, absent without leave.

## Summary Thoughts from Chapter 18, The Warriors

- As you grow in spiritual maturity, you will powerfully impact every relationship in your life and nullify Satan's influence.
- Besides the "heavenly host" of angels the Lord Sabbaoth commands, His redeemed people are also spiritual warriors.
- Our job is to declare the victory and help others join the ranks of the victorious Christ and the others He has rescued.

# 19

## SANCTIFIED SOLDIERS

**Boot Camp: Ephesians 4-6**

Being chosen by the King, and even being given a commission and adopted into the King's family, does not make me a competent warrior. Now that I know from Ephesians 1-3 who I am in Christ — a chosen, blessed, and spiritually endowed son or daughter of God — I am ready for boot camp and to see from Ephesians 4-6 that I am commissioned to impact the world around me by being who I am.

In Ephesians 4:1-16 we hear Paul say, "Grow up." In verses 17-32, he says, "Stop it!" referring to the pagan practices of the world. In 5:1-20, Paul says "Imitate God," a preposterous statement. If you are like me, you want to say, "Hold on, Paul, maybe King Agrippa was right — you have lost your senses; you're mad! Imitate God? Don't you recall that...

- Abraham was the friend of God, but he sinned.
- Moses met with God face-to-face, but he sinned.
- David was the man after God's own heart, and he sinned — a lot!
- And, we might add, Peter and Paul — both of them were self-declared sinners.

What possibly could have possessed Paul to write such a comment — "Imitate God"?

The stakes were high. The Church's reputation was on the line in Ephesus, "Sin City." Would the Christians be any different than other Ephesians? What would set them apart as belonging to God? They would need to emulate His character. It's the character of God, not His infinite attributes, that they were to imitate. And that is still important to God because the stakes are still high. Much of the world hates the Church.

- Modernists see the Church as hypocritical.
- Young people see the Church as irrelevant.
- LGBTQ's see the Church as intolerant.
- Muslims see Christianity as the evil religion.
- Communists see the Church as a threat.
- Many people believe Christians are "haters."

Should we be concerned about the reputation of the Church? Answer: Yes, but only before God. It's quite doubtful that God cares even a whit about what those under the authority of His enemy think about the Church. He knows Satan hates the Church; why would it be any different for those outside of the Church?

Part of being a warrior is being a fit, trained, loyal representative of the King we represent.

Then, why would God care about the character of His people? Precisely because we are His people, and as we reflect His nature, we fulfill His plan, rebuke His enemy, and please Him. Part of being a warrior is being a fit, trained, loyal representative of the King we represent.

So, how can we imitate God? Paul suggests three ideas in Ephesians 5, all using the word "walk," as translated correctly in the NASB. The precise way in which we are to imitate God is to walk as God walks. *Walk in love* is the emphasis in verses 2-7, *walk in light* is the theme of verses 8-14, and *walk wisely* is the topic of verses 15-20. The imagery of walking is important because it suggests progressive and purposeful movement. Part of the conditioning of military soldiers is walking, running and many other strenuous activities.

Paul alluded to this in admonishing Timothy, *Endure suffering with me as a good soldier of Christ Jesus* (2 Timothy 2:3).

Spiritual warriors live disciplined lives of love in their sacrifice, their sexuality and their speech.

*Therefore be imitators of God, as beloved children; and walk in love, just as Christ also loved you and gave Himself up for us, an offering and a sacrifice to God as a fragrant aroma.*

*But immorality or any impurity or greed must not even be named among you, as is proper among saints; and there must be no filthiness and silly talk, or coarse jesting, which are not fitting, but rather giving of thanks. For this you know with certainty, that no immoral or impure person or covetous man, who is an idolater, has an inheritance in the kingdom of Christ and God.*

*Let no one deceive you with empty words, for because of these things the wrath of God comes upon the sons of disobedience. Therefore do not be partakers with them.*

Ephesians 5:1-7

### The Weapon of Sacrificial Love

Maybe thinking of love as a weapon of warfare seems odd, but Dr. Martin Luther King, Jr. was right on target with this quote:

*Darkness cannot drive out darkness; only light can do that. Hate cannot drive out hate; only love can do that.*[131]

The reason love is the weapon is that our attention is not to be on the enemy of God, but on the people still in Satan's clutches. Loving the unconverted, as Christ does, is the major strategy of winning their freedom. More about this in Chapter 20 on the battle plan, but we pursue the idea here in our insights from Ephesians about walking.

---

131   Martin Luther King, Jr. From *Strength to Love*, a book by Martin Luther King, Jr. It was published in 1963 as a collection of his sermons.

Walking in love puts us on the path of sacrifice. Paul says that we are to walk in love *just as Christ loved us and gave himself up for us as a fragrant offering and sacrifice to God* (Ephesians 5:2). Biblical love always seeks to meet the true needs of others and usually entails sacrifice. Even with all the kind and merciful acts Jesus demonstrated to His contemporaries, had He stopped short of the cross He would not have loved us in the full sense of biblical love. Our need is salvation — deliverance from the penalty of our sins, which could be paid for only by His perfect sacrifice.

> Biblical love always seeks to meet the true needs of others and usually entails sacrifice.

God's basis for forgiving humans has always demanded sacrifice. In the Old Testament era the sacrifice usually involved an animal such as a lamb or an ox. In the New Testament era that sacrifice can be no less than the perfect sacrifice, Christ Himself, who is described as a *fragrant offering*. The reason for the fragrance is that, unlike all other sacrifices, Christ *gave Himself up*. He volitionally and voluntarily surrendered Himself to the painful fate of crucifixion, not as an act of masochistic martyrdom but because in His great love He bore God's judgment on our sins.

Some people think Jesus was a victim, that He was not really in on the planning. However, not only was Jesus in on the planning, but He drew up the mission statement: *For the Son of Man did not come to be served, but to serve, and to give his life as a ransom for many* (Mark 10:45). He gave Himself up for us knowing fully what the stakes were and what He had to do. Full love demanded full sacrifice. In Ephesians 5:25, Paul used the same terminology admonishing husbands to *love their wives as Christ loved the church and gave himself up for her.*

God receives this sacrifice as a pleasing aroma. It seems a bit odd that in the Old Testament economy God considered burning animal flesh to be a pleasing aroma. I doubt if we are far off in suggesting that the "nostrils" of God smelled not the physical aroma but the spiritual attitude behind the sacrifice. That is why in 2 Corinthians 2:14, 15 Paul wrote, *But thanks be to God, who always leads us in triumphal procession in Christ and through us spreads everywhere the fragrance of the knowledge of him. For we are to God the aroma of Christ amongst those who are being saved.*

The most important lesson we can learn about sacrificial love is that it must be given to people on their terms, that is, it must be perceived by them to be an act of love. Love that is convenient to give or self-oriented in its consideration (that is, love as *we would want to receive it*) is not biblical love. A ludicrous example of self-oriented love is a husband who gives his wife on her birthday the electric saw he has always wanted.

The Apostle Barnabas provided a good example of sacrificial love for the pilgrim converts who remained in Jerusalem after Pentecost. He sold all his land and used the proceeds to feed the new Christians in the early days of their orientation into their new faith.

### The Weapon of Sexual Purity

Another pathway for walking in love is through sexual purity. Ephesians 4 describes the gentile world without Christ. Ephesians 5:3 emphasizes this even more to the whole church: *There must not be even a hint of sexual immorality or of any kind of impurity, or of greed, because these are improper for God's holy people.* Try imagining a world without any Christian values. That was Ephesus in the days in which Paul was writing. The famous Temple of Artemis, or Diana, was a place where ritual prostitution was practiced regularly. Blatant sexual impurity almost always involves or invites demonic influence. Our sexual idols may not be named Diana, but they are every bit as seductive and addictive, as Anderson points out in *A Way of Escape*:

> Blatant sexual impurity almost always involves or invites demonic influence. Our sexual idols may not be named Diana, but they are every bit as seductive and addictive.

> *Satan, the god of this world, has orchestrated the subtle erosion of moral standards in our nation. He has numbed the senses [of] this generation to sexually explicit material so we no longer react to it. A Christian who dabbles in pornography is like a soldier marching blindfolded through a mine field. Sooner or later poor judgment and careless experimentation will explode in his or her face.*[132]

---

132  Neil Anderson, *A Way of Escape* (Eugene, OR: Harvest House Publishers, 1994), p. 21.

*So why is this ongoing cosmic battle between God's kingdom and Satan's kingdom, between righteousness and sin, so often waged in the arena of sex and sexual behavior? It dawned on me after years of helping people find their freedom in Christ that a person's sexual practices are a primary way by which seeds are sown in these two kingdoms. For example, most of the people who come to Freedom in Christ Ministries struggling against sin and Satan have some kind of sexual problem. In fact, every person who shared his or her story in my book,* Released from Bondage, *had either been sexually abused, sexually disoriented, or sexually promiscuous.*[133]

Why are people especially vulnerable to moral failure and sin by abusing God's great gift of sexuality? What does Satan see and use in sex to promote his heinous agenda of destroying people? Think about it. God created us to have intimacy with Himself. Satan exploited our intimacy drive and perverted it as Eve and Adam made bad choices. They both chose to listen to and heed the guidance of other creatures rather than God. Eve complied with the serpent, and Adam complied with Eve.

Choosing creatures over the Creator is called idolatry. Pornography is a modern form of idolatry, and men are especially vulnerable to choosing Eve over God. I believe there may be hundreds of thousands of Christians who are residents of MASH (Mobile Army Surgical Hospital) needing healing from the *fiery darts of the wicked one* in the form of addiction to pornography. Trapped in sexual sin, they may be believers in Christ, but they lack victory in their lives that would qualify them to be warriors for Him.

Satan doesn't require people to worship him; he is quite happy for people, especially those who should be Christ's warriors, to worship anyone or anything other than God and His Son Jesus Christ. After mentioning the pagan gods Molech and the Babylonian satyr, Anderson writes:

*There were many other pagan gods in biblical times whose worship involved sexual perversity. Chemosh, the national deity of the Moabites, required the*

133  Anderson, *Way of Escape*, p. 60.

*sacrifice of children, and Diana of Ephesus had an explicitly sexual nature. Devotion to anyone or anything less than the God and Father of our Lord Jesus Christ is idolatry, and idolatry always leads into some perfusion of moral purity.*[134]

The Ephesians demonstrated the truth that people tend to invent religious deities to their own liking when they are not guided by the objective, infallible Word of God. Rather than pleasing God, people invent religious

> Rather than pleasing God, people invent religious activities to please themselves.

activities to please themselves. Paul admonished the Ephesians not only to abstain from such practices but not to get so close that even a hint of these sexual sins could ever be suggested of the Christian church.

## The Weapon of Sanctified Speech

A further pathway for walking in love is through our speech. Ephesians 5:4 focuses on this and relates also to the previous idea of purity.

> *There should be no obscenity, foolish talk or coarse joking, which are out of place, but rather thanksgiving* (NIV).

Paul was also concerned that believers should not betray a wrong attitude toward sex. There should be no joking about sex, or use of lewd language, but in total contrast, anything having to do with sex should be viewed with honor, and thanksgiving.

*Obscenity* or *filthiness* (NASB) refers to shameful, disgraceful speech. Profanity, nearly an epidemic in our society, is well outside the bounds of sanctified speech. Analyzing why people swear in daily life leads one to believe it stems from anger or the desire to be "cool" and accepted by others who have similar lewd and coarse vocabulary. Profanity includes using God's name loosely, making common other sacred or fearsome realities, verbal condemnation, "barnyard" allusions, and trivializing of sex. The

---

134  Anderson, *Way of Escape*, p. 62.

adjective form of this word that is rare in the New Testament is found later in verse 12, saying, *It is <u>shameful</u> even to mention what the disobedient do in secret* (Ephesians 5:12, NIV).

*Foolish talk* — the Greek word, *morologia*, appears only in Ephesians 5:4, and could literally be translated "words of a moron." Jesus gave a similar warning in Matthew 12:36-37: *But I tell you that every careless (useless) word that people speak, they shall give an accounting for it in the day of judgment. For by your words you will be justified and by your words you will be condemned.* Obviously, words matter to God, since communication is an ability He shares with us.

As suggested earlier, imitating God — even God in the flesh, Jesus Christ — is an outrageous idea, but an imitation is not necessarily perfect. Just as little children may try to imitate daddy or mommy, but do so imperfectly and even humorously, as God's children we naturally admire Him so much that we want to be like Him, even in our speech. And, I believe, He loves that and enjoys even our imperfect attempts. Our motive is more important than our performance, and when godly love is our motive, we have our best chance of getting closer to imitating God.

So, in these verses in Ephesians 5, we have learned that walking in love requires sanctified sex and sanctified speech. Before leaving this chapter, let's remind ourselves what our identity in Christ entails. We were chosen (elected) before the foundation of the world. As God's (adopted) children, we are to imitate our Father in being holy and blameless. This will be done as we walk in love, in light, and in wisdom. Walking in love requires sexual purity and godly speech. All these attributes, attitudes, and activities are essential for our spiritual warfare. In the next chapter, we see other weapons of warfare.

## Summary Thoughts from Chapter 19, Sanctified Soldiers

- Part of being a warrior is being a fit, trained, loyal representative of the King we represent.

- Darkness cannot drive out darkness; only light can do that. Hate cannot drive out hate; only love can do that.
- Sacrificial love is the most potent weapon in spiritual warfare.
- People tend to invent religious deities to their own liking when they are not guided by the objective, infallible Word of God.

# SECTION THREE
# THE WARFARE

# 20

## THE BATTLE PLAN

One of the strange and lamentable curiosities of our day is how people devoted to non-Christian religions sometimes seem to be more ethical in their lifestyle than Christians are. I was reminded of this during an overseas trip.

My companion said to me, "The third world in some ways is way ahead of us, isn't it?" We were walking through the Bangkok airport *en route* from Malaysia to India when my traveling companion made that observation. As a pastor who had never been out of North America, my friend had a startling baptism of cross-cultural experiences in Southeast Asia. The paradox of dirt, stench, poverty, and confusion combining with beauty, elegance, dignity, and gentleness makes Southeast Asia an enigma, to say the least.

Another paradox had been a topic for us earlier: Why is it that the Christianized West is blatantly and shamelessly so sensually based and immoral and so violence-prone, while the pagan East, steeped in Buddhism, Hinduism, Shintoism, and Animism, seems to be far more Christian in lifestyle? Has it always been so? Or has the West changed?

We had no shortage of time to ponder the paradox, circumnavigating the planet from east to west in thirteen days. An answer emerged. Despite the false content in these religions, the East retains a strong awareness of the transcendent, which translates into reverence. Whether revering ancestors, sages, fearsome deities, or demons, most Asian people are convinced that a higher realm exists. Unfortunately, for many, they live in terror of the spirits or the insecurity of a vengeful god. Love, joy, and peace do not seem to be part of their religions. But reverence is.

**The Right Stuff**

A popular 1983 movie depicted the story of the Mercury 7 astronauts, recounting the dangers and frustrations of these NASA heroes. With their backgrounds as test pilots in the Army, Navy, and Marines, the astronauts had to have "The Right Stuff," the name of the movie, to be considered by NASA for the important space mission. Discipline, courage, and commitment were a few of the qualities they needed. Similarly, for God's military campaign, spiritual soldiers need special behavioral qualities, especially godly, sacrificial love, and that continues the theme of the previous chapter, and unfolds for us the battle plan developed, demonstrated and required by the Commanding Officer:

> ... *walk in love, just as Christ also loved you and gave Himself up for us, an offering and a sacrifice to God ...*
>
> Ephesians 5:2

> Sons and daughters of God should be walking billboards of the loving character of God.

So, how does *walking in love* fit into His battle plan? *Agape* love is the right stuff because people are attracted to real, selfless love. We all want to be loved, and when we see *agape* love in others, we are drawn. Sons and daughters of God should be walking billboards of the loving character of God. And we should take great satisfaction that by walking in love, we not only please the Father and draw others to Him, but we also do further damage to God's enemy. Satan hates the entire system of Christian ethics.

With a solemn warning which Paul rarely used — *for of this you can be sure* — Paul offered some motivations for walking in love:

*For this you know with certainty, that no immoral or impure person or covetous man, who is an idolater, has an inheritance in the kingdom of Christ and God.*

*Let no one deceive you with empty words, for because of these things the wrath of God comes upon the sons of disobedience. Therefore do not be partakers with them ...*

Ephesians 5:5-7

- The *kingdom of Christ and of God* excludes those who are immoral, impure or greedy. Paul mentioned that all of these sins are founded on the greater sin of idolatry. The first motivation to walk in love is not to be disqualified from the kingdom by putting anything or anyone higher than our loyalty and love for God.
- God's wrath is certain to come on those who are disobedient. Paul wanted to make sure that the Ephesians would not be deceived into thinking that if they continued in pagan ways they would be exempt from God's wrath. Verse 6 is similar to Hebrews 10:26-27: *If we deliberately keep on sinning after we have received the knowledge of the truth, no sacrifice for sins is left, but only a fearful expectation of judgment and of raging fire that will consume the enemies of God.*
- So concerned was Paul that the Ephesian believers not be involved in the lifestyle of the surrounding culture that he admonished them in verse 7 not even to be partners with people who participate in the sins he has just mentioned.

## Walk in the Light

With the platform firmly in place, namely, God's grace, the gospel, and His love for all people, including the Gentiles who were most harassed by the demonic world, we move forward into the battle plan, especially revealed in the letter to the Ephesians. Paul had established that platform in the first three chapters, but then in the next three chapters he turned his attention to the need for spiritual maturity for general Christian living, for effective ministry, and for spiritual warfare.

Having warned the Ephesians about the negative lifestyle to avoid if they are to imitate God, Paul then gave them a positive idea. They are able to walk in light (Ephesians 5:8) because they are now children of light rather than children of darkness.

The idea of walking in light suggests that we should live as though we are always being watched. A transparent life is characterized by goodness, righteousness and truth. These qualities are essential for fullness of fellowship, an idea promoted in 1 John 1:7: *If we walk in the light as he is in the light we have fellowship with one another, and the blood of Jesus his Son purifies us from every sin*

> The idea of walking in light suggests that we should live as though we are always being watched.

While the fruit of light encompasses goodness, righteousness and truth, Paul told the Ephesians to avoid the *fruitless deeds of darkness*. In fact, there is a two-fold admonition here. Believers are to abstain from and expose the fruitless deeds of darkness, according to Ephesians 5:11-13. The idea of exposing the sins of others demands much care, because it can be done with the worst of motives and results. John Stott gives good counsel at this point.

> *Unfortunately, however, it is not possible to live in the light and enjoy it without also adopting some attitude towards those who still live in the darkness and to their lifestyle. What attitude will this be? Negatively, take no part in the unfruitful works of darkness. While the light produces the fruit of goodness and truth, the works of darkness are unfruitful, unproductive, barren; they have no beneficial results. So we are to take no part in them, but instead, positively, expose them, "show them up for what they are" (NEB). We may not wish to do this but we cannot help it for this is what light invariably does. Besides, evil deeds deserve to be exposed, that is, to be unmasked and rebuked "for it is a shame even to speak of the things that they do in secret" (verse 12).*[135]

---

135 Stott, *God's New Society*, p. 200.

A phrase that might be helpful here is *disclosure with discretion*. If we are to imitate Christ, exposing sin is always directed against the sin itself. While it is true that in some ways the sinner cannot be separated from the sin, the spotlight of God's purity inevitably will expose unrighteousness (see John 3:19-21).

In all things, if believers are to be imitators of God, they must *find out what pleases the Lord* (verse 10, NIV). The things that please the Lord surely have to do with walking in light and abstaining from and exposing the darkness, while praying and working to bring light to those who *sit in darkness* (Luke 1:79).

## Walk Wisely

Walking in love and walking in light are like two legs of a stool. They are strong and essential, but inadequate. A third leg is needed, and that is supplied by Paul in Ephesians 5:15-20. Paul encourages the Ephesians to walk wisely. On one occasion Jesus told the disciples to be *as harmless as doves*. Walking in love and in light is like being as harmless as doves. But Jesus also told the disciples to be as *wise as serpents*. Walking wisely suggests that part of the formula.

It is one thing to avoid the evils of our culture and to imitate God by living sacrificially and transparently. These are somewhat passive attitudes. It is another thing, however, to be proactive in imitating God. Paul first suggests that we are to make the most of our time, or to use up every opportunity for God because we live in an evil day. It's all about opportunity management.

Using time effectively, a popular topic in business circles, is the first aspect of walking wisely. Time management experts offer seminars to help people gain skills to master their schedules. There are countless time management tools such as electronic organizers to help us manage our lives. For the Christian, time management means making the most of every opportunity, which can best be done by giving ourselves and our day to the Lord. Because *the days are evil*, we will have many opportunities for serving Christ effectively if we are looking at the world with God's values in mind.

Walking wisely entails developing flexible priorities each day beginning with the question, "What does the Lord want me to do today?"

Time management trainers suggest the wisdom of discerning between *effective* and *efficient*. Mary and Martha present a useful example of the difference. Martha represents **efficiency**, which is *doing things right*. She was an excellent hostess, concerned to meet the practical needs of her guests. In normal circumstances, her desire to delegate some of the responsibility to her sister was not unreasonable. Mary illustrates **effectiveness** because she *did the right things*. Jesus affirmed her by saying, *Mary has chosen what is better* (Luke 10:38-42, NIV).

Perhaps nowhere is this distinction more important than in the military. For example, a fighter pilot might be very efficient by watching all the instruments that indicate the "health" of his jet, but still fly off-course by ignoring the flight plan. So, too, may well-intentioned Christian warriors seek to intervene in spiritual warfare, but may not be effective in following the Commanding Officer's orders.

So, what happens on a day when I am not sure what the Lord expects of me in serving Him?

> A person who is living to imitate God will not view other people as interruptions.

I believe it is important that we keep our schedules flexible because we will not always know exactly who God might bring into our lives. *Seek first the kingdom of God* (Matthew 6:33) should apply to our daily schedule. A person who is living to imitate God will not view other people as interruptions. One prayer which I sometimes use is to ask God to screen from me any unnecessary interruptions. That way I can go through the day confidently knowing that every person I meet is a divine encounter. It is true, some people can monopolize our time in an unproductive way. Asking God to screen us from those people will help us immensely. Once we've made a prayer like that, we should then be alert for any opportunities that come our way and view them as appointments which God has put on our schedule.

In the realm of spiritual warfare, wise walking includes spiritual discernment.

*Spiritual discernment is our first line of defense against deception. The Holy Spirit has taken up residence in every believer, and He is not silent when we encounter the counterfeit. Discernment is that little "buzzer" that goes off inside when something is wrong. For example, have you ever visited someone's home where everybody is polite and everything external seems to be in order, but you can cut the air with a knife? Even though nothing visible confirms it, your spirit detects that something is wrong.*

*The motive for true discernment is never self-promotion, personal gain, or to secure an advantage over another person — even an enemy. The Greek word for discernment — diakrino — simply means to make a judgment or a distinction. Discernment has only one function: to distinguish right from wrong so the right can be acknowledged and the wrong can be disregarded. In 1 Corinthians 12:10, discernment is the divinely enabled ability to distinguish a good spirit from a bad spirit. It is a manifestation of the Spirit, which is to be utilized to edify the church.*

*Spiritual discernment is not a function of the mind; it's a function of the spirit. Our union with God is what makes spiritual discernment possible. We rightly divide the word of truth with our minds, but the Spirit helps us know what cannot be objectively verified. We can spiritually discern whether something is right or wrong, but we can't always objectively verify what it is.*[136]

## Knowing and Doing God's Will

Military intelligence comes from the Commanding Officer. Knowing His battle plan and our specific role is critical, but *knowing* without *doing* is dangerous. Besides making the most of all of our opportunities, a second aspect of wise walking includes knowing and doing God's will. Ephesians 5:17 admonishes us to know or understand what the Lord's will is. Many people have difficulty in knowing the will of God. In reality, we all know at least ninety-five per cent of God's will, which is clearly given to us in

---

136  Anderson, *Bondage Breaker*, pp. 178-179.

Scripture. God's will begins with living to reflect His glory. He puts us on the path of salvation and holiness. He encourages us to worship and to witness and to edify one another in the church. Besides those responsibilities, which are the general will of God for all believers, we may also learn His particular will for our lives. This comes through the guidance of the Holy Spirit as we earnestly seek to know and to do God's will.

Those who receive guidance from the Lord are those who are already predisposed to obey.

On one occasion Jesus was being challenged by Jewish leaders about His credentials to teach in the temple court. He replied, *Anyone who chooses to do the will of God will find out whether my teaching comes from God or whether I speak on my own* (John 7:17, NIV). Implied in this statement is that those who receive guidance from the Lord are those who are already predisposed to obey. To do otherwise is to *be foolish* (verse 17). Part of learning the Lord's will is the readiness to obey.

Being filled with the Holy Spirit is a third aspect of walking wisely. Verse 18 is widely known because many Christians are eager to be filled with the Holy Spirit. Notice first that Paul used the imagery of drinking so that we might get an understanding of what it means to be filled. We are not, he said, *to get drunk on wine, which leads to debauchery* but instead to *be filled with the Spirit*. The imagery suggests several things about the filling of the Holy Spirit.

First, we should note that filling is not the same as conversion, baptism in the Holy Spirit, or sanctification. Some theologians suggest that conversion, regeneration, and baptism in the Holy Spirit are synonymous and are one-time events which are not repeatable.[137] On a graph it would be viewed as a dot. Sanctification is the process of being made more holy. On a graph, sanctification would be a diagonal line moving upward.

Being filled with the Holy Spirit is a repeatable event suggested by the fact that a cup can be emptied and refilled many times. On a graph, being

---

137   See John Stott's *The Baptism and Filling of the Holy Spirit*, although my view is that the baptism in (or with) the Holy Spirit is the first instance of being filled with the Spirit, usually a subsequent experience of surrendering to Christ's lordship.

filled with the Holy Spirit would appear like jagged saw teeth, ever moving further upward along the line of sanctification. The reason for repeated fillings is that the purpose for being filled with the Holy Spirit is to engage in effective ministry and warfare. It is the same idea as anointing in the Old Testament. As we give of ourselves in effective ministry we need repeated fillings for the fight.

The preciseness of the Greek word for *filling* is helpful here. It is in the imperative mood, meaning it is not a proposal or a suggestion but an authoritative command. It is obligatory, not optional. Second, it is plural, meaning the whole Christian community, not an elitist few, are to be filled. Third, it is in the passive voice and rendered correctly by the New English Bible, *let the Holy Spirit keep filling you.* There is no technique to learn nor formula to recite. It is rather like opening the valve for a gas to be released. And, fourth, the word for *be filled* is in the present tense suggesting a continuously needed experience, rendered properly, *be being filled.*

The first time a person is filled with the Holy Spirit is likely to be a remarkable and memorable event. In *Keys to the Deeper Life*, A. W. Tozer said,

> *Neither in the Old Testament nor in the New, nor in Christian teaching as found in the writing of the saints as far as my knowledge goes, was any believer ever filled with the Holy Spirit who did not know he had been filled. Neither was anyone filled who did not know when he was filled. And no one was ever filled gradually. The man who does not know when he was filled was never filled (though of course it is possible to forget the date). And the man who hopes to be filled gradually will never be filled at all.[138]*

While Paul does not say in this section how to be filled with the Holy Spirit, other scriptures suggest several helpful ideas: Romans 12:1, 2 urges us to **submit and surrender** to God; Luke 11:13 admonishes us to **ask;** Acts 5:32 commands that we **obey;** and Galatians 3:2 tells us to **believe.**

The question each Christian should face when considering Ephesians 5:18 is not a theological question, but a personal one. *Am I filled with the Holy*

---

138   A. W. Tozer, *Keys to the Deeper Life* (Grand Rapids, MI: Zondervan, 1959), p. 52.

*Spirit?* That is, am I actively engaged in the work of God that I require being filled with the Holy Spirit? Many Christians live so remote from imitating God and so detached from what God is doing in the world that they hardly need to be filled, and one would have no adequate way of knowing whether or not they are filled. If you are unsure of your own filling for effective ministry, the four steps mentioned above — submit, ask, obey, believe — would be a great place to begin.

**Worship Warfare**

In the subsequent verses, Ephesians 5:18-20, Paul describes what it will mean to be filled with the Holy Spirit. First, it will affect our fellowship as we *speak to one another.* In Chapter 4 he gave instructions for changing our speech patterns generally; here he tells about our conversation in the church. This is the *koinonia* for which the early church was well known. The particular kind of speaking that Paul admonishes is through the use of *psalms, hymns, and spiritual songs.* That is, being filled with the Holy Spirit will result in a life of worship. Furthermore, that worship will not just be public as we speak to one another but it will also be personal and private as we *sing and make music in (y)our heart* (verse 19). And finally, being filled with the Holy Spirit will mean that we will live as grateful people. We are always to be *giving thanks to God the Father for everything, in the name of our Lord Jesus Christ.* Living this way exposes an attitude which pleases God, and makes us to be "Worshipping Warriors."

So, we who are the Church and the Battlefield are also the Warriors. Although we are not presenting in this book the secrets to demon exorcism or the five easy steps to success in spiritual warfare, be assured that as you are filled with the Holy Spirit, you have all you need to succeed in spiritual warfare.[139] With the authority Jesus has given us over the principalities, powers, rulers and unclean beings that plague His people and keep the

---

139   While not presenting formulaic or ritualistic methodologies, books by Neil Anderson and Charles Kraft, cited in the Bibliography, give useful insights for this level of spiritual warfare.

world frozen in sin, and besides the elements of the Christian life mentioned above, there are two offensive weapons that we have at our disposal but we may not recognize as weapons. One is prayer; the other is worship. We say more about prayer in Chapter 27 when we consider Paul's Prayer Concerns.

In my less sanctified days, I have to admit, I did not like Sunday mornings; afternoons were great because I was either playing sports or watching it. But mornings at church were boring to me. The key words here are "to me." That's because I did not know what was going on. I saw church as merely a religious service. I think that's true for a lot of people, which is why church attendance is down. That is why some people say church is boring. That is why some complain that they "didn't get anything out of it." Question: When did church become a shopping mall where we go to "get" what we think we need? Worship is not about getting, but about giving; we ... *bring the sacrifice of praise into the house of the Lord* (Jeremiah 33:11).

Today, Sunday morning is my favorite time of the week because now I "get it." Worship is the environment, culture, and activity of heaven, and it is what Satan hates. That is why he constantly lured Israel into the worship of false gods and idolatry. Satan still hates worship of the true God.

> Worship is the environment, culture, and activity of heaven, and it is what Satan hates.

When God's people gather in the presence of Jesus Christ and pour out their love in heartfelt, exuberant praise, Satan's defeat is re-enacted. Every week! For sure, when we take communion, but also in every hymn or praise song, in the fellowship of God's children, in the offering of their souls and their substance, and in the strengthening and equipping they get from His Word — all of these and other worship activities are punches in Satan's gut. He wants no part of it.

Here are some thoughts about worship that I hope will elevate your appreciation for this strategic part of our warfare:

- Worship is why we are; God created us to be worshippers, and only those who worship Him willingly will be in His eternal Kingdom.

- Worship is the only eternal activity that we know about; the book of Revelation seems to bear this out.
- Worship is in the heart of everyone. No cultures or people groups have been discovered who were not worshippers of someone or something.
- Worship takes devoted attentiveness. Earth is the warm-up place where we learn to "fix our eyes on Jesus."
- Worship is vertical; it calls us into the heavenlies where we join with the angels, cherubim and seraphim in adoring the glorious God who loves us.
- Worship is the atmosphere of revelation. As we worship, we grow in our understanding of God and insights into His Word.

Have you ever wondered what worship is like in heaven? I mean, if worship is our main eternal activity, what is heavenly worship like? The New Testament worship manual of the church, the book of Revelation, gives several glimpses into the heavenlies through John's visions.

There we find that worship:
- Focuses on the character of God, Revelation 4:8, 11; 15:3, 4
- Is repetitious, Revelation 4:8-11
- They sing NEW songs, Revelation 5:9
- It is LOUD, Revelation 5:11-12; 7:10; 19:1-3
- It causes people to fall down in reverence, Revelation 5:14; 7:11; 11:16; 19:4
- It is multi-cultural, Revelation 7:9

I can imagine that worship in heaven includes a lot more than these characteristics, but let us be warned that if these ideas are threatening to us, we may find ourselves to be uncomfortably awkward in heaven. Maybe, in His mercy, God will allow us to take a worship remedial course before joining heartily with all the other celestial beings!

David was a man passionate about worship and warfare. About some of his warfare I am baffled and need to leave to the sovereignty of God. But there's no doubting David's dual identity. Look at Psalm 144. In verse 1 he blesses God, who *trains my hands for war and gives my fingers skill for battle.* And then in verse 9 he decides to *sing a new song to you, O God! I will sing your praises with a ten-stringed harp.* Imagine those same fingers plucking bowstrings and harp strings! If that isn't a picture of the worshipping warrior!

For David, I am convinced, there was nothing contradictory about using his skill in battle and in worship because he viewed his enemies as God's enemies. Whether fighting for God or singing for God, David was doing God's will. As we move further into the topic of warfare, we will see the same thing; one of the most powerful weapons of spiritual warfare is worship.

## Summary Thoughts from Chapter 20, The Battle Plan

- The idea of walking in light suggests that we should live as though we are always being watched.
- Spiritual discernment is not a function of the mind; it's a function of the spirit. Our union with God is what makes spiritual discernment possible.
- Those who receive guidance from the Lord are those who are already predisposed to obey.
- There are two offensive weapons that we have at our disposal. One is prayer; the other is worship.
- Worship is the environment, culture, and activity of heaven, and it is what Satan hates.

.

# 21

## WARRIOR QUALITIES

Military soldiers are expected to be fit. The grueling weeks of boot camp are intended to tone muscles and increase endurance to battle-ready conditions. Similarly, in preparing for spiritual warfare, spiritual fitness is critical.

### Moral Qualities

After one's basic relationship with Christ, Paul put a strong emphasis on moral qualities in Ephesians 4:1-7. These qualities come under the broad category of *live a life worthy of the calling you have received*. A more literal translation of that phrase is *walk worthy of the calling with which you have been called* (NASB). In these seven verses Paul *entreats* us to *walk...with all humility and gentleness, with patience, showing forbearance to one another in love, being diligent to preserve the unity of the Spirit in the bond of peace.*

#### Humility and Gentleness

The first two moral qualities that are emphasized are humility and gentleness. Humility means lowliness. Prior to the example of Christ and Christian teaching, the Greek word for humility was a derisive term. Jesus and his powerful way of living humbly gave a positive connotation to this word. Biblical humility stands opposed to arrogance, self-conceit, and self-exaltation. Romans 12:3 gives a similar emphasis — *Do not think of yourself more highly than you ought* — and verse 16 says *Don't be proud but be willing to associate with people of low position. Don't be conceited.* The humility Paul writes about is the humble recognition of the worth and value of other people. We certainly see that demonstrated in the life of our Lord on nearly every page of the Gospels.

MacMillan warns us of the danger of spiritual pride corrupting even warriors who have successfully engaged the enemy. Almost as a grenade thrown behind as the devil flees from us (James 4:7), a sense of self-congratulation can destroy the humility that is necessary for further victories.

> *While belief thus introduces us to our place of throne power, only humility will ensure our retaining it. As we compare the abounding grace of God and our own utter unworthiness, the question arises: Should we need such a warning? Praise God, it becomes less necessary as the soul grows in grace and the likeness of the Son increases in us. But we know little of the plague of our own hearts if we think the danger is ever over. The forces against whom we contend, the principalities and powers, the world rulers of this darkness, the hosts of wicked spirits in the heavenlies, know us far better than we know ourselves. As we attack them, and authority is naught but a long-drawn-out warfare against them, their return stroke is often swift and crushing. With a strategy gained in long experience in spiritual battles, they know that the offensive is their best mode of defense. One of their tested weapons is spiritual pride, and too often it proves effective.*

> *With believers, the consuming desire to be independent is something which even the regenerated heart does not fully overcome. Often, just after some signal victory has been gained, there comes the subtle whisper of the enemy, and the overcomer is swiftly shorn of strength through feeling that he is strong.*

*With profound humility, however, there may go the greatest boldness in the Name. True boldness is faith in full manifestation. When God has spoken, to hold back is not humility but unbelief. In the exercise of authority, there is needed a divine courage that fears nothing but God and reaches out strong hands to bind and to restrain all that is contrary to Him. But with this courage, there must be a continual and close abiding in God, a spirit that is alert to every urge and check from Him and a mind that is steeped in the Word of God.*[140]

> In the exercise of authority, there is needed a divine courage that fears nothing but God.

Boldness, MacMillan's "divine courage," does not in any way eliminate the possibility of being gentle. Surely, we see both qualities in our Lord. *Gentleness* was the word used to describe an animal trained to obey. It is the gentleness of the strong whose strength is under control. It is the absence of the need to assert personal rights to man or God. The gentle person thinks as little of his or her personal claims as the humble person thinks of his or her personal merits. We see this in Jesus particularly in Matthew 11:29 where He said, *Take my yoke upon you and learn from me for I am gentle and humble in heart.* These two qualities are essential on the spiritual battlefield because by having them, one must be fully dependent on the Lord. Effective spiritual warriors know the truth of *...apart from Me you can do nothing* (John 15:5).

### Patience and Forbearance

Another duet of moral qualities is described by the phrase, *Be patient, bear with one another in love.* Patience is a disposition that leads to the suppression of anger. It describes the person who has the motive and power to take revenge but never does so. We might imagine a big, strong dog lying idly while a little puppy runs around it, furiously yapping trying to distract it or entice it into a fight.

Patience bears with the impositions and discourtesies of others.

---

140   MacMillan, pp. 34-36.

In Colossians 3:12-13, Paul exhorts believers to *Bear with each other and forgive whatever grievances you may have against one another*. This kind of tolerance is a willingness to suspend judgment hoping for the best in another person. We are to demonstrate these godly graces in love. This is the well-known *agape* love which William Barclay describes as, *that quality of mind and heart which compels a Christian never to feel any bitterness, never to feel any desire for revenge, but always to seek nothing but the highest good of every man no matter what men do to him.*[141]

### Unity

Having the right temperament through godly moral qualities is critical for spiritual warriors, but so is commitment to certain truths that Paul emphasizes. Ephesians 4:4-6 mentions these fundamental doctrines. Notice how few and simple they are. Verse 4 indicates that as sure as there is only one Holy Spirit, so is there only one body of believers who have the same hope — the hope of eternal life. They will live together forever.

Paul wants believers to understand that there is only one Holy Spirit. In today's church we need to reclaim this truth. Some churches need to remember that there is a Holy Spirit. I heard British preacher David Pawson observe that the Trinity for the Roman Catholic Church has become God the Father, God the Son and God the Holy Virgin, while the Trinity for the Protestant Church has become God the Father, God the Son and God the Holy Scriptures. And when the Holy Spirit is emphasized, all too often we have replaced the person of the Holy Spirit with His spiritual gifts. Surely the proper exercise of spiritual gifts should be encouraged, but the Holy Spirit calls us always to defer to others for the sake of unity rather than allow our perspective on the role and gifts of the Spirit to cause dissension.

Paul goes on to state that just as certain as there is only one Lord Jesus Christ, so is there only one basic belief by which we know Him and only one entrance into His Lordship (verse 5). The Galatian believers received

---

141  William Barclay, *The Daily Study Bible, The Letters to the Galatians and Ephesians* (Philadelphia: Westminster Press, 1954), p. 165.

Paul's full treatment on this issue when he wrote, *As we have already said, so now I say again: If anybody is preaching to you a gospel other than what you accepted, let him be eternally condemned* (Galatians 1:9, NIV).

Without any doubt Christology is a watershed doctrine. Full belief in the virgin birth, sinless life, atoning death, bodily

Without any doubt Christology is a watershed doctrine.

resurrection, ascension, and visible return of Jesus is essential for really knowing Christ. Failure to trust these factors about Him distorts His identity and will surely render one impotent in the face of spiritual forces that want us to deny these truths.

And just as certain as there is only one God, so there is only one Christian family over whom He is Father (verse 6). He is over all; that is, He is sovereign and transcendent. He is through all; that is, He is diffused through believers and the churches. And He is in all, meaning He is personal and immanent.

With this trinitarian expression of the person of God and with these most essential beliefs, Paul affirms that believers must come together in organic unity around these truths. There are many secondary doctrines which leave room for varying viewpoints and interpretations, but these ideas about the three persons of the Godhead are non-negotiable.

We need to remind ourselves often that Paul was not writing just to edify individual believers, but to the whole Church, the body of Christ. So, these injunctions are to help the entire church, at Ephesus and all churches, to apply these qualities for the sake of a higher goal, the achieving of unity.

In our day there is a strong movement to put unity ahead of truth, and, surely, we should strive for peace in the Church. Significantly, immediately after his plea for unity in Ephesians 1:3, the Apostle cites three essential truths about the Trinity:

> *There is one body and one Spirit, just as also you were called in one hope of your calling; one Lord, one faith, one baptism, one God and Father of all who is over all and through all and in all.*

> Ephesians 4:4-6

There are many warnings in Scripture about false prophets and teachers who will infect the Church with teachings that corrupt the purity of the gospel and distort the true identity of Christ, as we saw from Galatians 1:9, above. We are not to entertain or listen to such people.[142]

Paul also emphasizes that for us to walk strongly in our faith, we must learn to appreciate diversity. Verse 7 emphasizes this by saying, *But to each one of us grace has been given as Christ apportioned it.* God gives grace to all but in different measures. This is consistent with His love. A gift to be personal cannot be the same given to every person. God's grace does not come in a form letter. The people in Christ's body must learn to appreciate how different members function. This is emphasized in 1 Corinthians 12 where literal bodily parts are cited as being dependent on one another. Paul emphasizes the same idea in talking about spiritual gifts. Christians have been gifted individually by God. No one gift is normative or superior. This calls on Christians to learn to appreciate the diversity and honor others for the way God has gifted them.

**Prepared Personnel**

Some of the diversity in the body of Christ is seen in Ephesians 4:8-10 where Paul cites an Old Testament reference and then gives a little commentary about it. Psalm 68:18 is a Messianic verse which seems to apply to the post-death, pre-resurrection experience of Jesus who descended to the lower parts of the earth to release captives and then ascended on high, giving gifts to men. Actually, more consistent with the wording of Psalm 68:18, the gifts are the people themselves who have been given to the Church, and as leaders they have responsibilities for guiding its growth, proclaiming and guarding the truth, and caring for the flock.

> Satan likes nothing more than to disrupt and disqualify the church from its mission.

In the realm of spiritual warfare, it is important to have the proper personnel leading the church because Satan likes nothing more than to disrupt and disqualify the church

---

142  See, for instance, Matthew 7:15; 24:4; 2 John 10; and Jude 4.

from its mission. It is essential that these leaders walk in maturity but also walk in unity. One method of Roman warfare provides a good picture of this. Soldiers carried shields that interlocked with one another, and they marched as a wedge. Seemingly they would be invulnerable if the entire regiment would be strong enough to hold ranks in the midst of attack.

In Ephesians 4 the gifts Christ has given to the Church are people. They are not special abilities or talents, but individuals who are gifts to the Church.[143] Actually, Paul cites four (or five) offices within the Church which were held by gifted men.

First on the list are apostles — people sent forth with a message and authority to deliver it. These apostles were church planters or missionaries. They were the ones who took the gospel beyond its previous borders to introduce new communities to the Christian faith.

The original twelve apostles were historically unique. When the first apostles were seeking to replace Judas, Peter gave the job criteria this way: *… men who have been with us the whole time the Lord Jesus went in and out among us, beginning from John's baptism to the time when Jesus was taken up from us. For one of these must become a witness with us of his resurrection* (Acts 1:21, 22). These two criteria — eyewitnesses to the life and to the resurrected Jesus — are not historically repeatable. The enduring witness of the apostles to the Lord's resurrection is our New Testament. In that sense, there have not been and cannot be any new apostles since the days of the early church.

There are, however, many people who continue to exercise spiritual authority and missionary ministry much like the first-century apostles. In fact, besides the original twelve and Paul, the New Testament uses that term to describe Barnabas, James (the Lord's brother), Andronicus, Junia (a feminine name; a woman?), Epaphroditus, Apollos, Silas, and Timothy who are mentioned by name. Second Corinthians 8:23 implies a large band of people who did apostolic work, but did not have the credentials of the twelve.

---

143  These are not the same as the *charismata* of Romans 12 or the *manifestations* of 1 Corinthians 12.

The second category of gifts to the Church are the prophets or proclaimers of God's truth. The first-century prophets who may also have been used by God to communicate the revelation of scripture were also unique. The prophet's more evident role in the churches was to proclaim messages from God to those immediate communities. Scripture does not define the job of a prophet in a way that would preclude contemporary people from filling that role. For the most part, we find prophets today being preachers who have a ministry of proclamation. Usually the focus of their message is righteousness. The role of a prophet, even in Old Testament days, was not primarily foretelling but forth-telling. Prophets are not primarily predictors but proclaimers.

Third, Paul cites evangelists as being gifts to the church. Evangelists are heralds of the gospel. They are messengers who share the gospel either with individuals or groups of people. The word for evangelist is an expansion of the word *angel.* An angel is primarily a messenger for God. Philip, who is best known because of his ministry to the Ethiopian eunuch, is called *the evangelist* (Acts 21:8). While all believers should *do the work of an evangelist* (2 Timothy 4:5), some believers are especially gifted by God to be harvesters of souls. In the past century Billy Graham was surely the most prominently known evangelist.

Finally, Paul puts together two functions into one office: pastor and teacher. These are shepherds of local flocks. They are also ministers of the Word of God whose primary responsibility is to communicate and clarify God's truth. Most scholars believe Paul meant to mention them as one position because that is how they functioned. The pastors did the teaching and the teachers did the pastoring. For the most part, that is how it is today. In the local church some ministers emphasize their pastoral duties of caring for and shepherding their people. Other pastors emphasize their education responsibilities by providing enlightenment and guidance. Usually, both functions are the responsibility of church ministers.

In the early church all five of these functions were carried out by prominent Christians. Peter and Paul were apostles; James clearly was a prophet; Philip, an evangelist; Timothy, a pastor; and Apollos, a teacher. The apostles were like officers entrusted by the Commander to recruit (apostles and evangelists), train (prophets and teachers), and mobilize the troops (the laity) for battle. All the troops would need the spiritual armor Paul tells about in Ephesians 6 because as matured warriors they would all engage in battle. Among the leaders given to the Church, none are specifically designated for exorcism. In fact, in the book of Acts it seems that apostles and others did not intentionally engage in exorcism, but rather followed the example of their Lord who ministered deliverance in the course of His daily ministry.[144]

The reason God has given these people-gifts to the Church is *to prepare God's people for works of service* (verse 12). The concept of equipping the laity seemed to have been lost to the Church for many centuries. The professionally trained clergy took over the work of the Church, and less educated lay people were all too willing to let them. However, the ministry of the members is now being recovered in many places.

With the troops recruited, assembled, and trained, we are ready for further preparation for battle.

## Summary Thoughts from Chapter 21, Warrior Qualities

* After one's basic relationship with Christ, Paul put a strong emphasis on moral qualities.
* In the exercise of authority, there is needed a divine courage that fears nothing but God.
* Satan likes nothing more than to disrupt and disqualify the church from its mission.
* Among the leaders given to the Church, none are specifically designated for exorcism.

---

144   In fact, it appears in the Gospels that in only three cases did Jesus proactively expel demons; all other demonized people came to Him. The three exceptions were two who were muted by the demons and could not call out to Jesus (Matthew 9:32 and 12:22) and an elderly woman whom a demon had kept bent over for 18 years (Luke 13:10-17).

# 22

## MYSTERIES IN THE WAR

Back in Chapter 20 we mentioned that worship is a powerful strategy and weapon in spiritual warfare. As you read that, you might have been asking, "How so? I sit or stand in church on Sundays, along with the congregation, singing nice traditional or contemporary songs. It's all rather orderly and predictable, without any hint of warfare."

For us, it's true, our worship does not seem very confrontational. For God's enemy — he hates it. He hates when followers of Christ gather to praise and adore the Son of God, the One who has overcome Satan's evil efforts to subvert the plan of God to have an obedient, harmonious, worshipping family. Consequently, though he is a defeated foe, Satan continues to thrash about, much like the dead rattler I decapitated, mentioned in Chapter 1. So, the warfare continues, even if we are oblivious to it. We are strongly admonished in Scripture to **be alert** and **watch out**, words Jesus used frequently, as we will see in Chapter 29.

Spiritual warfare is an important topic, and one that makes many Christians nervous. We certainly see Jesus and His first-century followers casting out demons and imparting healings, and we surely want to embrace the worldview of Jesus, but ... most twenty-first-century western Christians are a little, or very, uncomfortable with the idea of such an evil-spirit-filled worldview. We hear of excesses that seem to be close to Christian animism, and truthfully, many people fear open use of spiritual warfare.

But Ephesians 6:10-18 will not let us dodge the issue. As discussed earlier, I believe that the entire Epistle to the Ephesians needs to be understood in the light of Acts 19 and the riot in Ephesus about the goddess Artemis. No wonder Paul wanted the church at Ephesus to recognize the officers in the warfare: Apostles, Prophets, Evangelists, Pastors /Teachers (Ephesians 4:11). I am not a military hero in the spiritual world, by any means, but an honest reading of scripture leads me to these observations:

**Ten Observations about Spiritual Warfare**
1. Spiritual Warfare is not a trendy, new church fad.

   *... for still our ancient foe does seek to work us woe* (*A Mighty Fortress Is Our God,* Martin Luther).
2. The Scriptures are saturated with a spiritual warfare worldview
   — from the serpent in Genesis 3 to the dragon in Revelation 20.
3. The beginning strategy for spiritual warfare comes from Paul's letter to the church most plagued by satanic presence — Ephesus.

   The strategy is PRAYER.
4. Jesus Christ put the primary responsibility for spiritual warfare into the hands of apostles.

   Matthew 16:17-19
5. The Church today is recovering the ministries most needed for this warfare, the five-fold offices of Ephesians 4:11.

   These offices are available *until we all ... become mature ...* (4:13).
6. Despite waging spiritual warfare without key "officers" for centuries, we have almost completed the job.[145]

---

145   See Patrick Johnstone, *The Church Is Bigger Than You Think* (Gerrards Cross, Bucks, UK: Christian Focus Publications Publishers / WEC, 1998).

7.  Many parts of the church are recovering a biblical understanding and use of apostolic ministry.

8.  Spiritual warfare engages local, regional, and global theatres of battle.

9.  The *schemes of the devil* include a hierarchy of evil spiritual beings. Ephesians 6:11, 12

10. While the armor is essential, those inside the armor must be prayer warriors who *pray at all times in the Spirit.* Ephesians 6:18

## Prerequisites for Spiritual Warfare

In preparing to receive our "orders" for spiritual warfare, we must make sure we are spiritually fit. In preparation for our heavenly role, the Apostle Paul encourages the Church with these words:

*And may you have the power to understand, as all God's people should, how wide, how long, how high and how deep his love is. May you experience the love of Christ, though it is too great to understand fully. Then you will be made complete with all the fullness of life and power that comes from God.*

Ephesians 3:18-19, NLT

As a result of the inner strengthening received through God's Holy Spirit and Christ's dwelling in their hearts through faith, Paul prays that the Ephesians would also be able to experience or comprehend with all other believers the breadth and length and height and depth of Christ's love. Paul purposely depicts Christ's love as three dimensional, using these four adjectives: broad, long, high and deep. We might view it as a cross reaching high, planted deep, spanning a length and being broad and strong enough to carry the weight of love which Christ conveys to us.

More important than experiencing and comprehending the love of Christ is to know that love which surpasses knowledge. This may sound like double talk but it is not. Paul uses an intensified form of the word for *know* to describe an experiential knowledge.[146] The Christian is not one who knows about God, Jesus, the Bible, the Church, etc., but one who knows God personally by experience with Jesus Christ.

> The Christian is not one who knows about God, Jesus, the Bible, the Church, etc., but one who knows God personally by experience with Jesus Christ.

Why was it so important to Paul for the Ephesian believers to have this intense personal knowledge of the love of Christ? In Ephesians 1:7-14 Paul emphasized the theological truths of our experience with Christ. These ideas cannot be understood adequately by the mind without being appropriated for personal blessing. Paul would not be content with that. He wants believers to know God's love experientially; that is, personally to be enveloped by the presence of Christ's love. This love is like a healing atmosphere in which we thrive. It communicates the fullness of God's forgiveness regardless of what deeds we might have done to offend Him. This love brings us into God's forever-family, a family consisting of those in heaven and earth (verse 15), a family of all the saints (verse 18), many of whom are experiencing now a much more immediate awareness of the love of Christ because He is not just in them, they are with Him.

> Satan surely enjoys assailing shallow disciples whose head-knowledge about the Lord provides them little protection.

In view of the present, real danger of the demonic atmosphere of Ephesus, Paul knew that with Christ truly present in the believers' lives, the devil would not have the opportunity to harass and beleaguer His saints. On the other hand, Satan surely enjoys assailing shallow disciples whose head-knowledge about the Lord provides them little protection.

The difference between knowing about God's wonderful love and appropriating it is illustrated by the crippled man who sat for years near the pool of Bethesda (John 5:1-15). Every time the water was stirred, someone else would get into the pool before him. Presumably, they were healed

---

146   *Epignosis*, not just *gnosis*.

because they entered into a full "knowledge" of the pool, an experiential knowledge.

The man crippled for thirty-eight years believed in the healing power of the pool when the water was stirred, but his knowledge did not translate into renewed health. His disability remained. And he never did get into the pool. Jesus had something better in store for him. We do not know what became of others who made it into the pool in time to be healed. Did they go on in life as devoted lovers of God? Did their healing change their heart? Were they ever able to get beyond the power of the pool to the Power behind the pool, and learn to worship God in purity and truth? The pool may have become an obstacle to right belief. This man, however, not only was healed but also met the Master, the One whose healing power could save entirely.

As part of the strategy of God's Battle Plan, Paul wants all of God's people to live in that atmosphere of full and complete acceptance and experiential love. He wants their entire lives to be permeated by a perpetual awareness of the love of Christ. Paul yearned that each believer would have a full, eternal, perpetual, all-encompassing, intellectual, emotional, experiential, filial, and transforming encounter with the love of Christ. Toward this end Paul prayed that God would grant believers the sense of His presence which is experienced only as we are empowered inwardly through God's Spirit. Christ's presence dwelling in our hearts through faith becomes the rooting and grounding of a rich experiential knowledge of the love of Christ.

Professor MacMillan richly elaborates on the blessings and benefits of this intimate, personal relationship with the Lord as a key in thwarting the schemes of Satan.

> ... the Epistle to the Ephesians (2:5-6) gives a wonderful breadth to the fact of the relationship of the Christian to his risen Lord. He is made alive with Christ through spiritual regeneration, raised up with Him in resurrection and made to sit with Him 'in heavenly places' where Christ is enthroned at the right hand of God. The Apostle Paul thus anticipates the message of the Savior to the seven churches (Revelation 2-3) and sets forth the basis of the

*victorious life of the 'over-comer,' which so few Christians understand or seek to enter into. It is throughout an appropriation by faith of that which the Spirit reveals as ours in Christ Jesus. It is a present-day experience received through yieldedness to the cross. It is the acceptance of that identification with Christ which brings His 'throne power' into the earthly ministry of the believer. It is a living 'by the faith of the Son of God, who loved us and gave himself up for us.' It is a practical exercising of the Lord's authority in matters which are met in His service. It is, moreover, workable and brings a blessing to the believer and to others who seek Him for help. Finally, it is all of God, 'who hath reconciled us to himself by Jesus Christ, and hath given to us the ministry of reconciliation' (2 Corinthians 5:18) and also the ministry of liberation of men from the powers of the air.*[147]

## The Mysteries

The Commander in Chief of the spiritual war has always had total command of the war. He knows the end from the beginning and all that happens in between. But only He knows. As the Apostle Paul asks, *Who has known the mind of the Lord?* (Romans 11:34, quoting Isaiah 40:13). God's ways are not our ways, and He reveals only what He chooses for us to know. He also chooses when, how and to whom He will reveal truth. Much of what occurs in the theater of battle has been kept from humans and Satan as *mystery.*

*Musterion* is an important New Testament word, which does not refer to a genre of literature or an unresolvable puzzle, as the English word usually connotes. Thayer's Greek lexicon shows several usages of the term, which appears 27 times in the New Testament. The predominant usages concern *a hidden purpose or counsel; secret will of God: the secret counsels which govern God in dealing with the righteous, which are hidden from ungodly and wicked men but plain to the godly.*[148]

---

147   MacMillan, pp. 171-172.

148   Thayer's Greek Lexicon, https://www.biblestudytools.com/lexicons/greek/kjv/epouranios.html.

Imagine, for example, as I did many years ago in a British pub, watching four people playing a card game with a small board in front of them, laying out cards one at a time and moving little pegs on the board. Later, I found out the game is called Cribbage, and I even learned how to play it. But seeing it initially baffled me completely, even though the players knew exactly what they were doing. To me, it was a mystery, not because I was not as smart as they, but because I didn't have the special knowledge they had. That is what a *musterion* is.

It should be quite evident to all believers that this warfare is not like an earthly battle. The opponents are spiritual beings, so traditional armaments and battle strategies are useless. What is not so evident is how this warfare is being waged. Even for the most enlightened soldier of the cross much of the imagery of Revelation, for example, remains mysterious. We will look at the *Apocalypse,* the Greek name for Revelation, and give some sanctified speculation about some of those images, but much mystery remains. What is not a mystery, however, is that we are engaged in the battle of the ages and the true Creator God has decisively won the war, even as the battle continues.

Some aspects of our realities remain a mystery, even to the believer. While we are told the time of fulfillment of this mystery, namely, *when the times will have reached their fulfillment,* we are not told when that will be. Humans are curious about that, but from God's perspective, apparently, we do not need to know.

However, the end of the war is alluded to in Revelation 10:4-7 where John was ready to write about something he saw, but he *heard a voice from heaven saying, "Seal up the things which the seven peals of thunder have spoken and do not write them."* Then John learned that *"in the days of the voice of the seventh angel, when he is about to sound, then the mystery of God is finished, as He preached to His servants the prophets."*

## Unlocking the Mysteries

Fifteen of the occurrences of *musterion* touch on the issues of God's grace, the gospel, and the Gentiles, and illuminate the secret plan used by

God to win the war. For example, Ephesians 1:9, *He made known to us the mystery of His will…that is, the summing up of all things in Christ, things in the heavens and things upon the earth.*

These three topics wherein believers are clued into the mysteries — grace, gospel, and Gentiles — remain mysterious to unbelievers because they do not have the apparatus to understand, namely, a spirit that is alive to God, the Holy Spirit. First Corinthians 2:14 makes this clear: *But people who don't have the Spirit can't receive these truths from God's Spirit. It all sounds foolish to them and they can't understand it, for only those who are spiritual can understand what the Spirit means.* The first disciples were confused about some of the teachings of Jesus, so He said to them,

> *I have much more to say to you, more than you can now bear. But when he, the Spirit of truth, comes, he will guide you into all the truth. He will not speak on his own; he will speak only what he hears, and he will tell you what is yet to come.*

> John 16:12-13, NIV

> The mysteries were held in the counsel of God until the Holy Spirit inhabited a people He could trust.

The mysteries were held in the counsel of God until the Holy Spirit inhabited a people He could trust. These truths were kept secret from the enemies of God who tried to subvert the plan of God, but after His ascension Christ had the faithful disciples remain cloistered until they received the power He sent, the Holy Spirit, from His privileged seat of authority at the right hand of the Father. With the Spirit of God now in His new covenant people, Jesus could reveal the mysteries of grace, the gospel, and the Gentiles.

## The Mystery of Grace

Unsaved people, especially entertainers, love to sing *Amazing Grace,* but unbelievers do not and cannot understand grace. For them, it is more than amazing; it is mysterious. They may be able to give a rational definition of grace, but grace is a truth that must be understood from the inside. Paul makes this clear:

*God decided in advance to adopt us into his own family by bringing us to himself through Jesus Christ. This is what he wanted to do, and it gave him great pleasure. So we praise God for the glorious* **grace he has poured out on us who belong to his dear Son**. *He is so rich in kindness and grace that he purchased our freedom with the blood of his Son and forgave our sins. He has showered his kindness on us, along with all wisdom and understanding.*

**God has now revealed to us his mysterious plan** *regarding Christ, a plan to fulfill his own good pleasure. And this is the plan: At the right time he will bring together under the authority of Christ — everything in heaven and on earth.*

Ephesians 1:5-10 (NLT), emphasis added

The source of the forgiveness is the blood of Jesus, according to Ephesians 1:7. Blood, being the most valuable substance in the world, is the ultimate payment for sin, and the perfect blood of Jesus Christ is the totally

> "There's Power in the Blood." No other substance, regardless of its value, is acceptable to God as a payment for sin.

potent weapon that defeats the devil. That's why we sing, "There's Power in the Blood." No other substance, regardless of its value, is acceptable to God as a payment for sin. The Cain and Abel story illustrates this vividly, as Cain was rebuked by God for bringing a bloodless sacrifice. Through that example — Cain trivializing the seriousness of his sin — the people of God learned that sin is of such serious consequence that only the shedding of blood would be acceptable to God for the remission of sins (see Hebrews 9:22). Cain-sacrifice is akin to all religious attempts to placate God through good works or human effort.

The motivation for offering the blood of Jesus was the riches of the Father's grace. He lavished his grace on those who were chosen and adopted in Christ in such a way that all their trespasses have been cleansed by the blood of Jesus. Satan's grip on the worst sinner cannot prevail when the blood of God's grace is applied.

As noted earlier, God's grace is at one and the same time unnecessary and essential. It is unnecessary from God's perspective in that nothing forced God to offer such a gift. No constraint or compulsion was on God to provide for man's forgiveness other than His eternal plan and love. We should not view the great cosmic warfare between God and Satan as merely God seeking revenge against His enemy, but rather as a loving Father intent on rescuing His children from eternal destruction. God was not compelled to rescue us; He chose to.

On the other hand, His grace is entirely essential if God is to redeem His fallen creation. The effects of sin are so great that no part of the creation, including mankind, retained enough value to merit God's good pleasure. Something from outside of creation needed to be offered to atone for the sins of mankind. Therefore, God, by His own free choice and kindly disposition, offered up His own Son, the second person of the Trinity, to shed His blood as the payment for our redemption.[149]

Satan clearly did not have a clue about what God was up to by this bizarre sacrificial act. Undoubtedly, Satan thought he had won the war. While Jesus did not succumb to Satan's temptations earlier, Satan invaded Judas and inspired him to betray the innocent blood (John 13:27 and Matthew 27:4). The idea of resurrection never occurred to Satan; for those still under his sway, disbelief in the resurrection of Jesus and refusal to bow before the resurrected One is the ultimate damning sin, as Peter boldly stated in Acts 4:10-12 (NLT) explaining how, or by whom, a crippled man was healed.

> Satan clearly did not have a clue about what God was up to by this bizarre sacrificial act. Undoubtedly, Satan thought he had won the war.

---

149 Some have questioned how, even with the virgin birth, Jesus did not inherit our sinful nature since Mary was also a daughter of Adam. Roman Catholic theology teaches that her conception was free from original sin by virtue of the merits of her son Jesus Christ. Perhaps just as speculative, but more likely is the view that the bloodline of Jesus came not from His mother, but His Father through the Holy Spirit by whom Jesus was sired. In fact, in both Matthew 1 and Luke 3 the genealogy of Jesus is traced back to Joseph, who *as it was being thought* (Luke 3:23, literally in Greek) was his father.

*Let me clearly state to you and to all the people of Israel that he was healed by the powerful name of Jesus Christ the Nazarene, the man you crucified but whom God raised from the dead .... There is salvation in no one else! God has given no other name under heaven by which we must be saved.*

Saved from what? From Satan's evil plan to destroy God's creation, especially the ones made in His image, human beings. Satan cannot tolerate the thought that worshippers of God will take his place in the heavenlies. His success in causing Adam and Eve to sin and break fellowship with God brought the entire creation under his bondage. Humans born since the fall of Adam and Eve are, by nature, under condemnation. God's judgment against sin has already been made.

There will be no sin or hint of unholiness in His eternal presence. Jesus made this clear to the Jewish leader Nicodemus, saying that, *There is no judgment against anyone who believes in him* (God's Son). *But anyone who does not believe in him has already been judged for not believing in God's one and only Son* (John 3:18). In other words, for the unbelieving, Satan's curse is in full force. The curse can be broken only by receiving the grace that enables us to believe.

Paul says that prior to grace we are dead because of or on account of our trespasses and sins, which cause us to fail to meet God's standards. That is the predicament of every human prior to receiving grace. In helping the Ephesians recall the dominance of sin in their lives, Paul reminds them about the *sins in which you used to live.* Literally, the phrase refers to walking in sin, that is, they were daily conversant with sin, devoted to it, surrounded by it and clothed with it.

Outside of the grace of God we are pawns to ungodly powers. There are the powers of this world or this age. We can be controlled by conformity to the value system of the cultures around us. The pressure to conform to societal values is seen in today's macro-concern about being *politically correct* in our speech. The Phillips translation of Romans 12:2 exhorts us this way, *Do not let the world squeeze you into its mold.* Political correctness is an example of that squeeze.

There is also the power of the devil who is described as *the ruler of the kingdom of the air*. The omnipotence and omnipresence of God obviously put limitations on the power the devil can exercise even in his realm. His power is often subtle and unperceived because the devil is a great deceiver. He manages to have us either disbelieve in his reality or become tyrannized by that reality. In either case, he has a firm grip. He is also described as *the spirit who is now at work in those who are disobedient*. Often those who are disobedient are rebellious against God, and they glory in their independence. Little do they know how controlled they are, that another spirit is at work in them. When they are released from that control (their sinful nature), it is because they have bought into another mystery, the Good News, a.k.a., the gospel.

Two powerful warfare acts are given to believers to declare their allegiance and affirm the grace that has saved them, the sacraments or ordinances known as baptism and communion. Chapter 38 of Michael Heiser's *The Unseen Realm* is titled "Choosing Sides," in which he demonstrates from three unlikely biblical passages, 1 Peter 3:14-22, 1 Corinthians 8:1-6 and 10:14-22, that these two church events are significant parts of spiritual warfare. I always knew that baptism was more than getting wet in Jesus' name and that communion was more than a small snack at the end of church once a month. Like many, I supposed they were liturgical symbols that we did in obedience to the Lord's command. But I did not apprehend their importance in the bigger scheme of God's attack on the forces of the dark rebellion. Exegeting the passage in 1 Peter, Heiser states:

> *Baptism, then, is not what produces salvation. It "saves" in that it reflects a heart decision: a pledge of loyalty to the risen Savior. In effect, baptism in New Testament theology is a loyalty oath, a public avowal of who is on the Lord's side in the cosmic war between good and evil. But in addition to that, it is also a visceral reminder to the defeated fallen angels. Every baptism is a reiteration of their doom in the wake of the gospel and the kingdom of God...Early baptism formulas include a renunciation of Satan and his angels for this very reason. Baptism was — and still is — spiritual warfare.*[150]

---

150   Heiser, *The Unseen Realm*, pp. 338-339.

If baptism is one's enlistment into the "army of the Lord" — a one-time act — ingesting the wafer and wine is a fresh declaration of war and a taunting reminder to the enemy that the sacrifice of Jesus on the cross satisfies God's justice as a judgment on our sin and releases us from Satan's clutches to become part of the divine family as joint-heirs with Jesus Christ. The fact that God's family gathers frequently in small groups all around the world to remember Jesus in His death until He comes again is an unwelcomed reminder to Satan that his efforts to corrupt God's creation have failed.

Earlier, when describing the biblical concept of mystery, we cited the Lord's Supper as an example. Surely, every sacred meal is like another arrow or missile in the spiritual war. Grace certainly is a mystery; in the next chapter we see two more mysteries.

## Summary Thoughts from Chapter 22, Mysteries in the War

- As part of the strategy of God's Battle Plan, Paul wanted all of God's people to live in that atmosphere of full and complete acceptance and experiential love.
- The mysteries were held in the counsel of God until the Holy Spirit inhabited a people He could trust.
- Satan's success in causing Adam and Eve to sin and break fellowship with God brought the entire creation under his bondage.

# 23

## PREPARING FOR WAR

To whom was this mystery made known most fully? And to whom did God make it known, and for whom was it a special surprise? All three questions are answered in Ephesians 3:1-6 (NIV):

*For this reason, I, Paul, the prisoner of Christ Jesus for the sake of you Gentiles —*

*Surely you have heard about the administration of God's grace that was given to me for you, that is, the mystery made known to me by revelation, as I have already written briefly. In reading this, then, you will be able to understand my insight into the mystery of Christ, which was not made known to men in other generations as it has now been revealed by the Spirit to God's holy apostles and prophets. This mystery is that through the gospel the Gentiles are heirs together with Israel, members together of one body, and sharers together in the promise in Christ Jesus.*

### The Mystery of the Gospel

The mystery was revealed to the Apostle Paul, and he revealed it to the Ephesians in his letter to them — and, undoubtedly, in person and to many other churches and people. And his special emphasis, much to their surprise and delight, no doubt, was the truth that God viewed the Gentiles on equal ground with the Jews. That by itself was good news, but that was not the gospel.

The gospel is good news -- really, it's great news! -- and for us humans it is about the salvation provided by God's grace, but God's purposes are much grander than earthly and human blessing. The fourfold hallelujahs sounded out in the heavenlies in Revelation 19 by *a great multitude* and heavenly beings are in response to the mighty voice of an angel exulting because *Fallen is Babylon the Great...a dwelling for demons and a haunt for every impure spirit...* (Revelation 18).

Paul wrote to the Colossians about Christ's victory as being about more than just our salvation; *having disarmed the powers and authorities, he made a public spectacle of them, triumphing over them by the cross* (Colossians 2:15). While the focus of the gospel is clearly about our salvation, our deliverance from Satan's tyranny, the whole cosmos also rejoices in the redemption that extends to all that Satan has stolen from God.

> *For the creation waits in eager expectation for the children of God to be revealed. For the creation was subjected to frustration, not by its own choice, but by the will of the one who subjected it in hope that the creation itself will be liberated from its bondage to decay and brought into the freedom and glory of the children of God.*
>
> Romans 8:19-21 (NIV)

Genesis makes it very clear that God said, "It is good" about everything He created. We know that the fall brought about by Satan's attack extends to all of creation, which exists in continuing decay, death and entropy, defined as a "steady deterioration of a system or society." From aging and death of all human, animal, and plant life to erosion of mineral formations and, perhaps, to cosmic cooling of astral bodies, all creation moves toward disintegration. Scripture is consistent in its view that nothing in the creation is permanent, except the word of God. It also looks forward to a new heaven and a new earth, which God will initiate (Revelation 21:1) after the final destruction of the devil and all that is represented by the beast and false prophet, who will be *tormented day and night forever and ever*, the same fate that awaits *anyone whose name was not found written in the book of life* (Revelation 20:10, 15).

In the light of such a horrific destiny, no wonder the salvation won by Jesus Christ is such good news. The reason, perhaps, that the gospel is considered a mystery is that, apart from divine revelation, such as the prophets and apostles received, including Paul,[151] the very idea of God, Creator of over two trillion galaxies, being personally aware of, interested in and loving individual humans seems preposterous. That is why the hymnist wrote,

> *'Tis mystery all: the Immortal dies:*
> *Who can explore his strange design?*
> *In vain the first-born seraph tries*
> *To sound the depths of love divine.*
> *'This mercy all! Let earth adore!*
> *Let angel minds inquire no more.*[152]

The hymn writer, no doubt, got this idea from 1 Peter 1:12 which says that angels are eager to look into this gospel.

It's important to understand that grace offered apart from the cross would be a great injustice. It would be a violation of the holiness of God. Sin could not just be swept under the cosmic rug; God had to deal with it, and He did so at the cross of Calvary. The good news of the gospel is that God's wrath against sin has been satisfied by the sacrifice of the Lamb who was without sin. The cross stands as the bridge between heaven and earth. It was also the scene of the determining battle of the warfare between God and Satan. Battles continue to rage, as Satan has not surrendered; he continues to attack the Church, but he will not prevail. He is on the defensive, as Jesus continues to, *build My church, and the gates of Hades shall not overpower it* (Matthew 16:18).

---

151   Those interested in knowing how Paul received "his gospel" are encouraged to study Galatians 1:11-23 and Ephesians 3:1-5.

152   Charles Wesley, *And Can It Be*, 1738.

The first nails that went into building Christ's Church went into His hands and feet, and this completely fooled Satan. Through his evil influence on Judas, Satan thought he had, at last, prevented the Son of God from achieving the messianic role. The grave was sealed, and so, Satan thought, was the doom of Adam's race. He did not know about the mystery of the gospel, revealed later to the apostles:

> The first nails that went into building Christ's Church went into His hands and feet, and this completely fooled Satan.

*Now to Him who is able to establish you according to my gospel and the preaching of Jesus Christ, according to the revelation of the mystery which has been kept secret for long ages past ...*

Romans 16:25

*... and pray on my behalf, that utterance may be given to me in the opening of my mouth, to make known with boldness the mystery of the gospel.*

Ephesians 6:19

*... praying at the same time for us as well, that God may open to us a door for the word, so that we may speak forth the mystery of Christ ...*

Colossians 4:3

Part of the mystery was that through the way of the cross God was in Christ Jesus reconciling the world to Himself, and the way of the cross continues to be a strategy of the battle plan. Jesus admonished His followers right after declaring the victory of the Church over Hades that, *If anyone wishes to come after Me, let him deny himself and take up his cross and follow Me* (Matthew 16:24). As MacMillan points out, the way of the cross does not end on the cross:

*The way of the cross is the appointed path to the realization of the experiential sitting with Christ, which the Father has ordained for the believer. Our blessed Lord died at Calvary, and the bands of death being broken, He has been exalted to the right hand of the throne. There [is] no other way for the disciple than to be as his Lord. It is not a method of fleshly works of self-denial, but the firm belief that God does as He says, as we walk in the light of His truth. Our part is the simple entering by faith into that which has already happened at the cross, the tomb and the resurrection. We yield ourselves unto God that the Spirit may work in us that which He has revealed in His Word as His divine purpose, a purpose which He can only fulfill as we abide in the faith that He is working in us to will and do of His good pleasure. We have died with Christ; we were buried with Him (not in the mere symbolism of water baptism, but in the apprehension of that work of the Spirit which baptism symbolizes); we were raised with Him in His resurrection out of that tomb in which all our sins and the old man, the root of all, were buried; and we have been made to sit with Him in the heavenlies, at the right hand of the Father. It is in the realization which this faith brings that we come to know that the Lord has Himself become the strength of our countenance as we see a new power working in us and through us in our ministry.*[153]

## The Mystery of the Gentiles

We have now seen that grace and the gospel are mysteries that God has revealed so that we can participate in His great plan of salvation. Jewish people, having lived with this God of the covenants given to their ancestors,

> When Jesus said, *For God so loved the world,* He meant all people, an idea quite foreign to the typical Hebrew mind.

were surely amazed at the outworking of His promises to Abraham and David, but were even more shocked when they learned of the third mystery: the gospel of grace is extended also to the Gentiles. When Jesus said, *For God so loved the world,* He meant all people, an idea quite foreign to the typical Hebrew mind.

Understanding this third mystery is so essential to our ability to be effective in spiritual warfare because a major battle has been won. Satan is not omniscient. He knows only what God chooses to let him know, and this part of God's plan was withheld from him as another mystery. God chose Paul to unwrap this mystery as reported to three of the churches,

---

153   MacMillan, pp. 75-76.

which had Gentile members. To the Roman Jewish and Gentile Christians, he gave a very thorough teaching about the role of the Gentiles in Romans 11, affirming that this part of God's plan was a mystery withheld until God chose to reveal it through the apostles.

*For I do not want you, brethren, to be uninformed of this mystery …*

Romans 11:25

*… the mystery which has been hidden from the past ages and generations; but has now been manifested to His saints, to whom God willed to make known what is the riches of the glory of this mystery among the Gentiles …*

Colossians 1:26, 27

A lengthier passage from Ephesians demonstrates the Apostle Paul's insight into the mystery of the Gentiles:

*For this reason I, Paul, the prisoner of Christ Jesus for the sake of you Gentiles — if indeed you have heard of the stewardship of God's grace which was given to me for you; that by revelation there was made known to me **the mystery**, as I wrote before in brief. By referring to this, when you read you can understand my insight into **the mystery** of Christ, which in other generations was not made known to the sons of men, as it has now been revealed to His holy apostles and prophets in the Spirit; to be specific, that **the Gentiles are fellow heirs and fellow members of the body, and fellow partakers of the promise in Christ Jesus through the gospel,** of which I was made a minister, according to the gift of God's grace which was given to me according to the working of His power.*

*To me, the very least of all saints, this grace was given, **to preach to the Gentiles** the unfathomable riches of Christ, and to bring to light what is the **administration of the mystery** which for ages has been hidden in God who created all things; so that the manifold wisdom of God might now be made known through the church to the rulers and the authorities in the heavenly places.*

Ephesians 3:1-10, emphasis added

What is the point of this? Presumably, Satan might have been content to allow God to have the Jews. In 2018, the Jewish population in the world was 14,511,000, which is less than 2 tenths of 1% (.00193) of the world's population of over 7.5 billion. But again, *God so loved the world.* The battle plan of God remained a mystery to Satan and the world, a mystery that expressed His love through grace that brought about the gospel, which has included the Gentiles. I would suppose that the vast majority of those reading this book are Gentiles, so I hope you can join my response to this with a hearty "Amen; hallelujah!"

Prior to Christ, the Gentiles were at a disadvantage not only because of their exclusion from any of the blessings afforded the Jewish people, but they were even more

> The best of lives without God is depressing because the specter of death haunts every man.

accursed because they had no hope and lived without any true sense of God. They had no hope because God is the only possible source for hope. The best of lives without God is depressing because the specter of death haunts every man.

We saw and heard this vividly in the train station in Toulouse, France, some years ago. During a delay, the college chorale we accompanied sang a few Christian songs. I watched a young Frenchman slouched on the bench at the other side of the terminal with his beret covering most of his face. I would have assumed he was sleeping, but he was chain-smoking. After the chorale sang a hymn that referenced heaven, he called out in a loud voice, "Yet we all must die!" He typified so many who live *without God and without hope.*

Prior to the incorporation of Gentiles into the body of Christ through baptism, many Jewish believers insisted that male Gentiles must first undergo circumcision. In other words, they believed that the only door of entrance into God's kingdom was through, first, being a Jew. The apostles, including James and Peter, dealt with this decisively at the Jerusalem Council, reported in Acts 15. Nevertheless, it became a custom later because of the high incidence of Gentiles who were contaminated by demonic presence and experience to have them submit to exorcism prior to baptism.

That was not an apostolic or biblical injunction, but a practical, pastoral ministry, which seems quite reasonable when we see Paul's perspective on the pre-Christian life of most Gentiles. He reminded the Ephesians about this in Chapter 2 of his letter.

*Don't forget that you Gentiles used to be outsiders. You were called "uncircumcised heathens" by the Jews, who were proud of their circumcision, even though it affected only their bodies and not their hearts. In those days you were living apart from Christ. You were excluded* (alienated) *from citizenship among the people of Israel, and you did not know the covenant promises God had made to them. You lived in this world without God and without hope.*

Ephesians 2:11-12 (NLT)

The strife between Jews and other people has a long history, going back to Ishmael and Isaac, the sons of Abraham. Gentiles of very many ethnic groups have persecuted Jewish people throughout history. And Jewish people have zealously sought to retain their ethnic individuality in ways which sometimes have contributed to the alienation.

That hostility was inspired by Satan and first expressed in the first human family as an older brother, Cain, murdered his younger brother, Abel. Brotherly hatred and warfare have continued down through the ages. Further Old Testament examples are Isaac and Ishmael, Jacob and Esau, eleven of Jacob's sons and Joseph. Much of the Semitic alienation seen in Scripture, such as seen in the Edomites, Moabites, Arameans, and Arabs, is rooted in these brotherly animosities, and Satan has been the instigator of it all.

In New Testament times the breach between Jews and Gentiles was extremely great. William Barclay notes:

*The Jews had an immense contempt for the Gentile. The Gentiles, said the Jews, were created by God to be fuel for the fires of hell. God, they said, loves only Israel of all the nations that he had made. The best of serpents crush, the best of Gentiles kill. It was not even lawful to help a Gentile mother in her hour of sorest need for that would simply be to bring another Gentile into the world ... If a Jewish boy married a Gentile girl, or if a Jewish girl married a Gentile boy, the funeral of that Jewish boy or girl was carried out. Such contact with a Gentile was the equivalent of death.*[154]

Surely, such ethnic animosity plays well into Satan's hand. Gentile hatred and anti-Semitism are not merely earthly social problems. They are weapons of satanic warfare that span the ages and the globe. Because God's attention through the covenants to Abraham, Moses, and David seemed to be all about the Jewish people, and since the gentile nations were steeped in idolatry, perhaps Satan assumed that Gentiles were already irrevocably bound in his kingdom. But not so! God's covenant with Abraham was that *... you shall be the father of a multitude of nations ... and in (you) all the nations of the earth will be blessed* (Genesis 17:4; 18:18).

The antagonism between Jews and Gentiles seemed to defy all possible mediation because by definition everyone who was not a Jew was a Gentile. There seemed to be no third party who was suitable to provide an effective bridge of communication. However, God, because of His great love for the Jews and Gentiles, found a way to destroy the hostility. Jesus Christ, whose death was conspired by both Jews and Gentiles, paid for the guilt of both parties.

Nonetheless, alienation is a huge problem in our generation. Racism, divorce, labor strikes, teenage rebellion, war, and even common arguments are expressions of alienation. Young people, alienated from the ideals of their parents and disillusioned with corrupt authority figures, rebel against the establishment and create their own hip-hop culture. They have been alienated from traditional society. Political extremists plot revolution in their cultures, and export terror to other lands, expressing a very intense form of alienation. Average citizens, dismayed by public or private moral failures by leaders, suffer alienation from systems and institutions they once supported. Alienation is the enemy of all relationships.

---

154   William Barclay, *The Daily Study Bible, Ephesians,* p. 125.

**Reconciliation**

Ephesians 2:17 says that Jesus came and *preached peace to those who were far away*, namely the Gentiles, and *peace to those who were near*, the Jews. This gave both Jews and Gentiles access to the Father by one Spirit. This reconciliation to God and to one another has been achieved through Christ's work on the cross, which has put to death the hostility between the two groups.

> Earthly war is traceable to the enemy of all mankind who suffers alienation from God and inflicts it on all human individuals and societies.

The Christian gospel has brought the possibility for reconciliation not only between God and man, but also between hostile ethnic factions. Apart from the gospel, the world is fragmented into thousands of alienated groups, which is usually the cause of human war. It is not stretching our thoughts very far to see that earthly war is traceable to the enemy of all mankind who suffers alienation from God and inflicts it on all human individuals and societies.

We might wonder how the cross has been effective in eliminating the hostility between Jews and Gentiles. Those who understand and appropriate the merits of Christ's death on the cross are the first ones to want to achieve reconciliation with God and with one another. It is the cross that draws all men to Christ, and those gathered at the foot of the cross who love Jesus cannot help but love each other.

So, we have seen that in the city most plagued by demonic activity, even though the Gentiles were previously alienated from God and from the Jewish community, the activity of Jesus Christ in dying for Gentiles as well as Jews has given them equal standing and total access to God. Not only that, but the Jewish/Gentile problem has been dissolved through the activity of Christ. But only in the Church do we see the Jewish/Gentile prejudices dissolved.

Christians have a great opportunity to demonstrate to the rest of the world the reality of Christ's divinity and victory over Satan by displaying a unity born out of our love for Him and for one another (see John 17:20, 21). Many leaders in the world and people of good will are striving to promote racial and ethnic harmony. Some degree of tolerance may be achieved, but without God's supernatural working in the human heart it is impossible to overcome our natural prejudices.

The great apologetic and evangelistic strategy which God has given the Church is breaking down the walls of hostility and building up communities of interracial and inter-ethnic *agape* love.

Breaking down the dividing walls of hostility is God's primary strategy for evangelism, which is the forerunner to God's summing up all things in Christ (Ephesians 1:10). The key mark of the kingdom of God and of a true church is unity of people who have no other reason to love each other than their relationship to Jesus.[155]

Christ's prayer was that they *may all be one ... that the world may still believe that you did send me* (John 17:21). He said, ... *all men will know that you are my disciples if you love one another* (John 14:35). Obviously, a major plank in Christ's platform for convincing the world of His truth-claims, and thus a major plank for evangelism, is the love that Christians have one for another, demonstrating the victory of God in creating a family in His image – the very thing all of God's enemies despise.

Having right relationships in God's family, the Church, is a huge emphasis in Paul's letter to the Ephesians because of the context of warfare they were in, which we have discussed earlier. When leaders, laity, marriages, families, and co-workers love each other as they should, as Paul discusses in Chapters 4-6, there is far greater potential for success in spiritual warfare, which we now move into more directly in the next chapter.

## Summary Thoughts from Chapter 23, Preparing for War

- The mysteries — grace, gospel, and Gentiles — remain mysterious to unbelievers and the rebel *elohim.*

---

155  For an outstanding treatise on this subject, see Francis Schaeffer's *The Church Before the Watching World* (Downers Grove, IL: InterVarstity Press, 1971).

- The first nails that went into the building of His church went into His hands and feet, and this completely fooled Satan.
- God's Word makes it clear that empowered laypeople, like fishermen and tax collectors, can be given "power from on high" to drive out the darkness.

# 24

## TAKING AUTHORITY

I n the Acknowledgments, I credit John A. MacMillan and Neil Anderson with being "field generals" in the Lord's army, not merely because of their insightful writings, from which I draw heavily, but also because of their practical experience in spiritual warfare. As we proceed now further into the heat of the battle, their insights become all the more important and prevalent in the succeeding chapters.

They are the first to agree that nowhere in Scripture does it state that ministering to those afflicted by satanic powers is restricted to apostles or any other office within the Church. What is evident, rather, is the importance of the role of authority in ministries of deliverance. The astonishment of the onlookers and listeners to the ministry of Jesus was that He carried such authority in word and deed. The demonized surely recognized His authority. He has given that authority to those who serve in His name and under the reign of His kingdom.

John A. MacMillan begins his book, from which we are quoting freely, with these comments on the meaning of authority:

> There are few subjects relating to the Christian life concerning which there is
> so little exact knowledge as that of the authority of the believer. This is not
> because such authority is the property of only a few elect souls. On the contrary,

*it is the possession of every true child of God. It is one of the 'all things' received in Christ. Its reception dates from the soul's contact with Calvary.*[156]

As you have been reading this book, perhaps you have been looking for the key idea or the formula for successful spiritual warfare. Maybe you or someone you care about is troubled by demonic influences, and you want to know how to engage in exorcism. Hopefully, you are not just interested in demonology as a theological doctrine. In any case, as an author, drawing extensively on thoughts from far more worthy authors than I, my hope is to help you see the authority you already have in Christ and to use that authority.

There is no magic bullet for spiritual warfare, but let's start with these very important ideas from Neil Anderson that help us narrow the range of strategies:

1. *We should derive our methodology for dealing with the kingdom of darkness primarily from the epistles rather than the Gospels and the Book of Acts....*[157]

2. *Because there are not instructions in the epistles to cast out demons does not mean that Christians cannot have spiritual problems. It means that the responsibility for living free in Christ has shifted from the specially endowed agent of authority to the individual believer. ...*

3. *Dealing with the demonic should be seen as a truth encounter rather than a power encounter....*

4. *The primary prerequisites for helping others find freedom are godly character and the ability to teach.*[158]

---

156  MacMillan, p. 5.

157  For Anderson's rationale about this idea, see *The Bondage Breaker*, pp. 26-27.

158  Anderson, *Bondage Breaker*, pp. 255-259. These four points are supported by important paragraphs in *The Bondage Breaker*.

## Wrong Conceptions

Anderson expounds more fully on the third strategy — *truth encounter rather than a power encounter* — as correcting a basic misconception in exercising spiritual authority:

> *Satan is like [a] yappy little dog: deceiving people into fearing him more than God. His power is in the lie. He is the father of lies (John 8:44) who deceives the whole world (Revelation 12:9), and consequently the whole world is under the influence of the evil one (1 John 5:19). He can do nothing about your position in Christ, but... he can deceive you into believing his lies about you and God.... You don't have to outshout him or outmuscle him to be free of his influence. You just have to **out-truth** him. **Believe, declare, and act on the truth of God's Word**, and you will thwart Satan's strategy.*

> You don't have to outshout him or outmuscle him to be free of his influence. You just have to out-truth him.

> *This concept has had a dramatic effect on my counseling. Previously when I exposed a demonic influence in a counseling session it would turn into a power encounter. With such a process, I saw counselees become catatonic, run out of the room, or become suddenly disoriented. I would attempt to take authority over the demon. My first approach was to get the demon to expose itself; then I would command it to leave. This exchange often resulted in a great deal of trauma for the counselee. Although some progress was made, the episode would usually have to be repeated.*

> *But I have learned from the Scriptures that **truth** is the liberating agent, and that has proven to be the case in every successful counseling session. Jesus is the Truth, and He is the One who sets the captive free. Power for the believer comes in knowing and choosing the truth. We are to pursue **truth**, because we already have all the power we need in Christ (see Ephesians 1:18, 19). Furthermore,*

> People in bondage are not liberated by what I do as the pastor/counselor, but by what they choose to believe, confess, renounce, and forgive.

THE LION, THE CHURCH AND THE WARFARE

*people in bondage are not liberated by what I do as the pastor/counselor, but
by what they choose to believe, confess, renounce, and forgive.*[159]

Besides the wrong idea that Satan has power over you, just cited from
Anderson, MacMillan adds other misconceptions people often have about
spiritual authority.

*The authority of the believer is by some confounded with the fullness of the
Spirit. It is taught that the coming of the gracious Spirit of God into the soul
in His divine fullness gives authority. But the believer's authority exists before
he seeks or realizes in any special way the Spirit's presence. It is certainly true
that the fullness of the Spirit empowers and enlightens the believer. By this
alone he is enabled to exercise authority. But the fullness is not the source of
the authority, but something apart from it.*

*Nor can authority be regarded as some special gift conferred, whereby the
recipient is endued with power, by virtue of which he performs mighty acts,
such as the casting out of evil spirits. Discernment of spirits and miraculous
powers are mentioned among the 'charismata'*[160] *of the Holy Spirit, but they
differ from authority.*

*By others, the authority of the believer is looked upon as nothing more than
prevailing prayer. We have heard men on their knees, when under a special
urge, giving thanks to God for the gift of prayer conferred at the time. But
later there has been no result seen from the agony or enthusiasm of intercession
through which they have passed. Personal blessing has resulted from the intense*

---

159   Anderson, *Bondage Breaker*, p. 24, emphasis added.

160   Here, I would disagree with MacMillan. Discernment of spirits and miraculous
powers are not in the list of *charismata*, which is found only in Romans 12:6-8;
rather they are manifestations (phanerosis) of the Spirit in the list in I Corinthians
12: 7-10. This confusion is due to an unfortunate supplying of *gifts* in I Corinthians
12:1. For a fuller treatment on this topic, see my book *Walking in Your Anointing*
(Indianapolis: AuthorHouse, 2007). However, I agree that spiritual authority,
generally, does not come from a special gift or manifestation.

*seeking of God's face, but a specific answer to their supplications has not been manifest.*[161]

## What Authority Is

Having seen some misconceptions about authority, continuing with MacMillan, let us look at the difference between power and authority and what biblical authority is.

*Let us first of all, define the difference between 'authority' and 'power.' In the New Testament the translators have not been uniform in the rendering of many words, and these two words have suffered among others. One notable instance is in Luke 10:19 where 'power' (KJV) is twice used, although there is a different Greek word in each instance. To have translated the first of these by the English word 'authority' would have given a clearer idea of the meaning of the passage.*

*One stands at the crossing of two great thoroughfares. Crowds of people are surging by: multitudes of high-powered vehicles rush along. Suddenly a man in uniform raises a hand. Instantly the tie of traffic ceases. He beckons to the waiting hosts of the cross street, and they flow across in an irresistible wave. What is the explanation? The traffic officer has very little 'power.' His most strenuous efforts could not avail to hold back one of those swiftly passing cars. But he has something far better. He is invested with the 'authority' of the corporation whose servant he is. The moving crowds recognize this authority and obey it....*

***Authority, then is delegated power.*** *Its value depends upon the force behind the user. ...*

*The believer who is fully conscious of divine Power behind him and of his own authority thereby, can face the enemy without fear or hesitation. Those who confront him bear the specific name of power and authority. We wrestle*

---

161    MacMillan, pp. 6-7.

THE LION, THE CHURCH AND THE WARFARE

*not against flesh and blood, but against principalities* (archas, *the first or preeminent ones), against powers* (exousias, *the authorities)' (Ephesians 6:12). But, behind the 'authority' possessed by the believer there is a 'Power' infinitely greater than that which backs his enemies, and which they are compelled to recognize.*[162]

## Using Authority in the Work of Deliverance

The believer has the authority, but the believer must believe in his or her authority.

Without any doubt, success in spiritual warfare is related directly to the authority of the believer. The believer has the authority, but the believer must believe in his or her authority.

*In the days of His flesh the Lord Jesus conferred on His disciples 'power against unclean spirits, to cast them out' (Matthew 10:1; Luke 10:19, etc.). This was done by the impartation of a divine power which accompanied them as they went forth preaching the gospel of the kingdom. Sometimes they failed (Matthew 17:19), and this He told them was due to lack of faith proceeding from failure to exercise themselves in spiritual approach to God. On one occasion, at least, an individual seems to have taken on himself the work of casting out demons in the name of Jesus (Mark 9:38). The disciples would have forbidden him; but our Lord passed the matter over with the statement that the individual who was not against them (as the rulers and many others were) was on their part.*[163]

*The spirits of evil are quick to recognize those who are armed with the authority of the Lord and who have knowledge of their devices. From such they will often seek to hide themselves. At times they will seem to have withdrawn from their victim, when the time for dealing with them has come. Commands for their departure will bring no response, and prayer seemingly has no effect.*

162    MacMillan, pp. 7-9, emphasis added.

163    MacMillan, p. 171.

The individual may have a period of apparent freedom and comfort, but it is deceptive. Or he will plead with the worker or workers to be let alone, control of the mind and will being held by the demons, although the possessed person seems to be expressing his own desire. Often the individual will profess willingness to unite in prayer or to join in singing or praise to God. But, almost invariably, if his assurance is accepted, there will be inability to take any spiritual stand.

The work of dispossession should always be preceded by prayer. If a group of believing persons can be gotten together to persevere in supplication, the result will be very helpful. Then, when the work of deliverance is taken up, the way has been prepared and the yielding of Satan's power is certain.

> The work of dispossession should always be preceded by prayer.

While demons will yield to the word of a single believer, when such a one knows how to use the name and authority of the risen Christ, it is well for two or three of like mind to work together. At times there may be struggling, when the power of the possessed person may seem superhuman. Or, at other times, the demons may cause the sufferer to attempt self-destruction, and it will be necessary to prevent this by force. Again, while one may undertake the exorcism of the spirits the others may pray either silently or aloud as the case may be. The united authority of the brethren will aid in the gaining of victory, although of course the power is entirely of God, and the ground of deliverance is the finished work of Calvary.[164]

The preceding comments by MacMillan demonstrate clearly what authority is not, what it is, and how we can invoke and use the authority God has given to us. Neil Anderson, below, gives practical advice on the qualifications that assure us of success in spiritual warfare, amplifying in his first point the analogy MacMillan used above. This section is worth

---

164   MacMillan, pp. 172-173.

THE LION, THE CHURCH AND THE WARFARE

citing in full because of the importance of the truth about authority that it conveys.

*I believe there are four qualifications for living in the authority and power of Christ:*

1.  *Belief. Paul talks about "His power toward us who **believe**" (Ephesians 1:19, emphasis added). Imagine a rookie traffic cop approaching a busy intersection to direct traffic for the first time. They told him at the academy that all he had to do was step into the street and hold up his hand and the cars would stop, but he's insecure. He stands on the curb, tweets his whistle weakly, and sort of waves at an oncoming car, which just roars by him. His authority is diminished by his lack of confidence.*

    *Now imagine a seasoned officer doing the same thing. He sizes up the situation, steps into the street carefully but confidently, blows his whistle, and stretches out his hand — and the car stops. There's no doubt in his mind that he's in control in that intersection, because he has the authority to direct traffic.*

    *In the spiritual realm, if you don't believe you have Christ's authority over the kingdom of darkness, you're not likely to exercise it.*

2.  *Humility. Humility is confidence properly placed. Humility is like meekness, which in the case of Christ was great strength under great control. In exercising our authority, humility is placing confidence in Christ, the source of our authority, instead of in ourselves. Like Paul, we "glory in Christ Jesus and put no confidence in the flesh" (Philippians 3:3).*
    *Pride says, "I resisted the devil all by myself." False humility says, "God resisted the devil; I did nothing." Humility says, "I assumed my responsibility to resist the devil by the grace of God." Apart from Christ we can do **nothing** (John 15:5), but that doesn't mean we're not supposed to do **something**. We humbly exercise His authority — in His strength and in His name.*

3. *Boldness. It is the mark of a Spirit-filled Christian to be strong and courageous. Joshua was challenged four times to be strong and courageous (Joshua 1:6, 7, 9, 18). "The wicked flee when no one is pursuing, but the righteous are bold as a lion" (Proverbs 28:1). When the early church prayed about their mission of sharing the gospel in Jerusalem, "the place where they had gathered together was shaken, and they were all filled with the Holy Spirit and began to speak the word of God with boldness" (Acts 4:31). Spirit-inspired boldness is behind every successful advance in the church. "God has not given us a spirit of timidity, but of power and love and discipline" (2 Timothy 1:7).*

4. *Dependence. The authority we're talking about is not an independent authority. We have the authority to do God's will, nothing more and nothing less. We don't charge out on our own initiative like some kind of evangelical ghostbusters to hunt down the devil and engage him in combat. God's primary call is for each of us to focus on the ministry of the kingdom: loving, caring, preaching, teaching, praying, and so on. However, when demonic powers challenge us in the course of our pursuing this ministry, we deal with them on the basis of our authority in Christ and our dependence on Him. Then we carry on with our primary task.*[165]

## Spiritual Responsibility

Perhaps not all believers are called to the deliverance ministry, and some may have such an encounter on only a few occasions. As with all the manifestations of the Spirit, exorcising demons will be done when and as He chooses. Exorcising demons is not a spiritual gift that we can choose and operate on demand. It is a work of God, sovereignly inspired by God, just as divine healing is. However, given the amount of evil bondage suffered by

> Exorcising demons is not a spiritual gift that we can choose and operate on demand. It is a work of God.

---

165  Anderson, *Bondage Breaker,* pp. 85-88.

so many, we may assume that the Lord would be pleased were there more spiritual warriors ready to engage battle at this level. We should not seek greater maturity primarily for sensational ministries, but strictly for the sake of knowing and fellowshipping more deeply with Christ. As we grow closer to Him, quite likely He will find us to have the strength of faith to join the ranks of others in the ministry of binding and loosing.

The early disciples knew who had given them authority, and in His name they went forth, succeeded, and returned to Jesus rejoicing. MacMillan fills out not only their responsibility but ours today:

> To the seventy who returned to Christ with joy (Luke 10:17, 19, ASV), saying, 'Lord, even the demons are subject unto us in thy name,' the Master replied: 'Behold, I have given you authority to tread upon serpents and scorpions, and over all the power of the enemy.' Lest any argue that this authority was given to them in a special time and is not now operative, we will refer to Mark 16:17, ASV, the scope of which cannot be questioned: 'These signs shall accompany them that believe; in my name shall they cast out demons,' etc. All that went before is included in this commission and a wider range is given to it; 'Them that believe' is the only limitation; he who believes and obeys has a wider ministry open to him than the vast majority of Christians have understood or exercised.

> Yet, while the foregoing is true, it is equally true that not all are called or equipped for the full performance of what is here outlined. Nevertheless, everyone who is named as a minister of the Lord and of the Word should examine himself as to whether he comes short of that to which he is commissioned. There are not a few serving congregations who are permitting conditions to exist among their people that are displeasing to the Head of the Church. There are others who face individual cases which need help and who realize that they are not instructed or ready for the task of deliverance.

> The civilized world as at no other time in history, save perhaps during the period when the Son of God was on earth, faces a working of demon power.

*The advance of so-called Spiritualism witnesses to this. But, in addition, there is manifest in the very congregations of Christians great numbers who need special understanding and help. Our national educational systems show the influence of what the apostle calls 'doctrines of demons.' To meet these sad conditions every minister of Christ needs a more intensive knowledge of what the Bible has to say about the impact of the unseen world on the seen.*[166]

*Upon pastors and evangelists rests the greatest measure of responsibility for the instruction of the flock of God. It is, in a special way, theirs to discern the signs of enemy-working and to deliver their people. It is theirs also to teach and to warn of the perils which threaten the spiritually minded. It must be realized that the 'heavenlies,' into which the saints are introduced by divine wisdom and grace, are in this present dispensation the habitat of 'the power of the air.' The believer who seeks the deepest experiences of the spiritual life may fall under deception unless he knows that Satan himself is transformed into an 'angel of light' at times and that the archenemy is at home in religious gatherings where earnest leaders are ignorant of his devices.*[167]

While those called to vocations of spiritual leadership certainly must be equipped and motivated to deal with the darkness that enshrouds even the Church and church members, MacMillan continues to show that all who are in Christ have authority and responsibility in this area:

*The question is often asked: Why does God permit this or that condition? Does not the answer lie here? God has planned that man shall, through the outworking of redemption, regain the place of authority in creation that he has lost. To this end, Christ, having conquered for man, sits as his Representative in the seat destined for him when redemption is fully manifested. In the interim, the wonderful provision exists that man shall be reckoned in Christ and shall,*

---

166   MacMillan, pp. 128-129.

167   MacMillan, pp. 141-142.

*to the limit of his spiritual understanding and obedience, be endowed with the authority of His name.*

*Accordingly, God throws upon man the responsibility for the continuance of the conditions which we question. We feel they ought not to be. We realize that they are the working of the enemy. We cry to God to rebuke the enemy and to alter things. Through the teaching of the Word, He replies: 'My children, rebuke the enemy yourselves. The authority over him is yours. Its responsibility I have committed to you. I desire you to learn in these things to prevail. I have purposed a high and holy ministry for you in the coming age. This is for you the time of testing and preparation. Be strong and of a good courage, and none shall be able to stand before you all the days of your life.'*[168]

If you believe God would have you be instrumental in releasing others from the bondage of demonic influence, Neil Anderson recommends four important steps and elucidates on them on pages 260-270 of *The Bondage Breaker.* You will want to read his entire presentation, but here are the four steps:

*1. Gather Background Information*
*2. Determine False Beliefs*
*3. Deal with the Individual, Not the Demons*
*4. Lead Them Through the Steps to Freedom.*[169]

---

168    MacMillan, pp. 52-53.

169    Anderson, pp. 277-284; the "Steps to Freedom" he refers to involve use of the "Confidential Personal Inventory" which is found in Chapter 13 of *The Bondage Breaker* and condensed here in Addendum 6 and offered freely for use or adaptation.

## Summary Thoughts from Chapter 24, Taking Authority

- Dealing with the demonic should be seen as a truth encounter rather than a power encounter.
- People in bondage are not liberated by what I do as the pastor/counselor, but by what they choose to believe, confess, renounce, and forgive.
- Exorcising demons is not a spiritual gift that we can choose and operate on demand. It is a work of God.

# 25

## SPIRITUAL ARMOR

At the end of Ephesians, starting with the word *finally* in Ephesians 6:10, Paul turns his attention to the enemy himself and how we should respond to him. Lest we become overly confident about our ability simply to change our lifestyle, add a few important character qualities, understand our identity in Christ, and thereby whip the enemy, Paul reminds us about the powerful threat of our foe. He gives us two important strategies for living and ministering effectively in the midst of a culture that is dominated by the kingdom of darkness. Verses 10-17 encourage us to go through three preparation exercises which are primarily defensive tactics, and then verses 18-24 instruct us about maintaining communication with our Commanding Chief.

### Readiness Alert: Be Strong

The readiness alert gives a confidence-builder — *be strong* — and two commands — *put on the full armor of God* and *stand firm*. The confidence-builder, described in verse 10, tells us that we may remain strong in the Lord with His mighty power. The three words, *strong, mighty,* and *power,* are three different Greek words which together are like a three-strand cable indicating great strength.

A quality which many great leaders share is the ability to get their troops, or team, or workers to believe in themselves. Sports followers are fascinated by inspiring half-time talks, during which a coach gives a rousing speech to inspire his team with confidence. Great coaches like Knute Rockne of Notre Dame were famous for their ability to stir their team to a great effort. Often, a speech like that turns the game around.

> In the case of spiritual warfare, we have seen that in Christ we are already stronger than our enemy. We need no rousing speech; it was uttered at Calvary: It is finished!

The same players are playing against the same opponent. Nothing has changed, except the players now believe in themselves. Confidence is an attitude of the human spirit; getting athletes to believe they are stronger and better than their opponents is an important part of achieving victory. In the case of spiritual warfare, we have seen that in Christ we are already stronger than our enemy. We need no rousing speech; it was uttered at Calvary: *It is finished!*

The strength which Paul mentions is *in the Lord* as these verses describe. We are to be strong *in the Lord*, in *his* mighty power, and we are to put on the full armor *of God*. As believers, even mature believers, we simply do not have the ability to compete with Satan in our own strength. A line in Martin Luther's great hymn, *A Mighty Fortress*, reminds us: *Did we in our own strength confide, our striving would be losing.*

After giving this confidence-builder about the tremendous strength that is available to us, Paul commands (verse 11) that as Christian soldiers we must *put on the full armor of God*. The Greek word for full armor is *panoplia*. The *panoplia* is intended to provide full protection.

### The Panoply of God: The Full Armor

MacMillan describes the full armor against the wiles of the devil and then the role of each piece of the armor.

> *To maintain his place against the wiles of the devil, the believer must be constantly arrayed in full armor. The different parts of this armor symbolize certain spiritual attitudes which he must maintain. It is most important to understand that the armor itself, when worn, constitutes the protection of the*

*believer and not his activity against the foe. Fully harnessed, he is fully kept and is unhampered in his ministry of authority. All that he need be concerned about is, like a good soldier, to keep his armor bright and well secured about him.*

*Let us note briefly the meaning of the various parts of the panoply: No item can be omitted. There is (1) 'The girdle of truth' (6:14), the clear understanding of God's Word, which, like a soldier's belt holds the rest of the armor in place. (2) 'The breastplate of righteousness' (6:14), not, as often stated, the righteousness of Christ, but rather the active obedience to the Word which he has received. (3) The 'feet shod with the preparation of the gospel of peace' (6:15), a faithful ministry in the heralding of the Word. (4) 'The shield of faith' (6: 16) (thureos, the large door-shaped shield covering the whole body), which indicates his complete refuge under the blood of Calvary, where no power of the enemy can penetrate. (5) 'The helmet of salvation' (6: 17) (called elsewhere 'the hope of salvation,' 1 Thessalonians 5:8). It is a remarkable fact that the hope of salvation, the coming of the Lord Jesus, is the only helmet that seems able to protect the head in these days of apostasy from the truth. (6) 'The sword of the Spirit' (6:17), which shows the Word of God used in an active sense, even as the 'girdle' shows it in a defensive one. (7) 'All-prayer' (6:18), the training of the faculties Godward by constant approach to God.*

*The emphasis in chapter 6 is laid on victory. Note the following paraphrase which brings out the full force of verse 13: 'Wherefore take up with you to the battle the whole armor of God, that you may be able to successfully withstand in the evil day, and having overthrown all foes, to remain unshaken.' There is no suggestion of defeat. Secure within his armor, the believer may disregard the enemy and give his entire attention to the exercise of the ministry to which he has been called.*[170]

---

170   MacMillan, pp. 37-39.

Some years ago in England I was pastor to a young man who served with Youth With A Mission (YWAM), an evangelical, independent mission. He told me that part of their spiritual preparation included prayerfully putting on all six pieces of the armor every morning. I was impressed by the importance of this discipline soon after that when I visited the Tower of London. There I saw displayed some interesting medieval suits of armor. Similar to the description of the *panoplia*, these suits of armor would provide protection for the entire soldier. So important is the spiritual armor that we give a fuller description of each piece here.

**Equipment Review**

While the next paragraphs may seem redundant to Professor MacMillan's treatment of the spiritual armor above, some added information is supplied, and in any case, a good soldier frequently reviews his equipment. Also, repetition is a strong element in learning, and we should be very informed about the six provisions God has given for spiritual warfare (see verses 14-17).

Some commentators suggest that Paul may have been chained to a Roman soldier as he wrote this letter. If so, he had a visual illustration of the armor he described. First on the list is the *belt of truth*, which was a foundational garment to be buckled around the waist. The belt gave both freedom and confidence. *Truth* is the quality describing this belt because truth is the foundation of our lives. As we have seen, Neil Anderson points out that when believers are beleaguered by the enemy, what is needed is not a power encounter, but a *truth encounter*. As the great deceiver, Satan has no weapons to fight against the truth. Jesus' use of Scripture three times during His temptations is a good illustration of Satan's impotence in the face of truth.[171]

The second piece of armor is the *breastplate of righteousness*. This piece of armor covers the body from the neck to the thighs. It is absolutely essential. Truth without righteousness is vulnerable. The righteousness that

---

171   See Matthew 4:1-11.

Paul talks about here is not our own integrity or our moral strength; it is the righteousness imparted to us, as he describes in Philippians 3:9: ... *not having a righteousness of my own that comes from the law, but that which is through faith in Christ — the righteousness that comes from God and is by faith.*

Righteousness speaks to us of an imputed integrity. A modern chorus rightly says, *He is all my righteousness, I stand complete in Him.* Without Christ's righteousness the first little doubt that strikes us may deeply wound us. Because we easily | Satan loves to remind us of past sins. remember some of those incidents when our behavior was not righteous, our confidence can easily be shaken. Satan loves to remind us of past sins. Christ's righteousness enables us to stand firm against temptations, accusations, and deceptions.

Third, Paul points to the feet, instructing believers to make sure they have on the *footwear of preparation which is the gospel of peace* (NASB). The emphasis here is not on the peace but on the preparation. We are to be ready always, in every skirmish, to inject the offer of peace, not peace *with* the enemy, but peace *from* the enemy's hold.

The Christian is always ready to move on orders. Part of our battle plan is to spread the gospel of peace. There's an interesting paradox here in that the Lord calls us into battle with Good News to proclaim peace. Certainly, peace will not be experienced unless the battle is won. Only as we are prepared to stand firm in the battle with our feet anchored in that gospel will we wage the war successfully. About the first three pieces of armor, Anderson notes:

> *It would appear from the verb tenses in Ephesians 6:14, 15 that three of the pieces of armor — belt, breastplate, and shoes — are already on you "having girded," "having put on," "having shod." These pieces of armor represent the elements of your protection made available when you receive Jesus Christ and in which you are commanded to stand firm.*[172]

---

172 Anderson, *Bondage Breaker*, p. 96.

Next Paul admonishes the believers to make sure they hold the *shield of faith*. This does not suggest the small, round shield, which was manipulated by the soldier's arms, but a huge, oval, door-like shield. In fact, the Greek word for this shield is *thurean* which means *door*. This door-like shield is described as faith because faith is able to extinguish any of the flaming arrows of the evil one. Our complete and perfect trust in Christ overcomes the world as described in Hebrews 11. The *flaming arrows of the evil one* are unholy, blasphemous, skeptical, malignant thoughts which are hurled at us by the enemy. They may quickly be extinguished by the shield of faith, which they cannot penetrate.

Our head is to be protected by the *helmet of salvation*. Helmets are used frequently in modern society, not so much in warfare, but in other semi-violent activities such as football, motorcycling, and construction. In the physical realm our helmet is our salvation. In the spiritual realm our salvation is our helmet. It protects our face and head. Charles Hodge notes, *That which adorns and protects the Christian which enables him to hold up his head with confidence and joy is the fact that he is saved.*[173]

*Finally, we must check to make sure we have the sword of the Spirit, which is the Word of God.* Another way of rendering this phrase is that we must have the sword which the Spirit gives. The Greek word here suggests the shorter mobile sword used in close conflict by brave soldiers. Wielding this sword requires agility and skill. The Word of God is described in Hebrews 4:12 as being *sharper than any double-edged sword, it penetrates even to dividing soul and spirit, joints and marrow* …. Paul tells young Timothy to be one *who correctly handles the Word of truth* (2 Timothy 2:15).

> The Word of God is the only offensive weapon in the armor of God. Paul uses "rhema" instead of "logos" for "word" in Ephesians 6:17 because he wants to emphasize the spoken word of God. There is only one Word of God, but the Greek word "rhema" brings in the idea of proclamation.[174]

---

173 Hodge, pp. 387-388.

174 Anderson, p. 100; see additional comments by Anderson on this page regarding Satan's inability to read your mind or know your thoughts; hence the importance of verbalizing the Word of God in your counter-attack.

As believers wield the sword of the Spirit, we are able to keep the enemy at bay because our use of the Word of God will prohibit even those that would try to get past the shield of faith. Sometimes when our faith weakens and our defenses are down, we need to take an aggressive, offensive mode to defeat the enemy, using the Word of God. In the three temptations of Jesus we see the successful use of the sword of the Spirit. Matthew 4:1-11 shows Jesus quoting Deuteronomy 8:3, 6:16, and 6:13 to combat each of Satan's appeals.

Attacks may occur at any point in our lives, which is why the armor described in this passage provides all-around protection. Paul instructs Christians to put on this armor. Anyone who refuses to take this verse seriously, seriously underestimates the *devil's schemes*. Anderson sums up:

> ... *as long as we are on planet earth, we are still on Satan's turf. He will try to rule our lives by deceiving us into believing we are still under his authority. As aliens in a hostile world, we need protection from this evil tyrant. Christ has not only provided protection, but in Christ we have authority over the kingdom of darkness. We also have the indwelling Holy Spirit who is the Spirit of truth (John 14:17), and He will guide us into all truth (John 16:13).*

> *Even though we are secure in Christ and have all the protective armor we need, we are still vulnerable to Satan's accusations, temptations, and deceptions. ... The fact that we have been instructed to put on the armor of God clearly reveals that we are vulnerable to some degree. Therefore, it is probable that every believer will be influenced by the god of this world. He can gain some measure of control over our lives if we are deceived and believe his lies. I have seen countless numbers of believers who are almost paralyzed by his lies. The oppression is so overwhelming that some can't seem to make the right choices and live responsible lives. They actually* **can** *make choices, but they don't* **think** *they can, so they don't.*[175]

The fact that we have been instructed to put on the armor of God clearly reveals that we are vulnerable to some degree.

---

175  Anderson, *Bondage Breaker*, p. 114.

297

Clearly, God has not left us powerless as pawns to the enemy. His provisions are manifold; our new nature in Christ that renders the sin principle powerless, the filling of the Holy Spirit to enable us to live the Christ-like life, and the spiritual armor — these are just some of His provisions. He has also given us some "spiritual muscle" that we might be *strengthened with power through His Spirit in the inner man* (Ephesians 3:16). We turn now to learn about this strength.

## Summary Thoughts from Chapter 25, Spiritual Armor

- God has given six pieces of spiritual armor and instructions about our warfare posture to ensure our success against the *wiles of the devil.*
- The fact that we have been instructed to put on the armor of God clearly reveals that we are vulnerable to some degree.

# 26

---○○---

# INSIDE
# THE ARMOR

---○○---

I n the previous chapter we looked at Paul's exhortation, in Ephesians 6:10, 14-17, to be strong, put on the panoply (or full armor) of God, and to review our equipment. Once inside the armor, the next command is that we stand firm with the armor on.

## Stand Firm

The concept of standing firm is expressed four times (verses 11, 13 and 14) in this short section. The injunction merely to stand firm might surprise us because we would expect that in warfare standing firm is not a particularly effective strategy. Why does Paul not say, *Fight bravely*? One answer is that the war has already been won. Victory has been gained. And all that the Christian warrior must do is to stand firm in that victory. It is true that the enemy will continue the skirmish, but we need not be overly concerned about that if we have the full armor on and if we stand firm. Another answer, as we suggested above, is that standing is the position of confidence. Some have rightly pointed out that there is no armor for the back, indicating that retreat is not an option.[176]

An analogy to this is a race in which all opponents have collapsed and you are the only one yet in the race. Nevertheless, you must cross the goal in order to gain the victory. So it is in the Christian life. The enemy has been beaten, but we are still called on to persevere to the end. The reason is that Satan has schemes, or wiles, which are indicated by the Greek word *methodos*. The methods of the evil one are to undermine our belief in Christ, but when he cannot do that Satan will try to undermine our belief in himself. If we begin to doubt Satan's existence or his activity, we will let down our guard or perhaps not put on the full armor.

One of his key methods to get us to not believe in him is allowing and encouraging the silly caricatures we see in books and in the media — the red devil image with horns, cloven hoofs, and pitch fork. Unbelievers are quick to laugh condescendingly at the naivety of educated people who believe in the devil. Such people would think otherwise had they spent any time in places like Haiti, India, and Nigeria where the demonic is so evident. Then they might also be able to see it in their own city.

An alternate scheme of Satan is to cause us to give him too much credit, which then plays tricks with our minds. If we ascribe to Satan and his minions authority which they do not have, by that very act we grant

---

176  Those who know this Ephesians 6 passage may wonder why the armor seems to be mostly defensive and why after putting on all the armor, the Christian warrior is not bidden to "wrestle," but merely to stand, mentioned in verses 11, 13, and 14. Two insights may help: while standing, the Christian is doing warfare as she or he prays in the Spirit, verse 18. We will look more deeply into this passage soon. Second, the idea of standing suggests active resistance. To kneel, bow, or prostrate oneself was a sign of being conquered. Standing fast suggests strength, composure, and confidence.

them that authority.[177] Animists are those who believe there are evil spirits all around us, inhabiting virtually anything and everything. These people, mostly in the so-called third world, live in terrible fear so they try to placate the spirits through sacrifices and many superstitions.

In Chapter 12 I reported about meetings in Nigeria where we saw amazing deliverances from demonic activity. One night after my message on "Knowing Jesus as My Lord," the host pastor left the platform and, with mic in hand, walked back and forth in front of the crowd of about 5000 people and began shouting into the heavenlies for about five minutes. Then he called on Christ to manifest His power and presence in the lives of all who were demonized. From the platform we could see dozens of people falling. The pastor then called on others to carry them to the front where about forty people were laid on the ground — some almost comatose while others were writhing in anguish. The pastors went to each one, standing over them and calling on Jesus Christ to release them from all demonic presence. One by one, they were silenced and almost all of them were set free. The pastor then exhorted them to forsake their idols, practices, and beliefs which are taught by demonized witch doctors. The power of Christ always prevails when people want deliverance in His name, as happened that night.

We see clearly in the Gospels and Acts and in contemporary life that the authority of Jesus Christ is vastly greater than the enemy's authority. People who want to be freed from Satan's grip and who look to Jesus will be delivered. Usually, another person will be involved in that ministry, but it is always the power of Jesus exercised through the authority of the believer that brings about the deliverance.

Churches today often go to one of two extremes in treating the subject of Satan and his realm. Most churches avoid the issue, either out of fear, disbelief, or the desire to appear sophisticated. This is unfortunate because many people who are demonically troubled would benefit greatly by

177  See Neil Anderson, *Victory Over the Darkness* (Ventura, CA: Regal Books, 1990), pp. 169-170.

receiving accurate teaching and a supportive ministry which effectively battle Satan's attempts to defeat believers and non-believers. Believers in Christ need to know that the enemy has no authority over the people of God which we do not grant him. Neil Anderson's books, *Victory over the Darkness* and *The Bondage Breaker*, provide outstanding and balanced treatments of how the Church might recognize and deal with demonic activity.

> Believers in Christ need to know that the enemy has no authority over the people of God which we do not grant him.

Other churches become overly absorbed by this issue. Some ministers and people in their congregations assume that demonic activity is responsible for every problem. We need to remember the three-fold source of sin as described in scripture: the world, the flesh, and the devil. Trying to treat toothache or broken arm by exorcising a demon may not be the most sensible way of handling the problem. Nonetheless, we are to be active, not passive, in spiritual warfare, as Anderson notes:

> *The first thing you should understand about God's protection is that our role is not passive. Notice* (in Ephesians 6:10-13) *how often we are commanded to take an active role.*[178]

> *Our "commanding officer" has provided everything we need to remain victorious over the evil forces of darkness. But He says, "I've prepared a winning strategy and designed effective weapons. But if you don't do your part, by staying on active duty, you're likely to become a casualty of war." In her classic book* War on the Saints, *Jessie Penn-Lewis stated: "The chief condition for the working of evil spirits in a human being, apart from sin, is passivity, in exact opposition to the condition which God requires from His children for His working in them." You can't expect God to protect you from demonic influences if you don't take an active part in His prepared strategy.*[179]

---

178   Anderson, *Bondage Breaker*, p. 93.

179   Anderson, *Bondage Breaker*, p. 94.

## Enemy Intelligence

Besides standing firm in the full armor of God, we also need a certain amount of enemy intelligence to successfully engage Satan. Notice, in verse 12, that we *struggle* or *wrestle* with this enemy. The word here does

> Excluding Christ from the skirmish by relying on psychological therapy or psychic power is fruitless and dangerous.

not suggest an all-out battle or fight but a skirmish. This does not minimize Satan's power but recognizes the superiority of Christ's power and the effectiveness of the armor which we wear. This skirmish is *not against flesh and blood*. We cannot engage the battle by using traditional, psychological, physical, or material methodologies. This would be like trying to kill germs by using bullets. We cannot see the enemy and therefore using material weapons is of no value. And excluding Christ from the skirmish by relying on psychological therapy or psychic power is fruitless and dangerous.

The enemy is described as *rulers, authorities, powers of this dark world*, and *spiritual forces of evil in the heavenly realms*. This four-fold description, which we discussed in Chapter 3, may suggest differing ranks of spiritual power within the demonic world. These ranks of evil certainly penetrate the cultures of this world, spreading much darkness and wickedness. They also penetrate into the heavenlies, which, thank God, is where Christ exists and successfully overcomes any advances of the enemy in that realm.

We are not invited by Scripture to be over-interested in these wicked beings, but we are made aware of their reality to help us grasp the seriousness and complexity of the demonic world so that we will fully depend on Christ when we find ourselves in battle. He fully understands these beings that He expelled from heaven.

Paul describes these enemies as powerful, wicked, and cunning. The Ephesian Christians had a first-hand knowledge of the enemy, as we find described in Acts 19:11-17. Paul had begun to defeat the powers of darkness by healing people with various illnesses and evil spirits. Others who were watching Paul tried to use the same tactics, even though they were not spiritually qualified to do so. The results were quite unpleasant, at least for the seven sons of Sceva. Undoubtedly, some of the Ephesian believers who were receiving this letter from Paul remembered that dramatic incident because *Many of those who believed now came and openly confessed their evil deeds. A number who had practiced sorcery brought their scrolls together and burned them publicly* (Acts 19:18, 19, NIV). These new believers, undoubtedly, became part of the Ephesian church.

To review: the strategy for waging an effective battle for the kingdom puts us on a readiness alert by reminding us of our confidence, instructing us to put on the *panoplia,* and exhorting us (four times) to stand firm. This strategy reviews the six important pieces of equipment for defense and offense in the battle. It also gives us enemy intelligence, describing the nature of the enemy and what his methods are. Finally, verse 18 instructs us to pray.

### Engaging Prayer

We might be tempted to think that, once we are wearing all the armor, we are fully prepared as Christian soldiers. This is not so. Armor does not make a soldier. If there isn't a robust heart pumping inside a healthy body, the armor is just so much scrap metal. Even the strongest soldier needs to communicate with the field general so that he fits in with the leader's strategy. This communication with the Commanding Officer is called prayer.

At the end of Ephesians Paul turns to the issue of prayer as a battle strategy for the kingdom. All the relationships we have observed in Paul's letter depend on prayer for their success. The essence of any relationship is communication. Since our most important relationship is with God, our most important communication is also with God. Inevitably, all our other communication, through speech and conduct, reveals the rapport we have with Him. The last verses of Ephesians reveal how effective prayer is characterized and what it concerns. We discuss prayer characteristics here and prayer concerns in the next chapter.

> Since our most important relationship is with God, our most important communication is also with God.

**Prayer Characteristics**

In Ephesians 6:18 we notice that prayer should be characterized by Spirit-control as Paul admonishes believers to pray in the Spirit. There is little use for praying if we are not doing so according to the instincts of the Holy Spirit.

*And pray in the Spirit on all occasions with all kinds of prayers and requests. With this in mind, be alert and always keep on praying for all the Lord's people.*

Praying in the Spirit, of course, implies being filled with the Holy Spirit, which Paul commands in Ephesians 5:18, as we saw in Chapter 10. Being filled with the Holy Spirit is extremely important for spiritual warfare and for effective prayer. Only the Spirit knows what is important to God, as Paul described in another situation:

*In the same way the Spirit helps us in our weakness. We do not know how we ought to pray but the Spirit himself intercedes for us with groans that words cannot express. And he who searches our hearts knows the mind of the Spirit because the Spirit intercedes for the saints in accordance with God's will.*

Romans 8:26-27, NIV

On another occasion, Paul emphasized the important role of the Spirit in prayer:

*The Spirit searches all things, even the deep things of God, for who among men knows the thoughts of a man except the man's spirit within him? In the same way no one knows the thoughts of God except the Spirit of God.*

1 Corinthians 2:10b, 11

Because of the essential and critical role of the Holy Spirit in our prayer life, our first prayer, after daily confession, should be for a fresh infilling of God's Holy Spirit. This will enable the rest of our praying to be effective, including putting on the armor of God.

Our prayer should also be characterized by alertness or watchfulness. Paul mentions in verse 18 that we should *be alert*, suggesting the imagery of someone on sentry duty. While visiting Windsor Castle in England, our family saw what must surely have been a very rare sight. One of the splendidly attired palace guards, who was standing guard in an inner courtyard, was nodding off to sleep. This was very visible because his tall headwear — the kind you see on the Buckingham Palace guards also — was bobbing lower and lower. Fortunately, his sleep was not deep enough to cause him to fall over. I thought of this as a picture of my prayer life all-too-often.

To what are we Christian soldiers supposed to be alert? Certainly, first and foremost, we must be alert to God. Our focus must be on Him. This might seem elementary and even trite to say that we ought to focus on God in our praying. But did you ever catch yourself in prayer just talking to yourself? This is easily done when we do not keep our minds fixed on the One to whom we are addressing our prayers. It is very difficult at first to keep one's focus on God in developing the life of prayer.

> To what are we Christian soldiers supposed to be alert? Certainly, first and foremost, we must be alert to God. Our focus must be on Him.

We also must be alert to what we are doing and what we are saying. Prayer, unfortunately, can easily be filled with clichés and religious jargon which have little meaning to us. Words like *bless* and *beseech*, which are used mostly in Christianese, should be avoided unless we truly mean what we are saying. We must also be alert to what God is saying. Prayer should include times of stillness, quiet and attentive listening to the Lord. During such times of quiet we should be alert to how we might be used by God to be part of the answer to the prayers that we have already uttered.

Finally, our prayer should be characterized by perseverance and persistence. Paul tells us that our praying in the Spirit should be *on all occasions with all kinds of prayers*[180] *and requests...and always keep on praying* (NIV). A

---

180    In my teaching on "Finding Your Charisma" fourteen kinds of prayer are listed. They are adoration, anointing, confession (personal and corporate), consecration, healing, intercession, petition, praise, praying Scripture, questioning/listening, rejoicing, spiritual warfare, supplication, thanksgiving.

parallel verse says *Devote yourselves to prayer* (Colossians 4:2), meaning literally, to hold up with strength in time of prayer. The early church had so much success because of their life of prayer. Notice particularly Acts 1:14, 2:42 and 6:4.

The Lord gave two great parables to emphasize the value of persistence in prayer. Luke 11:1-10 is about the friend who had visitors during the midnight hour and had nothing to set before them. Going to his neighborly friend to receive provisions, he was met by an initial refusal. But through his persistence he was able to receive what he needed.

Luke 18:1-8 tells about the persistent widow who was being mistreated. She appealed to the judge for justice. Even though the judge was unmoved by sympathy, he was very moved by her persistence and eventually gave her the justice that she requested. These two parables do not imply that God begrudgingly answers our prayers. They are parables of contrast.[181]

Most likely the one factor which undermines our persistence in prayer is that we do not receive our answers immediately. Sometimes this is due to asking with wrong motives, as James suggests: *You ask and do not receive because you ask with wrong motives so that you may spend it on your pleasures* (James 4:3). Other times we do not receive timely answers because our timing is wrong. Perhaps God has a lesson for us to learn first. Or, perhaps God has something better in store for us down the road.

The danger of not persisting and waiting but of acting on our own is illustrated many times in Scripture. Abraham's inability to trust God to give him a son is an example of preempting God. The result was Ishmael, the son of the handmaiden, whose descendants have continued to be enemies against the Israelites. Another Old Testament illustration is Saul. As king he was responsible to wait for the blessing of God to come through the priestly

---

181  Parables are not allegories where all the details of the story must be interpreted. Rather, they are intended to convey only one truth. For example, in the Luke 18 parable, the reluctant judge is not to be understood to be God; the lesson is about the importance of persistence in prayer. The **contrast** is between what the judge is like and what God is like.

ministry of the prophet Samuel prior to going to war. Saul showed no confidence in the presence and power of God but yielded to fear. Because Samuel was late in coming, Saul decided to fulfill the priestly role himself. God judged him severely because of this (1 Samuel 13).

Persistence in prayer is a key battle strategy. This is why four times in the previous section Paul admonished the Christian warrior to stand fast.

> In a deliverance ministry we should not be discouraged if our initial attempt is not successful.

In a deliverance ministry we should not be discouraged if our initial attempt is not successful. Immediately after the parable in Luke 11 about the persistence of the man seeking bread from his neighbor at midnight, Jesus said we are to *Ask, Seek and Knock*, implying persistence. The next passage tells about His expelling a demon from a mute man. While the demons seemed to respond immediately to His authority, that may not always be the case for us.

Our praying, then, should be Spirit-led, alert, and persistent.

## Summary Thoughts from Chapter 26, Inside the Armor

- If we ascribe to Satan and his minions authority which they do not have, by that very act we grant them that authority.
- Excluding Christ from the skirmish by relying on psychological therapy or psychic power is fruitless and dangerous.
- Since our most important relationship is with God, our most important communication is also with God.
- In a deliverance ministry we should not be discouraged if our initial attempt is not successful.

# 27

## PRAYER CONCERNS

### God's People

Paul wanted to make sure that the people prayed for Christians generally. Throughout his letters Paul wanted prayer for those who were new in the Lord, for those who were suffering, for those who were seeking God's will, and especially for those who were serving Christ. Even if you are not actively involved in deliverance ministry, if you know someone who is, please pray persistently for that person. Pray for their protection and effectiveness.

Let me encourage you specifically to pray for all pastors and church leaders you know. Satan is attacking them with fierce and violent assaults in many ways. You will be as alarmed as I was when first reading these statistics about pastoral casualties. The following statistics were presented by Pastor Darrin Patrick from research he has gathered from such organizations as Barna and Focus on the Family.

- Fifteen hundred pastors leave the ministry each month due to moral failure, spiritual burnout, or contention in their churches.
- Fifty percent of pastors' marriages will end in divorce.
- Eighty percent of pastors and eighty-four percent of their

spouses feel unqualified and discouraged in their role as pastors.

- Fifty percent of pastors are so discouraged that they would leave the ministry if they could, but have no other way of making a living.
- Eighty percent of seminary and Bible school graduates who enter the ministry will leave the ministry within the first five years.
- Seventy percent of pastors constantly fight depression.
- Almost forty percent polled said they have had an extra-marital affair since beginning their ministry.
- Seventy percent said the only time they spend studying the Word is when they are preparing their sermons.

These casualties are every bit as destructive to individuals, families, churches, communities, and our nation as the grim statistics we hear on the news during times of military wars. Without any doubt, lack of prayer and relation to the Commander-in-Chief is the primary reason for these casualties.

**God's Program**

Furthermore, Paul wanted prayer for God's program, the great work of spreading the gospel to everyone throughout the world. It is amazing that Paul, writing from jail as a prisoner in chains, did not ask the Ephesians to pray that he would be released, nor did he request prayer for comfort, but rather for further opportunity to proclaim the gospel. In Colossians 4:4 he said, *Pray that I might proclaim it clearly as I should.*

In fact, God even used imprisonment as a specific answer to prayer for furthering the gospel. The letter to the Philippians, which seems to have been written after Paul's first imprisonment, records this comment of Paul to the Christian church:

*Now I want you to know, brothers, that what has happened to me has really served to advance the gospel. As a result, it has become clear throughout the whole palace guard and to everyone else that I am in chains for Christ. Because of my chains, most of the brothers in the Lord have been encouraged to speak the word of God more courageously and fearlessly.*

Philippians 1:12-14, NIV

Praying for God's program can be as limited as requests for our own church or as expansive as praying around the world through a prayer manual each week. As we grow in our life of prayer, our concern for God's program will increase. And while such praying is not as dramatic as deliverance praying, clearly it is an important part of spiritual warfare. Satan's

> Rulers, powers, world forces of darkness, spiritual forces of wickedness in the heavenly places, can easily be applied to government and bureaucratic structures that are influenced by the demonic world.

influence in the world is not restricted to demonized people. A seminary professor alerted me to the idea that the Ephesians 6:12 designations, "rulers, powers, world forces of darkness, spiritual forces of wickedness in the heavenly places," can easily be applied to government and bureaucratic structures that are influenced by the demonic world. This is quite possible because Scripture indicates that God will be judging the nations, not just individuals. How He will do this is not known to us, but it would seem to be just that those in highest positions of authority and influence will incur stricter judgment. That is why we are told to pray for those in positions of authority.

Recently, I attended the Commencement of a Christian high school in South America and was greatly pleased to hear the American ambassador to that nation testify about his personal relationship to Christ. Imagine if every ambassador were serving not just our nation but also Christ! Maybe it would be good for us to pray this way.

Some time ago as a young man, I questioned the need and value for praying for God's program. In my mind was the objection, "Well, if it is God's program, He's going to do as He pleases anyhow. So why bother to pray?" I had been working for my father in the publishing business, and the Lord used my relationship to him as my father and my boss to give me insight and to correct my thinking about prayer.

The thought occurred to me that even though my dad made the decisions, talking with him was a tremendous blessing to me and a source of growth. Speaking with him about his business strengthened my concern for the business; it made me a company man. Those talks also gave him the opportunity to teach me. And I used those times to let him know my concerns. Often, I sensed that I was part of the decisions. At times I was able to persuade him to change his mind. Our talks also helped me to see how I fit in with his plans, and, most importantly, our conversations fostered our loving relationship as father and son. The Lord showed me that these are all advantages to engaging Him in meaningful prayer about His program worldwide.

Soldiers may not be best known for their lives of prayer, but we are not just soldiers. God views us as His sons and daughters. We are co-heirs with Jesus Christ, and His program is our program. We are part of His future. Our prayer life should reflect that intimate relationship which will draw us closer and closer to the heart of the Father throughout all eternity.

Some people have the erroneous notion that if you believe in the sovereignty of God, praying is done in vain. Just how important is prayer, really? Is anything really accomplished? Can we really engage in spiritual warfare when we pray?

Some time ago, I began a little intellectual exercise not knowing where it would take me. I began jotting down ideas about God in "If ... then" propositions. Here is my record of that exercise:

Proposition 1 - If God is real, then He is much greater than we consider Him to be, and worshipping God is the most basic reason we live.

Proposition 2 - If worshipping God is the most basic reason we live, then those who do not worship God are ultimately of no value to Him, and hell is a logical reality.

Proposition 3 - If hell is real, then Satan is real, and his primary goal is to have people worship false gods.

Proposition 4 - If Satan is set to cause people to worship false gods, then only the true God can conquer him, and our most important job is to pray.

Proposition 5 - If our most important job is to pray, then we must pray.

The message cannot be clearer.

### Intercessory Prayer

We conclude this chapter by taking us into the "war room" where our advisor, John A. MacMillan, details in depth the major weapon of spiritual warfare, intercessory prayer:

*For the greater struggles of our day and the thickening atmosphere into which we are entering, the Church needs **intercessors who have learned the secret of taking hold of the power of God and directing it against the strategic advances of the enemy**. She needs those who have understanding of the times to know what ought to be done amid the crashing down of old standards and the introduction of that which is uncertain and untried.*

> The Church needs intercessors who have learned the secret of taking hold of the power of God and directing it against the strategic advances of the enemy.

*God is waiting for those whom He can trust and use, who will have the discernment to foresee His steppings and the faith to command His power. **Authoritative intercessors are men and women whose eyes have been opened to the full knowledge of their place in Christ.** To them the Word of God has become a battle chart on which is detailed the plan of campaign of the hosts of the Lord. They realize that they have been appointed by Him for the oversight of certain sections of the advance, and they have humbly accepted His commission. Deeply conscious of their own personal unworthiness and insufficiency, they yet believe God's statement concerning their identification with Christ in His throne power.*

*Increasingly they realize that heavenly responsibility rests upon them for the carrying forward of the warfare with which they have been charged.* **Their closet becomes a council chamber from which spiritual commands go forth** *concerning matters widely varied in character and separated in place. As they speak the word of command, God obeys. His delight is in such co-working. They have caught His thought concerning the method of the advance of His kingdom. Through them He finds it possible to carry forward purposes and to fulfill promises which have been long held back for lack — not of human laborers nor of financial means — but of understanding spiritual fellow laborers.*[182]

"Authoritative intercessors" are very strategic in spiritual warfare, but MacMillan shows in these next paragraphs how direct-attack warfare praying threatens and conquers the enemy.

*As still further advancement in the knowledge of the Lord is given through the opening of the eyes of his understanding and [the believer] finds that he had been 'blessed with every spiritual blessing in the heavenly places in Christ' (Ephesians 1:3) there comes the startling realization that the very heavenly places into which he has been introduced are the habitat of the power of darkness. His acceptance of his seat with Christ Jesus (2:6), 'far above all principality, and power, and might, and dominion' (1:21), provides him with authority and power for full victory so long as he maintains his place, wearing the defensive armor and wielding the offensive weapons. But, unless at this stage of progress, there is received clear instruction as to the divine provision of overcoming, he is liable to spend many months or even years of fruitless struggle and defeat.*[183]

We move now, from what God has done and is doing through His people to defeat Satan and all rebellious spiritual beings, to be taken into

---

182   MacMillan, pp. 65-67.

183   MacMillan, pp. 82-83.

the heavenlies to see what this great victory has achieved. However, before we take up our final abode there, we are admonished to remain on the alert. The serpent's jaws are still snapping, and its coils still writhe.

## Summary Thoughts from Chapter 27, Prayer Concerns

- Satan's influence in the world is not restricted to demonized people.
- If Satan is set to cause people to worship false gods, then only the true God can conquer him, and our most important job is to pray.
- The Church needs intercessors who have learned the secret of taking hold of the power of God and directing it against the strategic advances of the enemy.
- Authoritative intercessors are men and women whose eyes have been opened to the full knowledge of their place in Christ.

# 28

## LAST DAYS

A re you worried about the future, not just your future, like your health, the grades you will get this semester, your teenagers, your job, paying your bills, aging and dying? What about the future of the world? I'm not sure what the disciples of Jesus were thinking as they crossed the Kidron Valley and looked back at the magnificent site of Jerusalem, but that short walk gave Jesus an opportunity to talk with them about the future. His main topic was not warfare but watchfulness. He was admonishing His followers to be alert to the times they were living in and to see the future through His eyes.

Disciples of the kingdom are forward-looking people. We live expectantly, believing that the future belongs to Jesus because He is coming back to possess it and all that His Father created. But there is more ahead than His return. The Bible frequently speaks about the end times. All three synoptic Gospels record Jesus' "Apocalyptic Discourse" (Matthew 24, Mark 13, and Luke 21). Perhaps the most famous of all prophetic writing is Revelation, the last book of the Bible. The apostles Peter, John, and Paul all added eschatological information in their New Testament epistles. And all New Testament teachings on eschatology draw heavily from Old Testament prophecies.

**Satan's Effort to Undermine Our Security**

As a college president for the past 25 years, I have been privileged to know thousands of young people who are increasingly aware of the dangers of our world. Recently, I was able to address this issue to some of them at a retreat, using Psalm 46, their choice. Their theme was on the importance of having a firm foundation in the midst of a shaky world. I shared with them an article that said,

*For the seventh straight year, the rate of students reporting they may harm themselves — and, in turn, who seek counseling — grew, according to a new report by the Center for Collegiate Mental Health (CCMH). The majority of students' distress can be reduced to manageable levels within two to 10 sessions at campus counseling centers, but many students need longer-term treatment of 20 or more visits.*

*The report summarizes data covering about 160,000 students and 1.25 million clinical appointments at nearly 150 colleges and universities for the 2016-17 academic year.*

*Counseling centers struggle to keep pace with this rising demand. Students may therefore face long waits for intake sessions or two- or three-week gaps between appointments. Colleges may also limit the number of sessions.*

*Institutions contradict themselves when they limit treatment but say they provide a supportive environment to sexual assault survivors and students struggling with sexual or gender identities, says Ben Locke, senior director of counseling and psychological services at Penn State University.*[184]

College life is stressful. Studies, classes, grades, papers, exams, finances, transportation, relationships, spiritual growth, career choice, job prospects ... the list goes on. And those issues threaten just personal security. What

---

184   University Business: Source: Center for Collegiate Mental Health 2017 Annual Report, tiny.cc/CCMH.

about national security? Computer security? Economic security? Social security? Eternal security?

In Maslow's pyramid of human needs, after physiological needs, such as food, water, sleep, etc., security and safety needs are most important. We are an insecure species. Always have been, but maybe more today than ever.

> Undermining our security is the nasty work of God's enemy, Satan, who enjoys keeping us detached from the only Source of every security we need.

Threatened by diseases, racism, bullying, uncontrollable nature such as hurricanes, hostile nations such as North Korea and Iran, in vain we look for security through our own efforts. Undermining our security is the nasty work of God's enemy, Satan, who enjoys keeping us detached from the only Source of every security we need.

Psalm 46 assures us that God, and only God, can provide security.

*God is our refuge and strength, always ready to help in times of trouble.*

*So we will not fear when earthquakes come and the mountains crumble into the sea.*

*Let the oceans roar and foam. Let the mountains tremble as the waters surge!*

Psalm 46:1-3, NLT

### Prophecies from the Messiah

Remember August 21, 2017? Probably not, but the whole country was in a stir about the very rare total solar eclipse that would be seen from 14 states that day. Imagine living in an earlier era or a pre-technological area of the world — how might you respond to seeing the sun disappear in midday? Or any cosmic or astronomical oddity that we can't explain? FEAR is the normal response. Many, if not most, people believe that some kind of apocalypse is on the horizon.

In His Apocalyptic Discourse, Jesus said there will be cosmic signs prior to His coming:

*"Teacher," they* [the disciples] *asked, "when will all this happen? What sign will show us that these things are about to take place?"*

*He replied, "Don't let anyone mislead you, for many will come in my name, claiming, 'I am the Messiah,' and saying, 'The time has come!' But don't believe them.*

*And when you hear of wars and insurrections, don't panic. Yes, these things must take place first, but the end won't follow immediately."*

*Then he added, "Nation will go to war against nation, and kingdom against kingdom.*

*There will be great earthquakes, and there will be famines and plagues in many lands, and there will be terrifying things and great miraculous signs from heaven.*

*But before all this occurs, there will be a time of great persecution. You will be dragged into synagogues and prisons, and you will stand trial before kings and governors because you are my followers."*

Luke 21:7-12, NLT

Then verses 13-24 refer to the immediate future of the disciples with the destruction of Jerusalem, which occurred in A.D. 70. And then Jesus continued His apocalyptic prophecies, affirming that cosmic upheaval will happen:

*"And there will be strange signs in the sun, moon, and stars. And here on earth the nations will be in turmoil, perplexed by the roaring seas and strange tides.*

*People will be terrified at what they see coming upon the earth, for the powers in the heavens will be shaken.*

*Then everyone will see the Son of Man coming on a cloud with power and great glory.*

*So when all these things begin to happen, stand and look up, for your salvation is near!"*

Luke 21:25-28, NLT

As Jesus said, *the nations will be in turmoil* and *Nation will go to war against nation.*

Besides the cosmic catastrophes that threaten us, what we might call "national bullying" can also intimidate us. As Jesus said,

***the nations will be in turmoil*** and ***Nation will go to war against nation.*** Verses 6 and 7 of Psalm 46 (NLT) say,

> *The nations are in chaos, and their kingdoms crumble! God's voice thunders, and the earth melts!*
> *The LORD of Heaven's Armies*[185] *is here among us; the God of Israel is our fortress.*

But Jesus assures the disciples that these fearsome signs will be followed by His return in power. And the psalmist affirms that the Lord of Hosts is here – our refuge in times of trouble.

The Lord Almighty, we know, does not need other warriors to be totally victorious. Just as He chooses to use humans in spiritual warfare, He also chooses to use angelic armies, but the omnipotent God does not need help. He delegates His authority to His followers, heavenly and earthly.

> *Come, see the glorious works of the LORD: See how he brings destruction upon the world.*
> *He causes wars to end throughout the earth. He breaks the bow and snaps the spear; he burns the shields with fire.*
> *"Be still, and know that I am God! I will be honored by every nation. I will be honored throughout the world."*
> *The LORD of Heaven's Armies is here among us; the God of Israel is our fortress.*

Psalm 46:8-11, NLT

**The *Eschaton***

The days Jesus was discussing with His disciples refer to the *eschaton.* In case you are not familiar with the term "eschatology," here is a simple

---

185 The name "LORD of hosts" occurs 261 times in the Old Testament. God is first called the "LORD of hosts" in 1 Samuel 1:3. The word *LORD*, capitalized, refers to Yahweh, the self-existent, redemptive God. The word *hosts* is a translation of the Hebrew word *sabaoth*, meaning "armies" — a reference to the angelic armies of heaven. Thus, another way of saying "LORD of hosts" is "God of the armies of heaven." The NIV translates YHWH *sabaoth* as "LORD Almighty."

definition: eschatology, which comes from the Greek word *eschatos*, occurs 54 times in the New Testament and refers to the last times or last days.

Although Jesus, in His humanity, said even He did not know when He would return (Matthew 24:36), He did understand the last times from God's perspective. Time is part of the created order; space, matter, and time are earthly properties in which we all live. God does not dwell in time. He is eternal. Yesterday, today, and forever are all the same to God. That's why Scripture says, a day is as a thousand years and a thousand years as a day to God. While we do not know much about God's view of earth's time, we know this: He created time, owns it, and will end it. So, eschatology is the study of the end times as best we can understand it.

Here it is important to give a word of caution. There have been and are many false prophets who have claimed to know when Jesus would return or when the world would end. These may have been total charlatans or may have been sincere Christians who truly believed their eschatology was correct. Thus far, all of them have been wrong. But more of that in the next chapter. William Barclay aptly comments:

*Jesus says that He does not know the day or the hour when He will come again. There were things which even He left without questioning in the hand of God. There can be no greater warning and rebuke to those who work out dates and timetables as to when He will come again. Surely it is nothing less than blasphemy for us to enquire into that of which our Lord consented to be ignorant.*[186]

What we can glean from God's Word is that the Old Testament writers assumed time would unfold in two distinct eras: these present evil days and the last days brought in by or leading up to the Day of the Lord. The coming of the Messiah would be the beginning of the last days, the *eschaton*, ushering in the new day.

Jesus taught, and Christians believe, that His coming as the Christ (Messiah) was the beginning of the last days. We already are living in the *eschaton*. However, we are in an in-between stage as two kingdoms on earth

---

186   William Barclay, *The Daily Study Bible, Mark*, p. 336.

co-exist, the kingdom of this world in which Satan has limited control, and the Kingdom of God. Jesus alluded to this in His comment to Pontius Pilate,

*My kingdom is not of this world. If My kingdom were of this world, then My servants would be fighting so that I would not be handed over to the Jews; but as it is, My kingdom is not of this realm.*

John 18:36

**The Commander's Eyes**

The next chapter discusses more fully the Apocalyptic Discourse. But first, let's set the stage. In fact, the context of the Discourse tells a lot about human nature. While the disciples were with Jesus in the temple in Jerusalem, Jesus was watching the rich people putting their gifts into the temple treasury. Seeing a poor widow put in two pennies, He commented to those around him, … *this poor widow has put in more than all the others. All these people gave their gifts out of their wealth, but she out of her poverty put in all she had to live on* (Luke 21:3-4, NIV). No comment from the disciples. Total silence on the topic. Rather, they began to discuss what really turned their heads: … *how the temple was adorned with beautiful stones and with gifts dedicated to God.* Jesus, our Commander, saw the spiritual richness of a widow's poverty; the disciples saw the material wealth of gifts given without sacrifice.

We have the same tendency of seeing the wrong things as we look toward the future. We seize on the sensational and the dramatic; Jesus wants us to see beneath the superficial to the deeper issues of "apocalypse" — God's purposes revealed.

The disciples were moved with awe and wonder as they viewed the magnificent architecture and ornate decorations of the temple compound. Most of them were country boys, from up north in rural Galilee; they continued to be impressed by the big-city sites.

And the Jerusalem temple was magnificent! Built between 20 B.C. and A.D. 35, Herod's temple covered one-sixth of old Jerusalem. Some of the stones were 40 feet long, 12 feet high, and 18 feet wide, and they were laid in an intricate pattern to show off their red and white coloring. This was the

THE LION, THE CHURCH AND THE WARFARE

same temple where Jesus was circumcised on his eighth day; where twelve years later He first confounded the scribes; where Satan took Him to tempt Him to jump off its pinnacle; where He chased out the merchants, calling it a den of robbers instead of a house of prayer; and where very recently He had silenced His opponents.

Now, in a most solemn and emphatic way as the disciples were admiring it, Jesus predicted the temple's destruction – a total devastation. And that sets the context for the disciples' question. Matthew records that Peter, James, and John questioned Him, *Tell us, when will these things be, and what will be the sign of Your coming and of the end of the age?* (Matthew 24:3, NIV). The disciples thought the destruction of the temple would usher in the Day of the Lord and the return of the Messiah. But Matthew's account shows that Jesus distinguished between the times questions: when the temple would be destroyed, and when He would return.

But that was not a topic Jesus pursued in the Apocalyptic Discourse. Mark 13 teaches that Jesus' purpose was not to satisfy the disciples' curiosity by teaching them eschatology, but to exhort them about their response to an uncertain future. He wanted them to be alert (verses 5, 9, 23, 33, 35, 37) to present realities, not to be anxious (verses 7, 11) about future events.

In fact, immediately before He ascended to heaven, the risen Christ was asked by His disciples, *Lord, are you at this time going to restore the kingdom to Israel?* Even then, they were still gripped by eschatology. He replied,

> *It is not for you to know the times or dates the Father has set by his own authority. But you will receive power when the Holy Spirit comes on you, and you will be my witnesses in Jerusalem, and in all Judea and Samaria, and to the end of the earth.*

> Acts 1:7-8, NIV

---

Jesus wants His people to concentrate on evangelism, not eschatology.

---

From this interchange, we may infer that Jesus wants His people to concentrate on evangelism, not eschatology. He does not require us to figure out the mysteries of the future, but to work toward preparing ourselves and others for that future.

## Summary Thoughts from Chapter 28, Last Days

- Undermining our security is the nasty work of God's enemy, Satan, who enjoys keeping us detached from the only Source of every security we need.
- We are in an in-between stage as two kingdoms on earth co-exist, the kingdom of this world in which Satan has limited control, and the Kingdom of God.
- Jesus wants His people to concentrate on evangelism, not eschatology.

# 29

## APOCALYPSE

In what is called "The Apocalyptic Discourse," Jesus taught that in both eras, their own generation and the end time, His disciples must be alert, even while busily serving Christ.

### The Apocalyptic Discourse

In Mark's account, verses 5-13 of Mark 13, Jesus gave five statements about future events, each of which contains a warning.

#### Many Will Come in My Name

First, disciples are not to be misled by false messiahs (verse 6). Jesus knew that the stresses of life and human impatience would cause people to latch on to deceivers who would claim "I am he." Gamaliel, "a teacher of the law," would later remind the Sanhedrin about two such men: Theudas, who drew four hundred followers, and Judas of Galilee, who led a band of revolutionaries (Acts 5:36-37). People of Samaria called Simon Magus "the Great Power" because of his wizardry (Acts 8:9-11). Not only Jews and Samaritans were waiting for a deliverer; the Romans, too, were expecting one. Seneca said that all men were looking *ad salutem* ("to a savior"). The times were indeed ripe for false messiahs.

THE LION, THE CHURCH AND THE WARFARE

In our generation we have seen several religious figures make messianic claims. I attended seminary with a Roman Catholic priest who had left the church to follow Sun Myung Moon, founder of the Unification Church, whom my friend believed was the most recent incarnation of the Messiah. Most new religions crown a new messianic leader or prophet, whether it be Maharishi Mahesh Yogi, Joseph Smith, or a New Age elephant. Often, desperate or gullible people make bizarre commitments to whomever or whatever will promise comfort and security, ignoring the clear teachings of Scripture.

> Jesus could not have made it any clearer: ... *if you do not believe that I am the one I claim to be, you will indeed die in your sins.*

Jesus told His disciples that they must first be strong in their own knowledge of who He is, so that when false prophets and deliverers appear, they will not be misled. We, too, need to be convinced that Jesus is the *only* Messiah, for there is no other way to know God. Jesus could not have made it any clearer: ... *if you do not believe that I am the one I claim to be, you will indeed die in your sins* (John 8:24). The buffet approach to religion, which allows you to choose what pleases your individual taste, will probably continue to permeate our society, but Christians must believe that Jesus Christ is exclusive, not one of several possible alternatives. Modern man does not like such limitations, but God, not man, sets the rules.

Scripture also asserts, and the early church fathers taught, that there would be many false teachers who would be inspired by demons. Admonishing his spiritual son Timothy, the Apostle Paul wrote,

> *The Spirit clearly says that in later times some will abandon the faith and follow deceiving spirits and things taught by demons.*
>
> 1 Timothy 4:1, NIV

Prompted by demons. Why? It is clearly the desire of God's enemy Satan to corrupt the truth of the gospel. He does it through human false teachers who believe they are right and may not know that they are influenced by

> *... deceptive spirits and teachings that come from demons. These people are hypocrites and liars, and their consciences are dead.*
>
> 1 Timothy 4:1b-2, NLT

The Apostle John also warned early believers about such false teachers, calling them antichrists in 1 John 2:18. These antichrists are seen to be spiritual frauds by continuing to live in sin, and about them John says:

*The one who does what is sinful is of the devil, because the devil has been sinning from the beginning. The reason the Son of God appeared was to destroy the devil's work.*

1 John 3:8, NIV

The reason the Son of God, the Commander, urges His soldiers to be alert and not be anxious is that He knows His work on the cross would destroy the devil's work. As the disciples, first-century and contemporary, face a frightening future for the world, those who are under the authority of the Commander know the cosmic events will be the final coiling and snapping of the serpent we met in Chapter 1. The battles may rage, but the outcome of the war is history.

### Do Not Be Frightened

Second, Jesus told the disciples not to be frightened by wars, revolutions, or natural disasters. These are not signs of the end times (verses 7-8), but merely *the beginning of birth pangs.* Political and cosmic upheaval have always been with us, and though they are frightening, they are only evidences that things are not right as they are.

Such disturbances were occurring in abundance in the first century. The Parthians were harassing the Romans; there were earthquakes in Laodicea and Pompeii; there was famine under Claudius. Every century has had similar shocks, but the heavy labor that will give birth to the *parousia,* the coming of Christ, is yet ahead. Disciples should not lose their composure during catastrophic times. Let the world panic, but God's people are to patiently trust in the Lord to deliver them.

> Disciples should not lose their composure during catastrophic times. Let the world panic, but God's people are to patiently trust in the Lord to deliver them.

I think there are four basic attitudes people can have about the future. I call this the "Apocalyptic Scale."

**APOCALYPTIC SCALE**

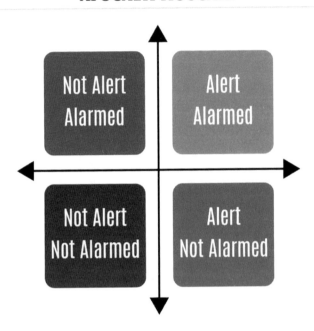

**Not Alert, but Alarmed** people are spiritually asleep with eyes on this world only; they are FRIGHTENED.

**Not Alert, but Not Alarmed** people are in a reality coma; they are the majority; comfortable, numbed down; they are PREOCCUPIED.

**Alert and Alarmed** people are on red alert; they are preparing for the worst, hoarding, as in turn-of-the-century Y2K days; they are PANICKED.

**Alert, but Not Alarmed** people are aware of biblical teaching and they are trusting in God; they are COMPOSED.

- Where are you on the apocalyptic scale?
- Not alert but alarmed (Frightened)
- Not alert or alarmed (Preoccupied)
- Alert and Alarmed (Panicked)
- Alert but not alarmed (Composed)

## They Will Arrest You and Flog You

Third, Jesus told His disciples not to be caught off guard by persecutions coming from established leaders (verses 9, 10). From the very beginning He made it plain to all who followed Him that persecution is part of discipleship. Now He tells them that religious and civil authorities will be the persecutors. The disciples will be treated as outlaws, but they must stand firm. God will give them wisdom when they are called to testify for Jesus before kings and governors.

In some countries of the world, Christians face this very situation today. Far from being commended for their piety, Christians are sometimes viewed as enemies of the state and are persecuted by guardians of the law. The day may not be far off when Christians in America will likewise be oppressed. Many who oppose abortion feel constrained to break the law to act on their convictions and suffer the consequences of fines, imprisonment, or both. Regardless of how we may feel about that, other issues will arise that will demand Christian activism and even civil disobedience.

There are times when Christians must actively defy a godless culture and state. Christians living in Nazi Germany, who passively watched as the Third Reich slaughtered millions of Jews and other innocent people, surely were not standing for Christ. Such a situation may seem remote from our life in America, but we need to ask what direction our society is headed and prepare to be faithful when persecution comes.

## Do Not Worry Beforehand

Fourth, Jesus told His disciples not to be anxious about what to say when they are called to stand before the courts, for He promised to give them wisdom and utterance that could not be refuted. Mark's account says,

*Just say whatever is given you at the time, for it is not you speaking, but the Holy Spirit* (verse 11b). As God had given Moses and Jeremiah words in Egypt's and Judah's courts (Exodus 4:12; Jeremiah 1:9), so He would do again for His people. And so He did. Stephen, Peter, Paul, and scores of Christian martyrs testified with such boldness and wisdom that it seemed as if the judges themselves were on trial.

Even in the most difficult times of persecution, disciples of Jesus must remember that the state is not the enemy, nor are government leaders. In godless contexts, although they likely do not know it, such leaders are merely pawns of Satan. In a sense, they are victims — willing ones, perhaps — but seeing them that way will enable believers to love their enemies and not become "haters," a label the world is all too eager to pin on Christians.

### You Will Be Betrayed

Fifth, Jesus said not to be surprised by hatred and rejection from their loved ones (verse 12). Perhaps the toughest thing about the gospel is that at times it divides families. No one wants to be alienated from family members, but when the choice comes down to loyalty to Christ *or* peace in the family, a disciple must choose the former. Jesus warned that the disciples would be betrayed *by parents, brothers, relatives and friends,* and that *all men will hate you because of me.* Those last three words are very important. Sometimes, believers — especially new Christians — by their ill-conceived and exuberant manner of witnessing, unnecessarily antagonize nonbelievers. The hostility is not about Christ, but about the aggressive way His gospel is presented by a self-righteous convert. The Apostle Peter made it clear that not all suffering that Christians endure stems from their right conduct (1 Peter 4:15).

As disciples, we need to understand why our witness may evoke a negative response, even in family members. The gospel is a rock. Some stumble on it; others build on it. In some, it evokes violent reaction; in others, it inspires belief. Because the gospel makes moral demands, no one can be passive about it. We are all under its judgment, and we must choose either to reject God's

The gospel is a rock. Some stumble on it; others build on it.

authority or submit to Him. Those who submit must not be surprised when others reject *us* along with the gospel.

Obeying Jesus' five cautionary commands is imperative, but compliance is easier if we are hopeful and alert. He says we must:

- not be misled by false messiahs
- not be frightened by wars or natural disasters
- not be caught off guard by persecution
- not be anxious about what to say
- not be surprised at rejection by loved ones

On a more positive note, He adds, *the one who stands firm to the end will be saved* (verse 13).

**Imminent Trouble**

Thus far, the disciples have received little comfort from Jesus' words about the future. To their question about when the temple would be destroyed, Jesus said that it would occur in their generation. He warned them to flee to the mountains when they saw Jerusalem being besieged. In this time of punishment, wrath, and distress, some people would be slain by the sword and others dispersed as prisoners. Jerusalem would be thoroughly trampled.

This prophecy of horror came true with a vengeance. The Jewish historian Josephus reported the grisly details that began in A.D. 70[187] when the armies of Titus, later to become emperor of Rome, laid siege to Jerusalem. Disease, starvation, and slaughter claimed 1,100,000 while 97,000 were deported as captives. Tales of ghoulish plundering, cannibalism, and diets of dung reveal how extreme the situation became. No wonder Jesus spoke with such passion as He urged His followers to flee Jerusalem. Many of the Christians took His advice, fled to the hills, and were saved.

---

187   Flavius Josephus, *The Works of Josephus*, Complete and Unabridged, translated by William Whiston (Peabody, MA: Hendrickson Publishers, Inc., 1987), p. 749.

**Ultimate Triumph**

The accounts in Matthew and Mark imply that the next events that Jesus described would take place in a different era. They respond to the question of the time of His return and the end of the age. Mark's account begins: *But in those days,* words that the Jews would easily identify with the Old Testament concept of the "Day of the Lord." Three things will then occur: great cosmic upheaval (the sun and moon will be darkened, stars will fall, and the heavenly bodies will be shaken), people *will see the Son of Man coming in clouds,* and *he will send his angels and gather his elect* (Mark 13:24-28, NIV).

The phrase *these things* in Mark 13:29-30 refers to the earlier events, which the disciples could surely see coming as easily as they could predict the coming of summer by the sprouting of the leaves of a fig tree. When they saw *these things,* they would know that "it" — the time of great trouble — was right at the door. But no one knows the actual timing of *that day or hour,* i.e., His return, not even the angels or Jesus Himself, but only the Father.

The triumph of Jesus has already been attained: He has provided a satisfactory sacrifice for our salvation by His crucifixion, and He has victoriously conquered death by His resurrection. The war has been won, but His triumphal march will not occur until His return. As His disciples, we eagerly await that moment. We want to see Him vindicated in the sight of both believers and scoffers. We long to see every knee bow before Him and to hear every tongue confess His lordship. And we will rejoice when He ends forever the devil's reign of terror on earth. But, in the meantime, we had better pay heed to the strong words He gave His followers about remaining alert.

**Watch and Work!**

> Because Jesus was concerned about giving exhortation more than information, He was emphatic about this: *Watch out ... keep watch ... be ready.*

Despite all the information about the future given by Jesus in the Apocalyptic Discourse, His main theme is a command for Christians to be watchful. Because Jesus was concerned about giving exhortation more than information, He was emphatic about this:

*Watch out ... keep watch ... be ready* (Matthew 24:4, 42, 44). As we have seen, Mark's Gospel uses similar wording: *Watch out ... So be on your guard ... Be alert!... keep watch ... Watch!* (Mark 13:5, 23, 33, 35, 37). The parallel verses in Luke 21 record the warnings as: *Watch out ... Be careful ... Be always on the watch* (verses 8, 34, 36).

What, then, does it mean for modern disciples to be watchful and alert? To simply sit on the sidelines as a spectator? No, it certainly does not mean that we should be idle or passive. Paul severely admonished the Thessalonians about this. Apparently, some were convinced that Jesus would return very soon, so they stopped working. The apostle warned them that they must follow his example and continue their labors so they *would not be a burden* to anyone (2 Thessalonians 3:7-8).

Jesus Himself told us how He expects His people to be watchful:

*Who then is the faithful and wise servant, whom the master has put in charge of the servants in his household to give them their food at the proper time? It will be good for that servant whose master finds him doing so when he returns.*

Matthew 24:45-46, NIV

In Mark's Gospel, Jesus expands on the concept by suggesting that His followers should be like one of the servants who would be assigned to keep watch at the door:

*...because you do not know when the owner of the house will come back ... If he comes suddenly, don't let him find you sleeping. What I say to you, I say to everyone: "Watch!"*

Mark 13:35-37, NIV

Just what is it, then, that we are to be doing in our alertness? Jesus wants us to be *working* — to be making disciples by witnessing in His name. This work, of course, includes spiritual warfare praying, as we saw in a previous chapter.

Over nineteen hundred years have passed since *these things* occurred, and we still do not know how many more years there will be before *those days*. Yet many people scoff at the idea that Jesus will return, believing that

His promise to return must be understood metaphorically, that perhaps He has already returned in His body, the Church.

Peter warned that

> ... *in the last days scoffers will come [saying], "Where is this 'coming' he promised? Ever since our fathers died, everything goes on as it has since the beginning of creation."*

2 Peter 3:3-4, NIV

Then in 2 Peter 3:8-9, Peter gave three facts that scoffers do not consider:

1. Everything has *not* been the same since the beginning of creation; God has already judged the world once (the great flood).
2. God does not live by man's calendar; one day with Him is like a thousand earth years, and vice versa.
3. God is patient, not wanting people to perish, but to repent.

A final idea comes from Jesus' words in Matthew's account of the Apocalyptic Discourse:

> *And this gospel of the kingdom will be preached in the whole world as a testimony to all nations, and then the end will come.*

Matthew 24:14, NIV

Scoffers fail to understand that God has a plan which He has been implementing from the beginning of time, and global evangelization is a big part of it. Scoffers will be overtaken by the return of Jesus just like Noah's neighbors were overtaken by the flood (see Matthew 24:36-39; 2 Peter 3:5-6). Believers should take no pleasure in that thought. Rather, living as alert disciples means warning the scoffers, convincing them of the reality of God's plan, encouraging them to repent, and teaching them to be disciples of Jesus Christ — all the while expecting His return.

"His last command – our first concern" is the motto of a great missionary church in Pennsylvania. And so it should be for all disciples of Jesus Christ. That last command was the Great Commission:

"His last command — our first concern."

> *Therefore go and make disciples of all nations, baptizing them in the name of the Father and of the Son and of the Holy Spirit, and teaching them to obey everything I have commanded you. And surely I will be with you always, to the end of the age.*
>
> Matthew 28:19-20, NIV

## Summary Thoughts from Chapter 29, Apocalypse

- Jesus could not have made it any clearer: ... *if you do not believe that I am the one I claim to be, you will indeed die in your sins.*
- The Spirit clearly says that in later times some will abandon the faith and follow deceiving spirits and things taught by demons.
- Disciples should not lose their composure during catastrophic times. Let the world panic, but God's people are to patiently trust in the Lord to deliver them.
- "His last command — our first concern."

# 30

---○○---

# THE
# CONCLUSION

---○○---

E arlier in this book we suggested that sometimes it is good to read the
last chapter first. The earliest Christians couldn't do that with the Bible,

which had not yet been completed. However,

Revelation is the conclusion —
Satan's conclusion.

it would have been good for Satan to have
known what was coming, for the Revelation is
the conclusion — Satan's conclusion. As the

Luther hymn said, *For, lo, his doom is sure.* Revelation 20:10 is his epitaph:

*And the devil who deceived them was thrown into the lake of fire and
brimstone, where the beast and the false prophet are also; and they will be
tormented day and night forever and ever.*

Revelation 20:10

So, we could conclude this book with a loud war cry to celebrate Satan's defeat. But that is not the mood of Revelation,[188] nor the primary outcome of the spiritual war. It's not about a defeat; it's about a victory that gets celebrated at the Marriage Supper of the Lamb (Revelation 19:9). But let's not rush to the feast. Let's join the early church in seeing how the victory will unfold.

**Ephesus Revisited**

In earlier chapters we looked in on the church in Ephesus as it developed during the ministry of the Apostle Paul. We saw the volatile beginnings of the church with the riot over the goddess Artemis, and then, perhaps a decade later, about A.D. 62, Paul wrote his letter to the Ephesians, quite likely from Rome, as an *ambassador in chains* (Ephesians 6:20). Several years later near the time of his death (martyrdom?) Paul wrote to Timothy, the pastor of the church at Ephesus, instructing him in his pastoral duties.

Then, we hear no more about the Ephesian believers until we open the book of Revelation and find another letter — this one from the resurrected, glorified Jesus Christ who wrote through John several decades later. In that brief letter, the first of seven written in Chapters 2 and 3 to churches in the province of Asia, Jesus commended the church in Ephesus for their deeds and perseverance, as well as their intolerance of evil men and false apostles. However, He said,

> But I have this against you, that you have left your first love. Remember the height from which you have fallen! Repent and do the things you did at first. If you do not repent, I will come to you and remove your lampstand from its place.
>
> Revelation 2:4, 5; paraphrase

---

188  Bible students know that the book of Revelation is a very different kind of literature than the rest of the New Testament. The genre is apocalyptic literature, a writing style that was popular from 200 B.C.-A.D. 150. This genre uses images, symbols, representative numbers, mysterious scenery, and graphic conflict to describe various stories and plots. Other biblical apocalyptic writings are found in the exilic prophets (notably Ezekiel, Daniel, and Zechariah) and in the apocalyptic discourses of Jesus, as noted in Chapters 28 and 29.

What had happened during the intervening years to warrant this hard rebuke from the Savior? Might their fall have been related to the morally and theologically corrupt environment of their city, which we have seen in Chapter 9? Almost certainly so, for infecting the church was the teaching of an apostate deacon, Nicolaus (or Greek., *Nikalaos*) whose deeds the church had come to hate. Thomas Keinath gives us insight about this:

> *In v. 6, as an extension of Christ's affirmations, we read of one specific heretical group that had troubled the Ephesian church, "But you have this in your favor: You hate the practices of the Nicolaitans, which I also hate." Only here and in Christ's message to the church in Pergamum, which was rebuked for having those who held to their teaching (2:15) is reference to the Nicolaitans found in the Bible. Extra-biblically, we have the assertions of several Church Fathers that this false movement was founded by Nicolaus, the proselyte of Antioch, one of the seven first deacons listed in Acts 6:5.*[189]

Keinath provides a quote from Irenaeus found in *Against Heresies*, Book 26, Chapter 26.3:

> *The Nicolaitans are the followers of that Nicolas who was one of the seven first ordained to the diaconate by the apostles. They lead lives of unrestrained indulgence. The character of these men is very plainly pointed out in the Apocalypse of John, [when they are represented] as teaching that it is a matter of indifference to practice adultery, and to eat things sacrificed to idols.*[190]

Recall the Apostle Paul's words to the Corinthians, *the things which the Gentiles sacrifice, they sacrifice to demons* (1 Corinthians 10:20), and those words from the apostles at Jerusalem in instructing Gentile converts:

> *For it seemed good to the Holy Spirit and to us to lay upon you no greater burden than these essentials: that you abstain from things sacrificed to idols*

---

189   Thomas W. Keinath, *Conquest & Glory* (Colorado Springs: Equip Press, 2018), p. 81.

190   Keinath, p. 107, quoting Alexander Roberts and James Donaldson, eds. "Irenaeus," *The Apostolic Fathers with Justin Martyr and Irenaeus, Vol. I. The Anti-Nicene Fathers*, Edinburgh, 1867, reprint, (Grand Rapids: Eerdmans), 1973.

*and from blood and from things strangled and from fornication; if you keep
yourselves free from such things, you will do well.*

Acts 15:28, 29, NKJV

Apparently, blatant disregard for these instructions had earlier infested
the church (as was still the case in Pergamum, Revelation 2:15). Even though
the Ephesians may have dealt with the Nicolaitans, the lingering effects of
their backsliding were that they had lost their first love. Thus, the Lord was
admonishing them to repent.

The other churches did not fare much better, except the one at
Philadelphia. Presumably, all these churches were birthed during the two
years Paul taught daily in the school of Tyrannus when *all who lived in Asia
heard the word of the Lord, both Jews and Greeks* (Acts 19:10).

**The Rome of Revelation**

Earlier, in Paul's letters we find a deep respect for government and
exhortations to the believers to be loyal and obedient citizens. Throughout
Acts, the Roman magistrate was often a safe refuge for Christian believers
against the hatred and fury of Jewish mobs. Paul was proud of his Roman
citizenship and used that privileged status on several occasions (Acts 18:1-
17; 19:13-41; 22:30-40; 23:12-31; 25:10, 11). He urged the Roman Christians
to be obedient to the powers who were ordained by God (Romans 13:1-7).
Peter urged the same respect for the emperor (1 Peter 2:12-17).

But in Revelation there is nothing but blazing hatred for Rome, which
is called *Babylon, the mother of harlots, drunk with the blood of the saints and the
martyrs* (Revelation 17:5, 6). What had happened to change so dramatically
the attitude of the apostles toward Rome? William Barclay notes that it was
"Emperor Worship."

By the time the Revelation was
written, Caesar worship was the one
religion which covered the whole
Roman Empire.

*By the time the Revelation was written,
Caesar worship was the one religion which
covered the whole Roman Empire; and it
was because of their refusal to conform to
its demands that Christians were persecuted*

342

*and killed. The essence of Caesar worship was that the reigning Roman Emperor, as embodying the spirit of Rome, was divine. Once a year everyone in the Empire had to appear before the magistrates in order to burn a pinch of incense to the godhead of Caesar, and to say: "Caesar is Lord."*[191]

Prior to the reign of Domitian (A.D. 81-96), no emperor, including the infamous Nero (A.D. 54-68), took his divinity seriously or insisted on emperor worship. Nero's persecution of Christians, it is generally believed, was to use them as scapegoats for the great fire of Rome which was part of his urban renewal project. Domitian, however, was a very egotistical and evil man who insisted that he be addressed as "Lord and God." He set the stage for many others well into the fourth century who relished their divine status.

This is the backdrop of the Revelation.[192] Christians were confronted with the choice of committing blasphemy or treason. The sentence for refusing to say "Caesar is Lord" was death. John wrote to encourage the Christians to maintain their faith in the midst of the persecutions and threats to their lives. His strong pastoral heart is evident. How many Christians were martyred by the Romans for their civil disobedience is not known, but estimates are 5,500-6,500. These occurred between A.D. 64 and 325. Toward the end of the first century, John, *your brother and companion in the*

---

191   William Barclay, *The Daily Study Bible, The Revelation of John,* vol. I, p. 19.

192   While undoubtedly the Roman persecution is the historical backdrop, there are four schools of interpretation that seek to explain the apocalyptic imagery of Revelation. They are 1) Preterist, which maintains that most of the book pertains to the period in which it was written; 2) Historicist, which interprets the material in terms of church history, assigning various items in the visions to different epochs from apostolic to modern times; 3) Futurist, that sees the central chapters as events of the end-time leading up to the return of Christ; and 4) Idealist or Spiritual View that sees the book more like a novel that sets forth the ageless struggle between the kingdom of God and the forces of evil. All four schools of interpretation see the spiritual warfare that is the theme of this book as a real conflict on earth and in the heavenlies.

*suffering*, (Revelation 1:9), referenced the martyrs he saw in his vision: *I saw under the altar the souls of those who had been slain because of the word of God and the testimony they had maintained* (6:9).

Author Thomas Keinath notes 30 references in Revelation to persecution and martyrdom.[193]

While the threat of martyrdom was a subplot of *The First Christian Drama*,[194] the title of John Wick Bowman's book on Revelation, clearly the main characters are not the Romans, nor even Caesar. Indeed, John studiously avoids using those terms, choosing instead words like "Babylon" and "beast." The main characters are not human; they are God, the glorified Son of God, angels, and Satan and his allies. Our interest here is to show how the spiritual and cosmic war that began in Eden comes to a conclusion.

**Rejoining the War**

From the dawn of human history and through the couple of thousand years of recorded biblical history, people who are open to the spiritual worldview expressed in the Bible have known about the war. They have known that good and bad, righteousness and evil, are not humanly invented categories. They have known that humans are spiritual beings who inhabit material bodies, and that the way we live — whom we worship and how we treat fellow humans — has eternal consequences.

During those years of revelation, the front stage, earthly battles often hid the heavenly, behind-the-scenes battles. God's people, the Israelites, were chosen to bless all other nations by showing how living under God's authority and rejecting all other gods would bring perpetual blessing. However, the true Creator God is too great, too magnificent, and too infinite to be depicted by any visual notion. To the Jewish people, He seemed too remote. The gods of the neighboring nations seemed much more available and less demanding. So, the battles raged. Prophets of

193   Keinath, pp. 294-295.

194   John Wick Bowman, *The First Christian Drama* (Philadelphia: Westminster Press, 1968.) Bowman sees Revelation as a seven-act drama, each act having seven scenes.

Yahweh kept holding up the Law, the teachings of the Torah, but except for occasional revivals, the people of Israel and Judah chose idolatry over the covenants of God. Behind the scenes, it seemed as though Satan was winning the war. Besides the prophets, God used floods, famines, exiles, and persecutions to awaken the Israelites to their waywardness. Even after the Babylonian exile when God restored the Judeans to their homeland and allowed the rebuilding of the temple and the city of Jerusalem, the Israelites rejected the ways of the Lord.

> Except for occasional revivals, the people of Israel and Judah chose idolatry over the covenants of God.

In final fulfillment of His covenants with Abraham, Moses, and David, in the *fullness of time* (Galatians 4:4), God came to earth permanently, first in His second person, Jesus Messiah, and then through His Spirit. During the ministry of Jesus, the hidden war became visible to all. Frequent victories over the ravages of sin, including demonic possession, demonstrated to all objective witnesses that the kingly reign of God was brought to earth and the battle strategy of Yahweh moved into a new campaign. The kingdom would now advance through empowered disciples who would take the good news of God's forgiveness to all people.

**The Command Center in Heaven**

After the letters from Jesus to the seven churches, recorded by John in Revelation 2 and 3, we are taken with John *in the Spirit,*

> *… and there before me was a throne in heaven with someone sitting on it. And the one who sat there had the appearance of jasper and ruby. A rainbow that shone like an emerald encircled the throne. Surrounding the throne were twenty-four other thrones and seated on them were twenty-four elders. They were dressed in white and had crowns of gold on their heads. From the throne came flashes of lightning, rumblings and peals of thunder. In front of the throne, seven lamps were blazing. These are the seven spirits of God. Also in front of the throne there was what looked like a sea of glass, clear as crystal.*

> *In the center, around the throne, were four living creatures, and they were covered with eyes, in front and in back. The first living creature was like a*

*lion, the second was like an ox, the third had a face like a man, the fourth was like a flying eagle. Each of the four living creatures had six wings and was covered with eyes all around, even under its wings. Day and night they never stop saying:*

"*Holy, holy, holy*
*is the Lord God Almighty,*
*who was, and is, and is to come.*"

Revelation 4:2-8, NIV

This is the most complete picture we have of the highest heaven. What comes next gives us a snapshot of the glorified Christ, whom we have described in Chapter 14 as The Commanding Officer of the warfare. He is described as *the Lion of the tribe of Judah, the Root of David* [who] *has triumphed.* When John looked at Him, he saw *a Lamb, looking as if it had been slain, standing in the center of the throne, encircled by the four living creatures and the elders* (Revelation 5:5-6).

After He had taken the scroll that represented the unfolding of all the history of the universe, past, present, and future,[195]

*the four living creatures and the twenty-four elders fell down before the Lamb. Each one had a harp and they were holding golden bowls full of incense, which are the prayers of God's people. And they sang a new song, saying:*

"*You are worthy to take the scroll*
*and to open its seals,*
*because you were slain,*
*and with your blood you purchased for God*
*from every tribe and language and people and nation.*
*You have made them to be a kingdom and priests to serve our God,*
*and they will reign on the earth.*"

---

195  See David Guzik, "Study Guide for Revelation 5" in *The Blue Letter Bible* internet app for other interpretations of the contents of the scroll.

*Then I looked and heard the voice of many angels, numbering thousands upon thousands, and ten thousand times ten thousand. They encircled the throne and the living creatures and the elders. In a loud voice they sang:*
*"Worthy is the Lamb, who was slain,*
*to receive power and wealth and wisdom and strength*
*and honor and glory and praise!"*

*Then I heard every creature in heaven and on earth and under the earth and on the sea, and all that is in them, singing:*
*"To him who sits on the throne and to the Lamb*
*be praise and honor and glory and power,*
*for ever and ever!"*

*The four living creatures said, "Amen," and the elders fell down and worshiped.*
Revelation 5:8-14, NIV

We have cited these images from John's vision to demonstrate the command center of the warfare so there can be no doubt about the locus of authority which assures the outcome of the war. Repeated doxologies in praise to God and Jesus occur throughout Revelation (7:12; 11:17-18; 15:3-4; 16:5-7; 19:1-8), which may be seen as victory chants exalting the Lord of Heaven's Armies.

> Repeated doxologies in praise to God and Jesus occur throughout Revelation.

## Back to the Dark Side

As encouraging as the visions of John may have been to the second and third generation churches which were being viciously attacked by Satan, they did nothing to deter Satan's assault. The first- and second-century believers had no doubt about the source of their persecutions. Their biblically informed worldview saw their earthly battles as merely part of the larger cosmic warfare between God and the rebellious traitors led by Satan. Aside from his influences on the seven churches, however, Satan does not personally come onto the stage of Revelation until Chapter 12. His domain, the Abyss, and perhaps other satanic identities are seen in Chapter 9 — *the angel of the Abyss, whose name in Hebrew is Abaddon, and in Greek, Apollyon* (9:1-11), which mean "Destroyer."

From this point, let us follow Dr. Thomas Keinath's narrative to describe Satan's last thrashings before his final demise:

*Satan, also identified as "the angel of the Abyss" (9:11); "Apollyon"/ "Abaddon"/ "Destroyer" (9:11); the devil; the dragon; and, "the ancient Serpent" (12:9, 14) is certainly a major figure in the end time drama. His personage is clearly defined as furious, murderous, accusatory, deceptive, and blasphemous; in fact, he invites the worship of rebellious humanity. It becomes clear by Chapter 12 that Satan is the driving force behind wickedness in the (second) heavens and in the earth. He deceives and leads astray all the nations of the earth (also 20:2, 8, 10) and he directs the evil activities of fallen angels (12:7), the first beast (13:2, 4, 7), and the second beast (13:11). His direct connection with Babylon is seen in that both appear "with seven heads and ten horns" (12:3; 17:3), which also associates him with wicked earthly rulers and end-time kings (17:10-13).*

*From the ancient past up until a determined period of time, Satan's rule issues from the "heavens" (12:3, 7). With defeat at the hands of archangel Michael and his angels, Satan and his angels are "hurled to the earth" (12:9, 10, 12). As the chief enemy of God, the dragon opposes and persecutes the following: "the woman" and the male child, Jesus, to whom she gives birth (12:4, 13, 15-17); Michael and his angels (12:7); Jesus, the Lamb (17:14; 19:19); and, God's holy people (12:11, 17; 13:7; 16:6; 17:6, 14; 18:24). Satan, in fact, does not prevail against any of these his foes. At the Revelation of Jesus, the devil will be bound in the Abyss, which is locked and sealed for one thousand years (20:2-6), keeping him "from deceiving the nations anymore" (20:3). At the end of this period, he is released for a short time (20:7), at which he once again leads a global rebellion (20:8, 9), which is immediately met with fiery judgment from Heaven (20:9). Satan is then personally judged by God and eternally consigned to "the fiery lake of burning sulfur" (20:10; cf. 19:20; 21:8).*[196]

## Hallelujah! and Maranatha!

Even though the outcome of the warfare was never in doubt, seeing its conclusion brought a great outpouring of joy and adulation to John and all the heavenly host who are part of this great drama. Whereas previous verses are peppered with words like "fallen" and "woe," from the moment of the enemy's final defeat there arises:

*what sounded like the roar of a great multitude in heaven shouting:*
*"Hallelujah!*
*Salvation and glory and power belong to our God,*
*for true and just are his judgments.*
*He has condemned the great prostitute who corrupted the earth by her adulteries.*
*He has avenged on her the blood of his servants."*

Revelation 19:1, 2, NIV

Hallelujahs and amens abound in these victorious chapters. The final two chapters of the Bible, Revelation 21-22, are the most glorious in the Bible. All else leads up to this great scene. What had begun in a beautiful garden with just two humans and was corrupted by God's adversary now ends in a glorious new Holy City with untold numbers in God's forever family.

> What had begun in a beautiful garden with just two humans and was corrupted by God's adversary now ends in a glorious new Holy City with untold numbers in God's forever family.

*The city does not need the sun or the moon to shine on it, for the glory of God gives it light, and the Lamb is its lamp. The nations will walk by its light, and the kings of the earth will bring their splendor into it. On no day will its gates ever be shut, for there will be no night there. The glory and honor of*

---

196    Keinath, pp. 297-298.

*the nations will be brought into it. Nothing impure will ever enter it, nor will anyone who does what is shameful or deceitful, but only those whose names are written in the Lamb's book of life.*

Revelation 21:23-27, NIV

We end this epic drama with perhaps the most beautiful vision ever seen by man and the most compelling prayer for Christ-lovers of all times: *I saw a new heaven and a new earth, for the first heaven and the first earth had passed away, and there was no longer any sea. I saw the Holy City, the new Jerusalem, coming down out of heaven from God, prepared as a bride beautifully dressed for her husband. And I heard a loud voice from the throne saying, "Look! God's dwelling place is now among the people, and he will dwell with them. They will be his people, and God himself will be with them and be their God. 'He will wipe every tear from their eyes. There will be no more death' or mourning or crying or pain, for the old order of things has passed away."*

*Maranatha! Come, Lord Jesus.*

Revelation 21:1-4 and 22:20

## Summary Thoughts from Chapter 30, The Conclusion

- The church at Ephesus, founded by the ministry of the Apostle Paul, was one of seven churches who received "letters" from Jesus encouraging them to regain their purity and to remain stable during the present stress.
- The Roman practice of emperor worship forced Christians either to commit treason by refusing to say, "Caesar is Lord," or blasphemy for saying it.
- In Revelation 4 we see the glory and majesty of worship before the throne of God depicted in dazzling colors. In

Chapter 5 we see the Lion/Lamb of God taking the scroll and receiving exuberant worship from other heavenly beings.

- Cosmic catastrophes occur through the sevenfold seals, trumpets, and bowls in Chapters 4-16, as God brings judgment to the earth and moves to God's ultimate victory.
- The ultimate victory of God through the conquering Christ results in an eternal embrace and intimacy in the new divine family in the new Jerusalem.

# BIBLICAL WORLDVIEW IDEAS AND SCRIPTURES[197]

David E. Schroeder, Ed. D.

- Genesis is the beginning of our story, not God's.
- Our story is just a part of a much larger and longer cosmic and celestial drama.
- Hints about the bigger worldview are sprinkled throughout the Bible.
- There is only one Creator God, who named Himself Yahweh.
- Jesus is part of the triune God, who is revealed as the Messiah and the only and unique Son of God.
- God made the divine council (see Psalm 82, for example, and the many references to "Us," such as Genesis 1:26) and shares governance with them.
- There are many gods and sons of God (*elohim*) which the Creator God made desiring to have a "family."
- Angels are not *elohim*.[198]

---

197  Many of these biblical worldview concepts are found in Michael Heiser, *The Unseen Realm* (Bellingham, WA: Lexham Press, 2015).

198  See footnote 31.

- God's earthly family is made in His image; they are His children.
- His purpose is to have a family of loving beings to live with in a perfect world.
- Some of the gods (*elohim*) rebelled at God's family expansion plan of creating humans.
- They intended and succeeded in corrupting God's new creation, including humans.
- Some of the rebellious sons impregnated human women (Genesis 6) creating *Nephilim* (giants), who occupied the Promised Land.
- The Israelites were to destroy this aberrant "race" of corrupted seed (Amalekites).
- Eventually, the *Nephilim* were destroyed physically, but some of their spirits continue to corrupt the world as demons.

**Select Passages that Reference the Biblical Worldview**

Psalm 29:1

*Ascribe to the LORD, O heavenly beings,* (Hebrew, *sons of God* or *sons of might*)
*ascribe to the LORD glory and strength.*

Psalm 95:3

*For the LORD is a great God,*
*and a great King above all gods.*

Psalm 82:1-8

*God takes His stand in His own congregation; He judges in the midst of the rulers.*
*How long will you judge unjustly And show partiality to the wicked?*
*Vindicate the weak and fatherless; Do justice to the afflicted and destitute.*
*Rescue the weak and needy; Deliver them out of the hand of the wicked.*

*They do not know nor do they understand; They walk about in darkness; All
the foundations of the earth are shaken.*
*I said, "You are gods, And all of you are sons of the Most High.*
*"Nevertheless you will die like men And fall like any one of the princes."*
*Arise, O God, judge the earth! For it is You who possesses all the nations.*

## Daniel 7:10

*A stream of fire issued and came out from before him; a thousand thousands
served him, and ten thousand times ten thousand stood before him; the court
sat in judgment, and the books were opened.*

## Job 38:7

*…when the morning stars sang together
and all the sons of God shouted for joy*

## 1 Kings 22:19-23

*Micaiah said, "Therefore, hear the word of the LORD. I saw the LORD
sitting on His throne, and all the host of heaven standing by Him on His
right and on His left. The LORD said, 'Who will entice Ahab to go up and
fall at Ramoth-Gilead?' And one said this while another said that. Then
a spirit came forward and stood before the LORD and said, 'I will entice
him.' The LORD said to him, 'How?' And he said, 'I will go out and be a
deceiving spirit in the mouth of all his prophets.' Then He said, 'You are to
entice him and also prevail. Go and do so.' Now therefore, behold, the LORD
has put a deceiving spirit in the mouth of all these your prophets; and the
LORD has proclaimed disaster against you."*

## 2 Kings 6:15-17

*Now when the attendant of the man of God had risen early and gone out,
behold, an army with horses and chariots was circling the city. And his servant
said to him, "Alas, my master! What shall we do?" So he answered, "Do
not fear, for those who are with us are more than those who are with them."
Then Elisha prayed and said, "O LORD, I pray, open his eyes that he may*

*see." And the LORD opened the servant's eyes and he saw; and behold, the mountain was full of horses and chariots of fire all around Elisha.*

## Jude 6

*And the angels who did not stay within their own position of authority, but left their proper dwelling, he has kept in eternal chains under gloomy darkness until the judgment of the great day.*

## 1 Peter 3:18-22

*For Christ also died for sins once for all, the just for the unjust, so that He might bring us to God, having been put to death in the flesh, but made alive in the spirit; in which also He went and made proclamation to the spirits now in prison, who once were disobedient, when the patience of God kept waiting in the days of Noah, during the construction of the ark, in which a few, that is, eight persons, were brought safely through the water.*

*Corresponding to that, baptism now saves you — not the removal of dirt from the flesh, but an appeal to God for a good conscience — through the resurrection of Jesus Christ, who is at the right hand of God, having gone into heaven, after angels and authorities and powers had been subjected to Him.*

## 1 Corinthians 6:3

*Do you not know that we are to judge angels?*

## Elohim

## Genesis 1:26-27 (NASB)

*Then God said, "Let Us make man in Our image, according to Our likeness; and let them rule over the fish of the sea and over the birds of the sky and over the cattle and over all the earth, and over every creeping thing that creeps on the earth."*

*God created man in His own image, in the image of God He created him; male and female He created them.*

Psalm 82:1

*God has taken his place in the divine council;*
*in the midst of the gods he holds judgment.*

Deuteronomy 32:17

*They sacrificed to demons that were no gods, to gods they had never known, to*
*new gods that had come recently, whom your fathers had never dreaded.*

## Notes about Satan and Fallen Angels

Scripture reveals much about God's adversaries, as documented here:

### Satan

His fall through pride - Isaiah 14:12; 1 Timothy 3:6; Luke 10:18
Appears in the form of a serpent - Genesis 3:14; Revelation 12:9; 20:12
The great red dragon - Revelation 12:3, 4, 12-17; 13:4, 14, 15
The prince of demons - Matthew 25:41; 1 John 3:8; Revelation 12:7
Accuser - Job 1:6-11; 2:1-6; Zechariah 3:1-2; Revelation 12:10
Resister - Ephesians 6:12; 1 Thessalonians 2:18
Tempter - 1 Chronicles 21:1; Matthew 4:1-11; Luke 22:3, 31; Acts 5:3; 1 Corinthians 4:4; Ephesians 2:3; 1 Peter 5:8; Revelation 2:10; 12:9
Deceiver and liar - Matthew 12:24-26; John 8:44; 2 Corinthians 11:14-15; Revelation 12:9
Afflicts - Job 1:12; 2:7; Luke 13:16; Acts 10:38
Overpowered - Luke 10:18; John 12:31; 14:30; 16:11; Romans 16:20; Revelation 12: 7, 8, 10, 11; 20:10

### Fallen angels / demons / *elohim*

Their fall and imprisonment - Luke 8:31; 2 Peter 2:4; Jude 6; Revelation 20:3

Recognized Jesus – Matthew 8:29; Acts 16:17; 19:15; James 2:19
Not closely confined – Ephesians 2:2; 6:12
Forms (vision) – Revelation 13:11; 16:13
Power (vision) – Revelation 9:5; 11:7; 13:12-13; 16:14
Possession – Matthew 12:43-45; Mark 5:2-5; Luke 8:27
Casting out – Matthew 12:26-29; Mark 3:23-27; Luke 9:49, 50; 10:17; 11:18-20
Identified with idols – Leviticus 17:7; Deuteronomy 32:17; 2 Chronicles 11:15; 1 Corinthians 10:19-21; 1 Timothy 4:1; Revelation 2:13; 9:20

## ADDENDUM 2

# BEING AND SOMETHINGNESS

David Eldon Schroeder, Ed. D.

We need to begin our inquiry into establishing a credible perspective on origins with the premise that nothing cannot make something. To believe otherwise requires a greater leap of faith than any proposition found in any religion. Therefore, if one does not want to call the maker "intelligent design(er)," at least the admission of a "creative impulse" or force must be allowed. And since all that we know in our dimensions of space and time seems to exist within a cause/effect nexus, the "creative impulse" must exist outside or independent of our material world, which breaks the dilemma of an infinite regress. (To be sure, it does require a faith assumption, but so does every attempted explanation of origins. The test of universal worldviews is not a question of faith versus some other basis of assumption, but their explanatory reasonableness [consistency, coherency, comprehensiveness and congruity; cf. James Sire, *The Universe Next Door*] in view of the evidence or effects that stimulate our inquiry in the first place.)

The purpose of this inquiry into origins is neither to find the answer nor to espouse a particular worldview. Rather, it is to challenge the empirically based view that it is impossible that there is intelligent design behind the origin of the universe and life. This brief treatise is more philosophical than theological; more perspective than polemic.

A second necessary premise for positing a credible perspective on origins is that non-life cannot generate life. To believe otherwise requires a leap of faith nearly as preposterous as the negation of the first premise. Therefore, the creative impulse must itself have life.

Third and fourth premises are that non-being cannot generate being and non-personality cannot generate personality. Therefore, the creative force responsible for life must be a being with personality. So, these four premises underlie the following remarks:

- nothing cannot make something
- non-life cannot generate life
- non-being cannot generate being
- non-personality cannot generate personality

Admittedly, these four premises may seem to be a rephrasing of Thomistic ideas, but they do not move toward teleology. Nor do they press for a faith position after establishing empirical or cosmological arguments. Instead, these premises expose the need for a faith perspective upfront – before any inquiry or commentary may be made about origins of the existence of matter, mind or spirit. Both radical skepticism and radical belief make an initial leap, or start with a presupposition about what may not or may be allowed as evidence. So, it seems to me, these four premises are foundational for any serious inquiry into reality.

Keen thinkers will at once, of course, see that these are meta-physical propositions. To restrict an inquiry into the realities surrounding the material (physical) world merely to physical statements or ideas is to settle for uncaused causes – brute nature, as some call it – without meaning, purpose or value. But worse, such denial of the validity and necessity of metaphysical propositions betrays and must reject the immaterial mind that is questioning its own source. Surely, the mind must seek to understand its own metaphysical nature. What has a new corpse lost - materially or physically - with the death of its mind? Weigh it! Measure it! Do the autopsy to find what's missing. Only one thing is missing – life, immaterial life. If the point is made that brain activity is merely matter (fuel) turned into energy (thought), we must ask, what is the operating system for stimulating the matter of the organism to convert the matter into mind. Is it not the mind itself? So, an honest, seeking mind will readily accept its metaphysical nature, and thus allow metaphysical premises in seeking an explanation for its source, and for all reality.

We do not minimize the enormity of the leap of faith that must be taken to accept the existence of a personal-being-creative impulse, and we accept it only because the negation of these properties requires an absurdly greater leap of faith, a leap with nothing (literally) to land on. And the reason critical thinkers accept the personal-being-creative impulse idea reluctantly is that the huge amount of evidence we have, our cosmos and the universe beyond, is circumstantial. Some may see so-called "fingerprints" of the maker in the design and grandeur of nature, but unless one posits celestial fingers, there can be no fingerprints, and the overwhelming amount of disorder and natural chaos do not point to very friendly fingers.

But we must deal with the circumstantial evidence, and we do so not as extraterrestrial, objective analysts, but as highly subjective and invested inquiring minds. We want to know, we need to know what reality is and how to live appropriately within what we perceive to be the really real. So having accepted four premises, the validity of making the propositions that those premises underlie, and the uncomfortable leap of faith that lands us in a hostile intellectual environment, let us fast forward to the end of our inquiry and work backwards. The end of our inquiry is, of course, the end of our lives — the most fearful point of our reality.

The question that most quickly springs from our subjectivity at that point — the subjectivity of intelligent beings about to be extinguished — is a good question. Assuming that the creative force behind our existence is an eternal life force, an assumption far more easily made than the four premises that have led us in this direction, why are we not also able to assume that a being exists for whom termination is not a necessity? Since the "termination" we all expect is the end of physical life, a truly metaphysical being may also transcend the limitations of life as we know it. One might name this being any name one chooses (let's use the name Being), but the attributes we have described — creative ability, intelligence, personality and timelessness — also describe the Being. Other attributes may also apply, but these are essential to our hypothesis.

Three possible relationships between this Being and humans may exist:

1. The Being has ceased to be aware of or involved with humans.

2. The Being is aware of but uninvolved with humans.

3. The Being chooses to remain aware of and involved with humans.

The first two positions are variations of deism, a faith position which is a reasonable response to evidence, or lack of evidence, in the world. These positions may or may not posit postmortem life for humans. What they exclude are transcendent purposes and meta-natural abilities or activities of humans (such as prayer, worship, or any truly spiritual activities that imply communication with the Being).

The third possible relationship between the Being and humans is some form of theism, which implies the active, interested involvement of the Being in its creation, especially humanity. Perhaps the communicative drives that have been observed in all cultures, such as prayer, worship, and sacrifice, do not necessitate the actual existence of an attentive Being at the other end, but it seems reasonable that these impulses reflect the nature of the Being who seemed to have had a relational reason for the genesis of humans. If the creative Being is also a communicator with mortals, that communication would seem to be spirit to spirit. Language would not seem to be either an obstacle or necessity. Thought patterns in language will obviously be needed from the human side, but presumably the inner impulses that underlie the content of the human's communication are perceived rather like a bar code at the other end. The symbols probably don't mean much except to the scanner. On the other hand, our ability to perceive the communication coming to us — if there is such — seems limited to the filter of our minds.

Critical thinkers may wonder at this point if we are not like children trying to cross a swamp by hopping from one weedy clump to another. We keep moving from one tenuous thought to another, but as we do so, hopefully we are navigating our way to a firm landing, and at least we are not cowardly quivering on the shore with life and death questions that we do not have the courage to address.

If, then, a creative impulse with personality has intentionally produced life which this Being seeks to relate to, it is quite reasonable to expect the immaterial aspects of our nature to seek this communicative connection and to anticipate a clearer comprehension beyond the limits of our material existence. Post-mortem life seems to be a *sequitur* rather than an absurdity.

Anticipating the possibility of life after death, we then rewind in our imaginations to the life we now experience and look for signs that will direct us to the other side of the swamp. We hear the voices of others farther along and read the accounts of those who pioneered the life of spirit. And while they all beckon us to live faith-fully as we move toward the other side, none of them (we assume) has actually appeared or spoken audibly to us since their crossing has been completed. Were their assumptions true and their expectations fulfilled? And because not all of them agreed on which path through the swamp would get us there, which voice or voices would be the best to follow? But these questions take us beyond the immediate inquiry.

What we are hoping to affirm credibly is the necessity of faith assumptions that point to the necessity of intelligent design, not just of present existence but also of future purpose. We are not seeking to establish just the validity of faith assumptions, and we are not seeking to establish just the plausibility of intelligent design, but the necessity of both. So, we affirm that Something or Someone has produced all that we experience as real, and that its product that we experience and call creation somehow reflects the nature of what we have called Being: intelligence, personality, purposefulness, and non-temporal and non-material existence.

This Impulse, Force, or Being we may also call The Life (source of living beings), whose existence is The Truth (Logos = explanation of reality and origins) and whose will is The Way (to transcend material finality). As human beings, our best expression of intelligent life is to pursue greater knowledge of the Being who is The Life, The Truth and The Way. Our inquiry should not be limited to the possibility of intelligent design in the universe, but accepting the four premises above, perhaps in our own best interest it will be wise to inquire into and conform to the spiritual, social and moral implications of the design.

# OUTLINE OF MATTHEW'S GOSPEL OF THE KINGDOM

David E. Schroeder, Ed. D.

Matthew's unique structure shows alternating sections of narrative (events) and discourse (teachings). However, in all sections, the dominant theme is the kingdom of God. At the end of each discourse, Matthew uses this verbal formula, *When Jesus had finished these words...*

1. Narrative One - Chapters 1-4: The **Kingdom** Unveiled
2. Discourse One - Chapters 5-7: The Principles of the **Kingdom** (Sermon on the Mount)
3. Narrative Two - Chapters 8-9: The **Kingdom** Confronts the Unclean
4. Discourse Two - Chapter 10: Service in the **Kingdom**
5. Narrative Three - Chapters 11-12: Opposition to the **Kingdom**
6. Discourse Three - Chapter 13: Parables of the **Kingdom**
7. Narrative Four - Chapters 14-17 (13:53-17:27): **Kingdom** Worldview for Disciples
8. Discourse Four - Chapter 18: Discipline in the **Kingdom**
9. Narrative Five - Chapters 19-22: **Kingdom** Citizenship
10. Discourse Five - Chapters 23-25: The Coming **Kingdom**
11. Narrative Six - Chapters 26-28: The Execution and Triumph of the **King**

## ADDENDUM 4

# THE MEANING OF CHRISTMAS[199]

## C. S. Lewis

*Enemy-occupied territory — that is what the world is.*

*Christianity is the story of how the rightful king has landed,*
*you might say landed in disguise,*
*And is calling us all to take part in a great campaign of sabotage.*

*God has landed on this enemy-occupied world in human form.*

*And now, what was the purpose of it all?*
*What did He come to do?*

*Well, to teach, of course;*
*But as you look into the New Testament or any other Christian writing*
*you will find they are constantly talking about something different —*
*about His death and His coming of life again.*

---

199    C. S. Lewis, *God in the Dock: Essays on Theology and Ethics* (London, Geoffrey Bles, 1970; published as *Deceptions*).

*It is obvious that Christians think the chief point of the story lies here.*

*They think the main thing He came to earth to do was to suffer and be killed. The central Christian belief is that Christ's death has somehow put us right with God and given us a fresh start.*

*We are told that Christ was killed for us,*
*That His death has washed out our sins,*
*and, that by dying, He disabled death itself.*

*That is the formula. That is Christianity.*
*That is what it has to be believed.*

*Now what was the sort of "hole" man had got himself into?*

*He had tried to set up on his own —*
*to behave as if he belonged to himself.*

*In other words, fallen man is not simply an imperfect creature who needs improvement: He is a rebel who must lay down his arms.*

*This process of surrender — this movement full speed astern —*
*is what Christians call repentance.*

*And here comes the catch.*
*Only a bad person needs to repent:*
*Only a good person can repent perfectly.*
*But the same badness which makes us need it,*
*makes us unable to do it.*

*But supposing God became a man —*

*Suppose our human nature which can suffer and die,*

*Was amalgamated with God's nature in one person —*
*then that person could help us.*
*He could surrender His will, and suffer and die, because He was man;*

*And He could do it perfectly because He was God.*
*You and I can go through this process only if God does it in us,*
*But God can do it only if He becomes man.*

*The Second Person in God,*
*The Son became human Himself:*
*Was born into the world as an actual man —*
*A real man of a particular height,*

*With hair of a particular color,*

*Speaking a particular language,*

*Weighing so many pounds.*

*The Eternal Being,*
*Who knows everything and who created the whole universe,*
*Became not only a man*
*But (before that) a baby,*

*And before that a fetus inside a woman's body.*

*If you want to get the hang of it,*
*think how you would like to become a slug or a crab.*

*The really tough work —*
*The bit we could not have done for ourselves —*
*has been done for us.*

*The perfect surrender and humiliation were undergone by Christ:*
*Perfect because He was God,*
*surrender and humiliation because He was man.*

*Now the Christian belief is that if we somehow share the humility and*
*suffering of Christ, we shall also share in His conquest of death*
*and find a new life after we have died*
*and in it become perfect, and perfectly happy, creatures.*

*God has landed on this enemy-occupied world in human form.*
*You might say landed in disguise.*

*Why is He not landing in force, invading it?*
*Is it that He is not strong enough?*

*Well, Christians think He is going to land in force;*
*We do not know when.*
*But we can guess why He is delaying.*

*He wants to give us the chance of joining His side freely.*

*God is going to invade, all right;*
*but what is the good of saying you are on His side then,*
*when you see the whole natural universe melting away like a dream,*
*and something else —*
*something it never entered your head to conceive — comes crashing in;*
*something so beautiful to some of us and so terrible*
*that none of us will have any choice left?*

*For this time it will be God without disguise;*
*something so overwhelming that it will strike either*
*irresistible love or irresistible horror into every creature.*

*It will be too late then to choose your side.*

# SATANIC WORKINGS
# THROUGH THE AGES AND THE NATIONS

David E. Schroeder, Ed. D.

W e live in a kingdom of darkness (see Colossians 1:13), presided over by an imposter prince (see Mark 3:22) who temporarily holds power over this world and those who are not in the kingdom of God. Knowing about this satanic usurper, the enemy of God, is also important for those of us who are in the resistance.

MacMillan describes how the dark kingdom was evident in the earliest times:

*We are sometimes prone to think that the saints of Old Testament times possessed little clear conception of the powers of the unseen world. But this is a misapprehension on our part. It is true that in the Book of Psalms the emphasis first appears to be laid upon visible and physical foes. Those the writer hates "with perfect hatred" (Psalm 139:22) because they were also the enemies of God. But we would be wrong in limiting the thought of the psalmist to what alone could be seen. It will be remembered that Satan is introduced in the very beginning of the Old Testament, and that he appears as the constant adversary of the people of the Lord. The facts also of possession by demons and contact with familiar spirits were well-known and often referred to with reprobation by the prophets and in the Law.*

*Furthermore, the book of Job was written long before the time of David and was unquestionably in his hands and those of the spiritual leaders of Israel. It was doubtless included among the Scriptures in which he meditated with great delight. In this remarkable narrative the veil of the invisible world has been drawn partly aside, and there is given a very startling view of the secret working of the great adversary who had been permitted to bring trouble upon God's champion. We see Satan so concealing his own working that the pious patriarch was actually deceived into believing that he had been set up as a mark for 'the arrows of the Almighty' (Job 6:4). Knowing these facts as they did, it is not too much to claim that David and his fellow saints realized that at least many of the bitter persecutions which they suffered originated from the same dread source that was responsible for the afflictions of Job.[200]*

Soon after David defeated Goliath, Israel would enter the international scene. It was necessary for the nation to realize that Yahweh was King even over the many other mighty nations. This kingship of the LORD of Hosts is vividly expressed in Psalm 24:10: *Who is this King of glory? The LORD of hosts, he is the King of glory!* (ESV). He is the glorious King of Israel, and Zechariah 14:6 tells us that He will be King of the world, over all the kingdoms of the earth (see also Isaiah 37:16).

Even though we experience the reality of evil in our world and in our day, we need to know that Satan has always corrupted societies, cultures, and nations throughout history. Looking at the bigger picture historically and geographically helps us see that the *fiery arrows of the devil* (Ephesians 6:16) that we face as individuals are mere salvos in the battle of the ages. God's enemy hates God and all He has created and called "good," including the nations of the world. Clearly, this is one of the primary truths that comes through the Old Testament, which we see most explicitly in Isaiah.

The historical setting of Isaiah 10-23 was 8th century B.C., the Assyrian threat against all the nations and cities of the Fertile Crescent. Isaiah, whose name means "Yahweh has given salvation," was the advisor to Judah's kings

---

200   MacMillan, pp. 69-70.

Uzziah, Jotham, Ahaz, and Hezekiah. The main message of this section of Isaiah is God's policy toward the nations that oppose Him, not just those who oppose Israel. To the "enemies" of God, Isaiah was to deliver separate messages, beginning with the most powerful empire of the day, Assyria (conquering west Iran, Iraq, Jordan, Syria, Lebanon, Israel, Sinai, Egypt). Assyria's capital was Nineveh, the wicked city that had repented earlier under Jonah's reluctant ministry. Jonah had resisted going there because he hated the powerful, evil empire. Unfortunately, Nineveh's repentance did not last long.

Isaiah's primary prophecies concern the nations of Israel and Judah, the twelve tribes that came from the lineage of Abraham, Isaac, and Jacob, but had split into two kingdoms after Solomon's reign. God would judge both nations, starting with Israel which fell to the Assyrians who destroyed Samaria in 722 B.C.

Assyria did not know or understand its role in God's sovereign ruling of the nations.

*What sorrow awaits Assyria, the rod of my anger. I use it as a club to express my anger.*

*I am sending Assyria against a godless nation, against a people with whom I am angry. Assyria will plunder them, trampling them like dirt beneath its feet. But the king of Assyria will not understand that he is my tool; his mind does not work that way. His plan is simply to destroy, to cut down nation after nation...*

*After the Lord has used the king of Assyria to accomplish his purposes on Mount Zion and in Jerusalem, he will turn against the king of Assyria and punish him — for he is proud and arrogant.*

Isaiah 10:5-7, 12, NIV

**Truth #1: From this, it is evident that the rulers of nations are pawns in God's hands to achieve His purposes, even in disciplining His people.**

*The LORD Almighty has sworn, "Surely, as I have planned, so it will be, and as I have purposed, so it will stand.*

*I will crush the Assyrian in my land; on my mountains I will trample him down. His yoke will be taken from my people, and his burden removed from their shoulders."*
*This is the plan determined for the whole world; this is the hand stretched out over all nations.*
*For the LORD Almighty has purposed, and who can thwart him? His hand is stretched out, and who can turn it back?"*

Isaiah 14:24-27, NIV

The fulfillment is given in Isaiah 37:33-37, NLT:
*"And this is what the LORD says about the king of Assyria: 'His armies will not enter Jerusalem. They will not even shoot an arrow at it. They will not march outside its gates with their shields nor build banks of earth against its walls.*
*The king will return to his own country by the same road on which he came. He will not enter this city,' says the LORD.*
*For my own honor and for the sake of my servant David, I will defend this city and protect it."*
*That night the angel of the LORD went out to the Assyrian camp and killed 185,000 Assyrian soldiers. When the surviving Assyrians woke up the next morning, they found corpses everywhere.*

**Truth #2: Ultimately, God will destroy enemy cultures to protect His own.**

Before God's judgment came on Assyria, however, He used that vile nation to judge other nations. Damascus (Isaiah 17) was (and still is) the capital city of Syria (Aram), just north of Israel. It also would be destroyed by an invasion of Assyria. But, there are hints of a remnant (verse 6) and repentance (verses 7-8). Though Israel, under King Ahaz, at first aligned with Assyria, Isaiah rightly predicted that God would use Assyria to punish both Syria and Israel, which He did by destroying their capital cities, Damascus in 734 and Samaria in 722 B.C.

The Philistines, who occupied the Gaza strip (now occupied by Palestinians) along the eastern shores of the Mediterranean, were the perpetual pesky neighbor to the west of Israel/Judah. Isaiah 14:28-32 predicts that famine and a northern power will destroy Philistia, and that happened in 721 B.C., when the Assyrians conquered them. Isaiah 2:6-8 describes Philistines as "fortune-tellers and idolaters." 1 Samuel 5 tells about their god and idol Dagon, whom Yahweh humiliated.

The people of Moab (east side of the Dead Sea, central Jordan) were the descendants of Lot, Abraham's nephew. Ruth, King David's great-grandmother, was a Moabitess. Seeing the Assyrian threat and the coming devastation of Moab, Isaiah urged them in Isaiah 15 and 16 to take shelter in Judah, but the outcome is seen in 16:11-14, NLT:

> My heart's cry for Moab is like a lament on a harp. I am filled with anguish for Kir-hareseth.
>
> The people of Moab will worship at their pagan shrines, but it will do them no good. They will cry to the gods in their temples, but no one will be able to save them.
>
> The LORD has already said these things about Moab in the past.
>
> But now the LORD says, "Within three years, counting each day, the glory of Moab will be ended. From its great population, only a few of its people will be left alive."

**Truth #3: God does not hate our neighbors, but as idolaters they receive the same judgment as their gods.**

Arabia (Jordan, Saudi Arabia, Kuwait, and Yemen) consisted of nomadic Arabs (Kedar was the second son of Ishmael). Arabia would also be overrun by the Assyrians: Isaiah 21:13-17.

Egypt, Isaiah 19, as the competing power to Assyria for empire dominance and pagan practices, receives the harshest prophecies because with Israel worshipping Yahweh in their midst for 400 years, they had the greatest chance to know the true God. First, civil war (19:1-4) and occultism, then economic disaster (19:5-10), then political folly (19:11-15), then spiritual panic and eventual revival (19:16-25) are parts of the prophecies to Egypt. Cush (Ethiopia) would fare no better through her alliance with Egypt (Isaiah 18 and 20).

**Truth #4: God uses economic and political events to judge nations.**

God's message to Babylon was given in Isaiah 13:1-14:23 (modern Iraq, Jordan, Syria, and Lebanon). More than any other world power, Babylon is depicted as the most hostile to God, from the tower of Babel in Genesis 11 to the great mother of prostitutes in Revelation. Babylon stands for all that arrogantly opposes God. Two hundred years after Isaiah's prophecy, Babylon, which conquered Assyria in 612 B.C., and then destroyed Jerusalem in 586, was conquered by the Persians in 539.

The prophecy against Jerusalem is in Isaiah 22:1-14. Isaiah rebuked their frivolous attitude in the midst of national crisis, and their cosmetic attempts to prepare for a siege. Human political efforts rather than repentance and trust were the strategies of Jerusalem according to verses 12 and 13. Though Jerusalem would be spared from Assyrian conquest, seen in Isaiah 37:36, the Babylonians would totally destroy the sacred city and carry off most citizens into exile in 586 B.C.

**Truth #5: Nothing short of true repentance will avert God's judgment on His apostate people.**

**What's the main message behind all this?** God is very much involved in political, military, and international affairs. He uses nations to judge nations, and then judges them. He is sovereign. That is why David could say in Psalm 46:8-11, NLT:

*Come, see the glorious works of the LORD: See how he brings destruction upon the world.*

*He causes wars to end throughout the earth. He breaks the bow and snaps the spear; he burns the shields with fire.*

*"Be still, and know that I am God! I will be honored by every nation. I will be honored throughout the world."*
*The LORD of Heaven's Armies is here among us; the God of Israel is our fortress.*

God is not a respecter of persons or of nations. His first disposition is to love and forgive Jews and Gentiles, but He will not tolerate sin. God will always judge sin, which is exactly what He did at Calvary. Eventually, Yahweh of armies will put down all rebellion (Isaiah 24:21-23) and establish His Kingdom from Mount Zion (Isaiah 31:4-5; 34:12). As the LORD of hosts, God is the all-powerful Ruler over the entire universe. All power and authority are His. He alone intervenes to provide victory for His people as they are faithful to Him. He alone brings world peace. At the same time, He is available to hear the prayers of His people (Psalm 80:19). The sovereign LORD of hosts has the grace to always be there for the one who comes to Him through faith in the Lord, Jesus Christ. There is no other God like this.

The King of glory commands the armies of heaven and will eventually defeat all the rebellion of all His enemies in this world, including Satan. God's kingdom conquers them all.

# CONFIDENTIAL PERSONAL INVENTORY[201]
## Neil Anderson

## I. Personal Information

Name _____    Telephone (_)_____
Address _____    Church affiliation    _____
Schools attended    _____
Highest grade completed    _____    Degrees earned    _____
Marital status _____    Previous marriage/divorce _____
Vocation:
       Present    _____
       Past    _____

## II. Family History

### A. Religious
1. To your knowledge, have any of your parents, grandparents, or great-grandparents ever been involved in any occultic, cultic, or non-Christian religious practices? Please refer to the Non-Christian Spiritual Experience Inventory and indicate what their involvement was.

---

201   Condensed from *The Bondage Breaker*, pp. 277-284.

THE LION, THE CHURCH AND THE WARFARE

2.  Briefly explain your parents' Christian experience (i.e., were they Christians, and did they profess and live their Christianity?).

**B. Marital Status**

1.  Are your parents presently married or divorced? Explain.
2.  Was there a sense of security and harmony in your home during the first 12 years of your life?
3.  Was your father clearly the head of the home, or was there a role reversal in which your mother ruled the home? Explain.
4.  How did your father treat your mother?
5.  To your knowledge, were any of your parents or grandparents ever involved in an adulterous affair?

**C. Health**

1.  Are there (were there) any addictive problems in your family (alcohol, drugs, etc.)?
2.  Is there any history of mental illness?
3.  Is there any history of the following ailments in your family (please circle)?      tuberculosis (TB)      heart disease diabetes      cancer      ulcers      glandular problems other
4.  How would you describe your family's concern for: a) diet b) exercise c) rest

**D. Moral Climate**

During the first 18 years of your life, how would you rate the moral atmosphere in which you were raised?

|  | Overly Permissive | Permissive | Average | Strict | Overly Strict |
|---|---|---|---|---|---|
| Clothing | 5 | 4 | 3 | 2 | 1 |
| Sex | 5 | 4 | 3 | 2 | 1 |
| Dating | 5 | 4 | 3 | 2 | 1 |
| Movies | 5 | 4 | 3 | 2 | 1 |
| Music | 5 | 4 | 3 | 2 | 1 |
| Literature | 5 | 4 | 3 | 2 | 1 |
| Free Will | 5 | 4 | 3 | 2 | 1 |
| Drinking | 5 | 4 | 3 | 2 | 1 |
| Smoking | 5 | 4 | 3 | 2 | 1 |
| Church Attendance | 5 | 4 | 3 | 2 | 1 |

## III. History of Personal Health

### A. Physical

1. Describe your eating habits (i.e., junk food addict, eat regularly or sporadically, balanced diet, etc.).
2. Do you have any addictions or craving that you find difficult to control (sweets, drugs, alcohol, food in general, etc.)?
3. Are you presently under any kind of medication for either physical or psychological reasons?
4. Do you have any problem sleeping? Are you having recurring nightmares or are there other reasons?
5. Does your present schedule allow for regular periods of rest and relaxation?
6. Are you adopted?
7. Have you ever been physically beaten or sexually molested? Explain.

## B. Mental

1. Which of the following have you struggled with in the past or are you struggling with presently? (please check)

| | | |
|---|---|---|
| -daydreaming | -lustful thoughts | -thoughts of inferiority |
| -thoughts of inadequacy | -worry | -doubts |
| -fantasy | -obsessive thoughts | -insecurity |
| -blasphemous thoughts | -dizziness | -headaches |

2. Do you spend much time wishing you were somebody else or fantasizing that you were a different person? Do you imagine yourself living at a different time, in a different place, or under different circumstances? Explain.

3. How many hours of TV do you watch per week? List your 5 favorite programs.

4. How many hours do you spend each week reading?_____ What do you read primarily? (newspaper, magazines, books, etc.)

5. Would you consider yourself to be an optimist or a pessimist? (i.e.: Do you have a tendency to see the good in people and life or the bad?)

6. Have you ever thought that maybe you were "cracking up"? Do you presently fear that possibility? Explain.

7. Do you have regular devotions in the Bible? Where and when, and to what extent?

8. Do you find prayer difficult mentally? Explain.

9. When attending church or other Christian ministries, are you plagued by foul thoughts, jealousies, or other mental harassment? Explain.

10. Do you listen to music a lot? What type do you enjoy the most?

## C. Emotional

1. Which of the following emotions have you had difficulty controlling or are you presently having difficulty controlling? (please circle)

| | | | |
|---|---|---|---|
| frustration | anger | anxiety | loneliness |
| hatred | worthlessness | depression | bitterness |
| fear of death | fear of losing your mind | fear of hurting loved ones | |
| fear of committing suicide | fear of_____ | | |

1. Which of the above listed emotions do you feel are sinful? Why?

2. Concerning your emotions, whether positive or negative, which of the following best describes you? (please check)

_____ readily express them

_____ express some of my emotions, but not all

_____ readily acknowledge their presence, but am reserved in expressing them

_____ tendency to suppress my emotions

_____ find it safest not to express how I feel

_____ tendency to disregard how I feel since I cannot trust my feelings

_____ consciously or subconsciously deny them; it's too painful to deal with them

3. Do you presently know someone with whom you could be emotionally honest (i.e., you could tell this person exactly how you feel about yourself, life, and other people)?

## IV. Spiritual History

A. If you were to die tonight, do you know where you would spend eternity?

B.  Suppose you die tonight and appear before God in heaven, and He asks you, "By what right should I allow you into My presence?" How would you answer Him?

C.  I John 5:11, 12 says, "God has eternal life, and this life is in His Son. He who has the Son has the life; he who does not have the Son of God does not have the life."

    1.  Do you have the Son of God in you?

    2.  When did you receive Him (John 1:12)?

    3.  How do you know that you received Him?

D.  Are you plagued by doubts about your salvation?

E.  Are you presently enjoying fellowship with other believers, and if so, where and when?

F.  Are you under the authority of a local church where the Bible is taught? Do you regularly support it with your time, talent, and treasure? If not, why not?

# ABOUT MASTERWORKS, INC.

## info@MasterWorksInc.org

MASTERWORKS began as a discipling ministry of men in 1987 when Rev. David Schroeder began small group ministries using material he had written based on the discipleship passages found in the Gospel of Luke. The name "MasterWorks" is based on Ephesians 2:10, *For we are His workmanship created in Christ Jesus for good works.* Using the imagery of the workbench of Jesus, who is shaping us to be in His image, Dr. Schroeder's books and teaching seek to lead people into lives of holiness, service, and leadership to bless their churches. In 1991 MasterWorks was incorporated in the Commonwealth of Pennsylvania.

**MasterWorks exists to help local churches and leaders to make, motivate, and multiply mature disciples of Jesus Christ.** Through writing, publishing, distributing, and teaching biblically-based materials, and through mentoring and consulting with individuals and churches, MasterWorks contributes to fulfilling the Great Commission Jesus gave to His first disciples and the Church.

Being aware that western culture is rapidly drifting from its historic Judeo-Christian foundation, the vision of MasterWorks is to **equip, inspire, and encourage Christ-followers to love, serve, and imitate Jesus Christ.** Toward this end, MasterWorks:

- Presents in group settings the teaching materials of Dr. David Schroeder, which include:
  - *Follow Me\** and the *Follow Me Group Guide\*,* a biblically-based disciple-making strategy

- *The Broken God: Power Under Control in the Passion of Christ*
- *Walking in Your Anointing: Knowing that You are Filled with the Holy Spirit**
- *Frontiers of Faith: Exploring Changeless Truth in a Changing World*
- *Bible Alive,* a certificate program that teaches context, content, ministry possibilities, and personal application of all sixty-six books of the Bible*
- *The Lion, the Church, and the Warfare: Spiritual Warfare and the Church*

*available in Spanish

Dr. Schroeder and other MasterWorks associates also:
- Provide in-depth church consulting, teaching, and coaching on a variety of themes:
  - Follow Me Discipleship
  - Local Church Renewal through the *Finding Your Charisma* seminar
  - Healthy Marriage and Pre-marriage counseling
  - Financial Freedom
  - Biblically-based Child Discipline
  - Leadership for Church and Mission
  - Empowerment for Ministry for Women
  - Leadership Lessons in
    - Vision-casting
    - Corporate character
    - Strategic planning
    - Conflict management
    - Change processing
    - Mentoring the next generation
- Serve as a spiritual covering by providing
  - Organizational affiliation
    - Licensing and mentoring for pastors and other spiritual leaders

# BIBLIOGRAPHY

Anderson, Neil T. *Victory over the Darkness.* Ventura, CA: Regal, 1990.

_____*The Bondage Breaker.* Eugene, OR: Harvest House, 1990.

_____*Walking Through the Darkness.* San Bernardino, CA: Here's Life Publishers, 1991.

_____*A Way of Escape.* Eugene, OR: Harvest House, 1994.

Barclay, William. *The Letters to the Galatians and Ephesians* in *The Daily Study Bible.* Philadelphia: Westminster Press, 1954.

_____ *The Revelation of John,* Volumes 1 and 2 in *The Daily Bible Study Bible Series,* second edition. Philadelphia: Westminster Press, 1960.

Bowman, John Wick. *The First Christian Drama.* Philadelphia: Westminster Press, 1968.

Bruce, F.F. *The Book of Acts* in *The New International Commentary on the New Testament.* Grand Rapids, MI: Wm. B. Eerdmans Publishing Co., 1954.

Bryant, David. *Christ Is Now.* New Providence, NJ: New Providence Publishers, Inc., 2017.

Davis, Chuck. *The Bold Christian.* New York: Beaufort Books, 2013.

Heiser, Michael T. *Supernatural.* Bellingham, WA: Lexham Press, 2015.

_____*The Unseen Realm.* Bellingham, WA: Lexham Press, 2015.

_____*Reversing Hermon.* Crane, MO: Defender Publishing, 2017.

Hodge, Charles. *Systematic Theology,* 1981 edition. Peabody, MA: Hendrickson Publishers.

Kraft, Charles H. *Christianity with Power.* Ann Arbor, MI: Servant Publications, 1989.

MacMillan, John A. *The Authority of the Believer.* Camp Hill, PA: Christian Publications, Inc., 1997.

Murphy, Ed. *The Handbook for Spiritual Warfare.* Nashville: Thomas Nelson Publishers, 1992.

Stott, John. *God's New Society.* Downers Grove, IL: InterVarsity Press, 1979.

Tozer, A.W. *Keys to the Deeper Life.* Grand Rapids, MI: Zondervan, 1959.

Unger, Merrill F. *What Demons Can Do to Saints.* Chicago: Moody Press, 1977.

Vine, W.E. *Vine's Complete Expository Dictionary.* Nashville: Thomas Nelson Publishers, 1996.

Wagner, Peter C. *Confronting the Powers.* Ventura, CA: Regal Books, 1996.

Warner, Timothy M. *Spiritual Warfare.* Wheaton, IL: Crossway Books, 1991.